THE COMMON PEACE

Participation and the criminal law in seventeenth-century England

CYNTHIA B. HERRUP

Assistant Professor of History,
Duke University, North Carolina

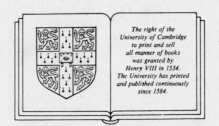

The right of the
University of Cambridge
to print and sell
all manner of books
was granted by
Henry VIII in 1534.
The University has printed
and published continuously
since 1584.

CAMBRIDGE UNIVERSITY PRESS

Cambridge
New York   Port Chester
Melbourne   Sydney

Published by the Press Syndicate of the University of Cambridge
The Pitt Building, Trumpington Street, Cambridge CB2 1RP
40 West 20th Street, New York, NY 10011, USA
10 Stamford Road, Oakleigh, Melbourne 3166, Australia

First published 1987
First paperback edition 1989

Printed in Great Britain at the University Press, Cambridge

British Library cataloguing in publication data

Herrup, Cynthia B.
The common peace: participation and the
criminal law in seventeenth-century
England. – (Cambridge studies in early
modern British history)
1. Criminal law – England – History –
17th century
I. Title II. Series
344.205'09   KD7850

Library of Congress cataloguing in publication data

Herrup, Cynthia B.
The common peace.
(Cambridge studies in early modern British history)
Bibliography
Includes index.
1. Criminal courts – Great Britain – History.
2. Criminal justice, Administration of – Great Britain –
History. I. Title. II. Series.
KD8276.H47 1987   345.41'01   344.1051   86–24968

ISBN 0 521 33313 X hard covers
ISBN 0 521 37587 8 paperback

CONTENTS

FIGURES AND TABLES

ACKNOWLEDGMENTS

This project has allowed me the luxury of following my curiosity to its natural end, and it is a pleasure to thank those who have made it possible. Graduate fellowships from the Fulbright-Hays program, the American Association of University Women, and Northwestern University helped to underwrite the early stages of my research and writing. The American Council of Learned Societies, the Horace H. Rackham fund of the University of Michigan, and Duke University provided later sustenance, computer support and time away from teaching duties.

The staff of the East Sussex Record Office showed me exceptional kindness during this project; Christopher and Margaret Whittick in particular have proved that in Lewes seventeenth-century ideals of hospitality live on. The staffs of the West Sussex Record Office, the Kent Archives Office, the Public Record Office, the Bodleian Library, the British Library, and the Institute of Historical Research were always helpful. The personnel of the Inter-Library Loan offices of Northwestern University and Duke University were courteous and resourceful. The editors of *The Historical Journal* have kindly allowed me to print a revised version of my article, "New Shoes and Mutton Pies: Investigative Responses to Theft in Seventeenth-Century East Sussex," which first appeared in their December 1984 issue.

The secretarial staff at the University of Michigan typed the early chapters of this manuscript, and when it turned out that northern and southern computers could not communicate easily with one another, Dot Sapp of Duke University typed three chapters yet again. She has overseen the final revisions of this manuscript and has in the process given new meaning to the phrase "the patience of Job."

I would also like to thank Richard Cust for making copies of the Grosvenor MSS available to me; John Farrant for sharing with me his wealth of information on early modern Brighton; Christopher Whittick for providing me with a typescript copy of his calendar of the Lewes manorial courts; J. M. Beattie, J. S. Cockburn, Lincoln Faller, Thomas Green, and Philip Jenkins for giving me access to their scholarship before publication; Henry Binford, Steve

Grossbart, and Terry McDonald for never letting me abandon the quest for computer literacy.

So many scholars have responded to part or all of this study that I cannot thank them individually. My teachers at Northwestern University and my colleagues at the University of Michigan and Duke University have given generously of their criticism and their encouragement. Geoffrey Holmes and Lacey Baldwin Smith were among my first teachers in English history; they have been examples as supervisors and as scholars. Conrad Russell and Geoffrey Elton are justly famous for the academic havens they provide for North Americans in England; my experience with each of them more than confirms their reputations. The perceptive criticisms of John Beattie, Judith Bennett, James Cockburn, Tom Green, Christopher Whittick, and Keith Wrightson saved me from numerous errors, challenged me to better explanations, and condemned me to more revisions than I would have thought possible. At a late stage, the constructive skepticism of Bill Reddy reminded me of the peculiarities of the English and spared me, I hope, from the most obvious signs of parochialism.

Personal debts are among the most pleasant to acknowledge. The support and companionship of Judith Bennett provided diversions that made the most intractable problems seem manageable. And, in an academic generation as famous for its casualties as for its accomplishments, I have been most fortunate to count Geoff Eley, Jim Epstein, Jan Ewald, Leon Fink, Susan Levine, Terry McDonald and Don Reid among my colleagues. Their friendship is a reminder of the real meaning of a community of scholars.

Durham, North Carolina

GLOSSARY

The definitions here are not meant to be exhaustive, but rather to provide accessible explanations for some of the technical terms used below.

Arraignment: to call someone to answer in form of law.

Assizes: the sessions held periodically in each county of England by judges acting under certain special commissions, for the purposes of administering justice.

Bail: the freeing of one arrested or imprisoned upon any charge, civil or criminal, on surety taken for his appearance at a specified place and time.

Bailiff: an officer of justice under a sheriff, who executes writs and processes, distrains and arrests (similar employed by king or lords).

Belly, Benefit of: the practice of postponing until after delivery the execution of any pregnant felon.

Bond: a written obligation binding one person to another to pay a sum of money to do some act; a surety.

Burglary: the crime of breaking by night into a house with intent to commit felony.

Case: a cause or suit brought into court for a decision; herein taken to mean one such accusation against one individual for one alleged crime and, hence, not synonymous as a unit with an indictment.

Clergy, Benefit of: originally the privilege of exemption from trial by a secular court allowed to or claimed by clergymen arraigned for felony; in later times the privilege of exemption from sentence which, in the case of certain offenses, might be pleaded on first conviction by everyone who could read. Abolished after earlier modifications in 1827.

Clerk of the Assize: an officer who records judicial decisions given by judges on circuit. *Clerk of the peace:* an officer who prepares indictments and keeps a record of proceedings at sessions of the peace.

Close: an enclosed place; an enclosure.

Commission of the peace: the authority given under the Great Seal empowering certain persons to act as justices of the peace in certain specified districts.

Common pleas: actions at law brought by one subject against another.

Constable: an officer of the peace. *High, Head,* or *Hundred Constable:* an officer of a hundred or other large administrative district appointed to act as conservator of the peace within his district and to perform various other duties. Abolished in 1819. *Parish,* or *petty constable, headboro, tithingman:* an officer of a parish or a township appointed to act as conservator of the peace and to perform a number of public administrative duties in his district. Abolished, except as incorporated into the county police system, in 1872.

Court leet: a court of record held periodically in a hundred, lordship, or manor before the lord or his steward, and attended by the residents of the district.

Cutpurse: one who steals by the method of cutting purses, a common practice when men wore their purses at their girdles; hence a pickpocket.

Examination: formal interrogation, especially of a witness or an accused person. The statements or depositions made by a witness or accused person when examined; the record of such statements.

Felony: a capital offense. Traditionally a crime perpetrated with an evil intention.

Felonious killing: a criminal homicide without malice aforethought.

Gaol delivery: the clearing of a gaol of prisoners by bringing them to trial, especially at the Assizes.

Homicide: the action by a human being, of killing a human being; see felonious killing, infanticide, murder.

Hue and cry: outcry calling for the pursuit of a felon, raised by the party aggrieved, by a constable, etc.

Hundred: a subdivision of a county or shire; the organizational unit for many of the obligations of early modern administration.

Ignoramus: the endorsement made by a grand jury upon a bill presented to them when they consider the evidence for the prosecution insufficient to warrant the case going to a petty jury.

Impanel: to enter the names of a jury on a panel or official list; to enrol or constitute a body of jurors.

Indictment: the legal process in which a formal accusation is preferred to and presented by a grand jury, the legal document containing the charge.

Infanticide: the crime of murdering an infant after its birth, perpetrated by or with the consent of its parents, especially the mother.

Judge: one who has authority to hear and try cases in a court of justice; used herein to refer to the men charged with administering the law at the Assizes.

Judgment: the sentence of a court of justice.

Jury: a company of men sworn to render a true answer upon some question or questions officially submitted to them: in modern times, in a court of justice, usually upon evidence delivered to them touching the issue; but, in the earliest times, usually upon facts or matters within their own knowledge. *Grand jury:* a jury consisting of from twelve to twenty-three "good and lawful men of the county," returned by the sheriff to every session of the peace and of the Assizes to receive and inquire into indictments before these are submitted to a trial jury, and to perform such other duties as may be committed to them. *Petty jury:* a jury which tries the final issue of fact and pronounces its decision in a verdict upon which the court gives judgment. *Jury of matrons:* a jury of women impaneled to inquire into a case of alleged pregnancy.

Justice of the peace: a member of the commission of the peace, a number of whom preside over the meetings of the court of Quarter Sessions.

Larceny: the felonious taking and carrying away of the personal goods of another with intent to convert them to the taker's use. *Grand larceny:* the larceny of goods valued at twelve pence or more. *Petty larceny:* the larceny of goods valued at less than twelve pence.

Liberty: traditionally a district within the limits of a county exempt from the jurisdiction of the sheriff and having a separate commission of the peace, but in seventeenth-century Sussex a district exempt only from certain administrative and financial obligations.

Magistrate: a justice of the peace.

Mens rea: mental guilt.

Mitigation: abatement or relaxation of the severity of a law or penalty.

Murder: to kill a human being unlawfully with malice aforethought; in early use often with the additional notion of concealment of the offense.

Neck verse: a verse (usually the beginning of the 51st psalm) set before one claiming benefit of clergy, by reading which he might save his neck.

Nisi prius: the trial or hearing of common pleas by the judges of Assize.

Oyer and terminer: the Anglo-French phrase "to hear and determine" partly Anglicized; a commission formerly directed to the king's judges, sergeants, and other persons of note, empowering them to hear and determine indictments on specified offenses, such as treasons, felonies, etc.

Pardon: an act of grace on the part of the proper authority in the state, releasing an individual from the punishment imposed by sentence or that is due according to law.

Passport: a license granted by any person in authority, for the safe passage of a person from one place to another.

Pleas of the crown: actions at law in which the king is one of the offended parties.

Presentment: a statement on oath by a jury of facts within its own knowledge.

Quorum: originally certain justices of the peace, usually of eminent learning or ability, whose presence was necessary to constitute a bench; latterly the term was loosely applied to all justices.

Rape: one of the six administrative divisions into which Sussex is divided, each comprising several hundreds.

Recidivist: one who relapses; especially one who habitually relapses into crime.

Recognizance: a bond entered into and recorded before a court or a magistrate, by which a person engages himself to perform some act or to observe some condition; also a sum of money pledged in surety for such performance and rendered forfeit by neglect of it.

Remand: to send back a prisoner into custody.

Reprieve: to respite or rescue a person from impending punishment.

Sessions: a sitting of justices in court upon a commission. *Petty sessions:* a court held by two or more justices exercising summary jurisdiction in minor offenses within a particular district. *Quarter Sessions:* a general court held quarterly by the justices of the peace in every county to hear matters touching the breach of the peace and to deal with other problems as specified by statute.

Surety: a person who makes himself liable for the default or the performance of some act on the part of another.

Sworn: appointed or admitted with a formal or prescribed oath to some office or function.

Theft: the felonious taking away of the personal goods of another; see burglary, cutpurse, larceny.

Trespass: any transgression of the law less than treason, felony or misprision of felony, but most commonly used for a wrong or damage done by one private individual to another.

True bill: a bill of indictment found by a grand jury to be supported by sufficient evidence to justify the hearing of the case.

ABBREVIATIONS AND CONVENTIONS

Albion's Fatal Tree	Douglas Hay, "Property, Authority and the Criminal Law," in Douglas Hay, Peter Linebaugh, John G. Rule, E. P. Thompson, Cal Winslow, eds., *Albion's Fatal Tree: Crime and Society in Eighteenth-Century England* (New York, 1975): 17–63
APC	*Acts of the Privy Council 1542–1628*, ed. John Roche Dasant, 43 vols. (London, 1890–1949)
ASSI	Assize files, Public Record Office, London
Babington	Zachary Babington, *Advice to Grand Jurors in Cases of Blood* (London, 1677)
Barnes, *Somerset*	Thomas G. Barnes, *Somerset 1625–40: A County's Government during the "Personal Rule"* (Cambridge, Mass., 1961)
BIHR	*Bulletin of the Institute of Historical Research*
BL	British Library, London
Blackstone	Sir William Blackstone, *Commentaries on the Laws of England*, 4 vols. (Chicago, 1979)
Bodleian	Bodleian Library, Oxford
C	Chancery files, Public Record Office, London
Cockburn, *Assizes*	J. S. Cockburn, *A History of English Assizes 1558–1714* (Cambridge, 1972)
Cockburn, *Calendar*	*Calendar of Assize Records: Home Circuit Indictments. Elizabeth I and James I*, ed. J. S. Cockburn, 10 vols. (London, 1975–85)
Cockburn, *Introduction*	*Calendar of Assize Records: Home Circuit Indictments. Introduction* (London, 1985)
Cockburn, "Trial by the Book"	J. S. Cockburn, "Trial by the Book: Fact and Theory in the Criminal Process 1558–1625," in J. H. Baker, ed., *Legal Records and the Historian* (London, 1978): 60–79

Crime in England	J. S. Cockburn, ed., *Crime in England 1550–1800* (London, 1977)
CSPD	*Calendar of State Papers. Domestic*, ed. M. A. E. Green, 11 vols. (to 1625, London 1857–72), ed. John Bruce, 23 vols. (to 1649, London, 1858–97)
Dalton, *Countrey Justice*	Michael Dalton, *The Countrey Justice*, 5th ed. (London, 1635)
E	Exchequer classes, Public Record Office, London
EcHR	*Economic History Review*
EHR	*English Historical Review*
ESRO	East Sussex Record Office, Lewes
Fletcher, *Sussex*	Anthony J. Fletcher, *A County Community in Peace and War: Sussex 1600–1660* (London, 1975)
Hawarde	John Hawarde, *Les Reportes del Cases in Camera Stellata 1593 to 1609*, ed. W. P. Baildon (London, 1894)
Herrup, diss.	Cynthia Brilliant Herrup, "The Common Peace: Legal Structure and Legal Substance in East Sussex 1592–1640" (Ph.D. dissertation, Northwestern University, 1982)
HJ	*Historical Journal*
JBS	*Journal of British Studies*
KAO	Kent Archives Office, Maidstone
Lambard, *Constables*	William Lambard, *The Duties of Constables, Borsholders, Tithingmen and Suche Other Lowe Ministers of the Peace* (London, 1591)
Lambard, *Eirenarcha*	William Lambard, *Eirenarcha, or of the Office of the Justice of the Peace in Four Books* (London, 1591)
Lawson	Peter G. Lawson, "Crime and the Administration of Criminal Justice in Hertfordshire 1580–1625" (D.Phil. dissertation, Oxford University, 1982)
LPS	*Local Population Studies*
Morrill, *Grand Jury*	John Morrill, *The Cheshire Grand Jury 1625–49: A Social and Administrative Study* (Leicester, 1976)
P & P	*Past and Present*
Pollock & Maitland	Sir Frederick Pollock and Frederic Maitland,

	The History of English Law before the Time of Edward I, 2 vols., reissue (Cambridge, 1968)
PRO	Public Record Office, London
Q/R/E	Quarter Sessions files, East Sussex Record Office, Lewes
Q/R/WE	Quarter Sessions files, West Sussex Record Office, Chichester
SAC	*Sussex Archaeological Collections*
Samaha, "Hanging for Felony"	Joel Samaha, "Hanging for Felony: The Rule of Law in Elizabethan Colchester," *HJ*, 21 (1978): 763–82
Samaha, *Law and Order*	Joel Samaha, *Law and Order in Historical Perspective: The Case of Elizabethan Essex* (New York, 1974)
SAS	Sussex Archaeological Society, East Sussex Record Office, Lewes
Sharpe, *Essex*	J. A. Sharpe, *Crime in Seventeenth-Century England: A County Study* (Essex) (Cambridge, 1983)
Smith	Sir Thomas Smith, *De Republica Anglorum* (London, 1609)
SP	State Papers, Public Record Office, London
SRS	*Sussex Record Society*
STAC	Star Chamber files, Public Record Office, London
TRHS	*Transactions of the Royal Historical Society*
VCH	*The Victoria History of the County of Sussex*, 6 vols. (London, 1905–53)
WSRO	West Sussex Record Office, Chichester

A NOTE ON TRANSCRIPTION

Quotations have been modernized. Dates throughout are given in New Style, the year being taken to begin on 1 January.

A NOTE ON STATISTICAL SIGNIFICANCE

The measure of a significant statistical relationship used throughout this work is the Chi square test. The smaller the number produced in this test, the more likely that the relationship between two variables is *not* random. A significant relationship has been generally defined herein as one producing a result smaller than .001. The strength of a significant relationship can be deduced from a second test, Cramer's V; the higher the number, the stronger the statistical relationship between two variables. The records extant from eastern Sussex are not full enough to allow the proper use of more sophisticated measures such as regression analysis.

❧ 1 ❧

The criminal law in early modern England

As recently as fifteen years ago, scholars considered the criminal law of Tudor and Stuart England barbaric, the backwater of an increasingly sophisticated legal culture. They saw crime in early modern England as a simple, largely stable tableau of saucy thieves outwitting bumbling constables. Neither generalization stands today. As scholars have looked beyond the proscriptions of the law into its practices, notions of both the law and crime have been transformed. Rather than a subject with but a "miserable history," the criminal law appears now as a responsive mechanism of considerable flexibility (albeit one without the subtlety of its private counterparts). Rather than the province of Shallow and Dogberry, crime and its control appears now as a ground on which villagers struggled over basic definitions of morality and power. Criminal law and crime have rightfully earned a new respectability in the study of early modern England.[1]

However, if recent research helps to explain what individuals in early modern England called crime or criminality, it has been less useful in uncovering how people arrived at their definitions. Whether interpreting verdicts as measures of criminal behavior or as measures of social discipline, scholars have generally treated the procedures of the law as background. Although no one who has worked with the legal records of this period would deny the complexity of the legal structure, the structure itself is often seen as secondary to its products. Too frequently legal process appears collapsed from a series of decisions into one judgment and from a multivoiced production into the solo of a single genteel tenor. Historians of law tell us how the legal process was to work and historians of crime tell us what the legal process was to do, but the interaction between legal and social forces has too

---

[1] The bibliography of the new legal history is voluminous, but some sense of the shifts in attitude can be seen by comparing S. F. C. Milsom, *Historical Foundations of the Common Law* (London, 1969), to *The Reports of Sir John Spelman*, ed. J. H. Baker, Selden Society, vols. 93–4 (London, 1977–8); and Sir Leon Radzinowicz, *A History of English Criminal Law and its Administration from 1750*, vol. 1 (New York, 1948), to J. A. Sharpe, *Crime in Early Modern England 1550–1750* (London, 1984).

1

often been shortchanged. The absence of any single center of power in decision-making was a crucial characteristic of early modern criminal prosecution, and the process itself, its forums, rules and personnel, is worthy of study.

This book is a social history of criminal process in England in the late sixteenth and early seventeenth centuries. As such, it examines not the accomplishments of the criminal courts but how they functioned. Since prosecution relied upon a series of choices, the ways in which results arose from the specific range of possibilities are as important as any categorization of final verdicts. The background of the decision-makers, the circumstances in which they worked and the social norms they saw themselves as enforcing affected the sequence of events. Laboring folk and gentlemen are a part of the tale told here, but the middling sort – yeomen, husbandmen and established tradesmen – hold center stage. Because this is the story of the standards used to label crimes, criminals and punishments, it is the story of the men who believed that they defined these categories more than the story of those who lived within those definitions or challenged them. Similarly, while gentlemen cannot be excluded from this sort of analysis, the fact that men of middling status, not gentlemen, were both the victims most likely to prosecute complaints and the men most frequently obliged to participate in enforcement justifies a shift away from the attention traditionally accorded to the views of local magistrates.[2] Only by taking into account the complexities of applying the law in specific situations and the diffusion of authority among propertied members of local communities can we hope to translate into contemporary terms notions of both hegemony and justice. Some sense of the reactions and the ideals of the middling sort is crucial to an understanding of either the legal or the social context of law enforcement.

The English criminal process was rooted in the common law of felony, which differed from private law in three important ways.[3] A felonious act hurt someone deliberately; the wrong was malicious, not mistaken. This intentional component, or *mens rea*, characterized crimes in early common law.

---

[2] Among crimes reported to the courts in eastern Sussex between 1592 and 1640 (1,631), gentlemen were listed as victims for 127 incidents. The proportion of genteel victims was equally modest in reports of felonies; they accounted for 4 percent of the known victims in homicides and 20 percent of the known victims in felonious thefts. In petty larcenies, gentlemen accounted for 21 percent of the known victims. These percentages exaggerate the prominence of gentlemen in routine process because prosecutions with genteel victims were more likely than any other sort to end in confession without trial.

[3] The following discussion on the nature of the criminal law, except where noted, relies on Pollock & Maitland, 2: 448–557; Milsom, *Historical Foundations*, 2nd ed. (London, 1981), pp. 403–28; J. H. Baker, *An Introduction to English Legal History*, 2nd ed. (London, 1979), pp. 411–36; Blackstone, 4: 1–19.

Moreover, felonies violated basic Biblical injunctions; they were sinful acts as well as crimes. Because they ignored basic ideas of right and wrong, they were not only harmful but also offensive. One hundred and nineteen criminal cases indicted in eastern Sussex between 1592 and 1640 ended with orders for execution; of these, all but two concerned direct transgressions of the Ten Commandments. The influence of divine proscriptions in common law was more direct in criminal matters than in any other area of jurisprudence. The relationship was emphasized initially by the early medieval ordeal, which left the determination of guilt in crime to God rather than to humanity. In the thirteenth century, trial by jury replaced the ordeal and eliminated direct divine intervention from the immediate judicial process, but crime remained closely linked to sin, deliberate evil, and moral weakness. Last, since a felony was both intentional and immoral, it struck at the very heart of a community. Because criminal acts threatened the peace of society, criminal justice could not be simply the concern of victims or their families. The prosecution of felonies belonged to the commonwealth, and by extension, to the monarch. The injury in crime transcended the loss of any single individual. It was the king who stood as the symbolic victim, and who had to be revenged.

Nonfelonious crimes – trespasses and violations of regulatory statutes – shared two of these three characteristics. Trespass was a catch-all for acts that violently shattered the local peace but were not serious or malicious enough to fit the definition of felony. Statutory transgressions threatened the peace through disobedience but were not necessarily violent. All three kinds of crime – felony, trespass, and violation of statute – were viewed as sinful acts and all were prosecuted as communal rather than personal grievances. Evil intention probably affected prosecutions in some instances of trespass and violation of statutes, but only felony assumed malice.

The criminal law was qualitatively different from its private counterpart. While lawsuits publicly arbitrated private disagreements, criminal prosecutions publicly reinforced the behavioral precepts of God, king and community. The position of the amateur in the enforcement of the criminal law probably best exemplifies the distinction between criminal process and other legal avenues of social regulation. Trained lawyers were essential to most procedures, but professional counsel was rare in criminal trials until the eighteenth century. Since contemporaries punished a crime as a moral and social lapse as well as a legal one, acquittal did not rely on professional ability or technical knowledge. As William Hawkins, a sergeant at law, wrote of criminal proceedings in 1716:

that requires no manner of skill to make a plain and honest defense . . . the simplicity and innocence, artless and ingenuous behavior of one whose conscience acquits him, having something in it more moving and convincing than the highest eloquence of persons speaking in a cause not their own.

Innocence, like character, was self-evident; one needed no special training to express it. Similarly, the control of criminals in early modern England was left to non-professionals. Diligence, not legal education, was supposed to produce good constables, jurors, and justices. The propertied community shared the obligation to identify and investigate criminal suspects. Concerned individuals and temporary officeholders divided the duties of criminal prosecution and punishment. Although a handful of professionals presided over the final stage of criminal prosecution, the link between justice and morality in theory made criminal law the moral inheritance of every resident. Since criminality allegedly arose from a flaw within the individual, and not society, other private individuals were the logical guards against disorder.[4]

Legal subtleties were out of place in criminal trials because the overriding issue was the character of the accused. The attributes of a good life – love of God and monarch, belief in obedience and neighborliness – were the traits that ensured social quiet. The lurking temptations of a bad life – sloth, greed, and pride – were the road to the gallows as well as the path to immorality. The central message of the homilies heard in churches and the speeches heard in courtrooms was strikingly similar; individuals must struggle constantly against their weaknesses. Those who were winning this unending battle were qualified to judge the progress of others in the same contest. A handbook on holding courts in the middle of the seventeenth century contended that the law was an "invitation which commands, constrains, and bridles us to come to God." Since crime was sinful, the struggle against criminality was the collective equivalent to the personal struggle for good character – a continuing battle between the weakness of humanity and its potential. Touchstone said it simply and logically in *Eastward Ho!* (1605):

Of sloth comes pleasure, of pleasure comes riot, of riot comes whoring, of whoring comes spending, of spending comes want, of want comes theft, of theft comes hanging . . .

Opportunity, not character, distinguished laziness from criminality. A sinner was a sinner.[5]

---

[4] Hawkins, *Pleas of the Crown*, c. 39, cited in Julius Goebel and T. R. Naughton, *Law Enforcement in Colonial New York: A Study in Criminal Procedure 1664–1776* (New York, 1944), p. 555. Some sense of this sentiment can be taken also from charges given to juries at the Assizes or the Quarter Sessions: PRO SP 12/46/150–1; Sir Edward Coke, *The Lord Coke, his Speech and Charge* (London, 1607); *William Lambarde and Local Government: His "Ephemeris" and Twenty-Nine Charges to Juries and Commissions*, ed. Conyers Read (Ithaca, 1962); see also John Brewer and John Styles, eds., *An Ungovernable People: The English and their Law in the Seventeenth and Eighteenth Centuries* (London, 1980), pp. 11–20.

[5] John Kitchin, *Jurisdictions or the Lawful Authority of Courts Leet, Courts Baron, Court of Marshalsea, Court of Piepowder and Ancient Demesne* (London, 1651), pp. 3–4; Ben Jonson, George Chapman and John Marston, *Eastward Ho!*, ed. C. G. Petter (London, 1973), 4: ii, 91; see also, Coke, *The Lord Coke*; *William Lambarde and Local Government*;

Communal participation in the control of criminality reinforced social pressure for moral conformity. It reminded persons of the frailty of social stability and provided a public display of the dangerous results of loose personal discipline. Chastisement allowed the community to exact revenge and to reaffirm local power against anarchy. At the same time, the courtroom provided a public forum for repentance. In fact, contemporary arguments against capital punishment emphasized not the brutality of execution, but its swiftness. Death by hanging, it was complained, came too quickly after conviction either for a felon to be penitent, or for spectators to absorb the social lesson of misconduct.[6]

The power of amateurs over prosecution made the criminal law seem closer to absolute justice than when lawyers or legal technicalities prevailed. Criminal verdicts depended in theory upon a single general issue: did the accused do the deed or not? Extenuating circumstances or special pleadings found no formal place before juries. Punishment, in theory, was equally simple: every felon deserved execution. The exclusion of lawyers from criminal procedure may have stunted the formal development of the criminal law, but that exclusion reaffirmed the ultimate validity of the law itself. The external forms of criminal process changed only slightly between the thirteenth and the eighteenth centuries, and some legal historians see barbarity in this conservatism much as they have seen immaturity in the reliance of the law upon amateurs. But the stability of criminal procedure, just like the wide participation of lay persons in the law, confirmed the moral substructure of criminal prosecutions. Unchanging process reflected the continuous fight of good against evil. The charge of barbarity might be justified if enforcement had adhered to every rule and formula, but in fact the formal intractability of the law reflected its absolute moral authority, not its actual practice. Rigidity cloaked fluctuation and sensitivity to circumstance. The guise of moral justice provided a solid backdrop for discretion while escaping the danger of trivializing the law with constant emendations.

Robert Greene, "Black Book's Messenger" in *The Elizabethan Underworld*, ed. A. V. Judges (London, 1930), pp. 263–4; *England as Seen by Foreigners in the Days of Elizabeth and James I*, ed. W. B. Rye (New York, 1967), p. 269; PRO SP 12/46/150–1; ESRO FRE MS 520; Edward Coke, *The Third Part of the Institutes of the Laws of England* (London, 1644), pp. 244–5; *An Homily Against Disobedience and Wilful Rebellion* (London, 1571), and, in another context, *D'Ewes Journal*, cited in Thomas Wilson, *A Discourse upon Usury*, ed. and intro. R. H. Tawney (New York, 1925), p. 150, as well as the sources cited in Cynthia B. Herrup, "Law and Morality in Seventeenth Century England," *P & P* 106 (February 1985): 109.

[6] Bodleian Tanner MSS 76/18/160; 233/7/134; Bodleian Rawlinson MS D399/90; BL Harleian MS 1603/30v–1.

The peculiar nature of the criminal law, its dependence on amateurs for enforcement and its need to reflect moral values, makes its application in the Assizes and the Quarter Sessions a particularly sensitive barometer of social ideals. Legal decisions reflected not the values of the gentry but the common ground between the values of the legal elite, the gentry and local men of middling status. As these ideals changed with the pressures of the age, the agreed sense of the best uses for discretion in the law changed as well. The particular concerns of the late sixteenth and early seventeenth centuries guided the social values of the enforcers of the law as powerfully as did their positions in local society.

While hardly a random sample of contemporary mentalité, the personal memorabilia of propertied men in the seventeenth century reveals a vision of social duty that obliged active and vigorous participation in governance. Godly magistrates such as Sir John Newdigate in Warwickshire, clergymen such as Ralph Josselin in Essex, and middling men such as John Everenden in Sussex echoed similar concerns. Life was a test of character and resolve. The conventional assurances of status, family, or good fortune could assuage only temporarily the anxiety of the reality of human frailty and vulnerability to temptation. Traditional boundaries between religious business and secular business, between minor weaknesses and major flaws of character, even between the behavior of one individual and another, paled before belief in a common propensity to sin and in a common fate for the majority of sinners.[7] As recent scholarship on Essex suggests, such activism was often a mixed blessing; along with a great concern for social problems, it could produce a great concern for a "culture of discipline." The chapters below, while they confirm the public influence of the godly so clear in Essex, also suggest that in shires such as Sussex, which was more stable, more evenly prosperous and

[7] See, for example, ESRO FRE 520, 4223; Anthony J. Fletcher, *Puritanism in Seventeenth-Century Sussex* (Studies in Sussex Church History, 1, London, 1981), pp. 141–55; *William Lambarde and Local Government*; Richard Cust and Peter G. Lake, "Sir Richard Grosvenor and the Rhetoric of Magistracy," *BIHR* 54 (1981): 40–53; V. M. Larminie, *The Godly Magistrate: The Private Philosophy and Public Life of Sir John Newdigate 1571–1610* (Dugdale Society, Occasional Papers, 28, Oxford, 1982); "The Diary of Robert Beake, Mayor of Coventry, 1655–1656," ed. Levi Fox (Dugdale Society, *Miscellany*, 1, Oxford, 1977): 111–37; *The Life of Adam Martindale Written by Himself*, ed. Richard Parkinson (Chetham Society, old series, 4, Manchester, 1845); Adam Eyre, "A Diurnall or Catalogue of all my Accions and Expences from the 1st of January 1646," pp. 1–118 of Eyre's diary, ed. H. J. Morehouse, in *Yorkshire Diaries and Autobiographies in the Seventeenth and Eighteenth Centuries* (Surtees Society, 65, Durham, 1875); *The Journal of Nicholas Assheton of Downham*, ed. F. R. Raines (Chetham Society, old series, 14, Manchester, 1848); *The Diary of Ralph Josselin, 1616–1683*, ed. Alan Macfarlane (British Academy, Records of Economic and Social History, new series, 3, London, 1976); Paul S. Seaver, *Wallington's World: A Puritan Artisan in Seventeenth-Century London* (Stanford, 1985).

more religiously diverse than Essex, the activism implicit in godliness could bring quite different results.[8]

The definition of the common law as common justice and the identification of both with ideals of virtue infused the legal and the social structures of early modern England. The intimate interweaving of criminal law and morality found expression not only in the courts but also in contemporary sermons, literature and legal dicta. Legal obligations were everywhere in early modern life and law was a vernacular outside as well as inside of the courtroom. Participation in some level of the processes of the law, willingly or not, was perhaps the most important unifying characteristic of men of property. Among the more modest ranks of the propertied, it was the criminal law that touched most deeply and made the most frequent demands.

Studying the behavior of such men through the records of the Assizes and the Quarter Sessions has several practical advantages. Because these courts involved so many men so regularly in the process of enforcement, their records offer a broad base for prosopographical studies. Because the jurisdiction of these courts was so broad, they reveal how the application of ideals of respectability varied when the potential punishment was execution rather than any lesser penalty. And, because the work of these tribunals cut across a variety of modern administrative categories, their meetings often encompassed not only law and morality but also conventional politics. The Assizes and the Quarter Sessions were occasions both local and national, coercive and responsive, elitist and participatory. For yeomen, husbandmen, and even most gentlemen, they provided the broadest as well as the most distinguished direct audience available to hear complaints of all sorts. The unity of administrative, didactic and disciplinary responsibilities so typical of early modern governance rightly earned these forums the epithet parliaments of the shires.[9]

Although comparisons with other shires have been included wherever possible, this book reconstructs the specific operation of the criminal law in a single region. It is based upon an analysis of 2,412 cases heard in the Assizes and the Quarter Sessions in eastern Sussex between 1592 and 1640. Sussex

[8] The phrase is used by William Hunt in *The Puritan Moment: The Coming of Revolution in an English County* (Cambridge, Mass., 1983). On Essex, see also Keith Wrightson and David Levine, *Poverty and Piety in an English Village: Terling 1525–1700* (New York, 1979); cf. Victor Skipp, *Crisis and Development: An Ecological Case Study of the Forest of Arden 1570–1674* (Cambridge, 1978); Patrick Collinson, *The Religion of Protestants* (Oxford, 1982), c. 4–6; A. L. Beier, "Poor Relief in Warwickshire, 1630–1660", *P & P* 35 (December 1966): 77–100; Paul Slack, "Poverty and Politics in Salisbury, 1597–1666," in Peter Clark and Paul Slack, eds., *Crisis and Order in English Towns* (London, 1972), pp. 164–203.

[9] On the liminal position of these courts and the value of that position, see Cynthia Herrup, "The Counties and the Country: Some Thoughts on Seventeenth Century Historiography," *Social History* 8 (1983): 169–81.

was not typical of the Southeast, but, of course, the Southeast was not typical of England. Since most of the current scholarship on crime and on enforcement has focused upon Essex, the study of a shire such as Sussex provides an important basis for contrast as well as for comparison.[10] Assessing the specific influence of economic, social and religious conditions upon the application of the criminal law demands a compact area of study. The difficulties of travel within Sussex encouraged eastern and western Sussex each to hold virtually independent Quarter Sessions. Eastern Sussex alone, then, had as many meetings of criminal tribunals as most shires. This peculiarity allows the study of a relatively contained area in exceptional detail. The surviving records fall into clusters rather than a linear sequence. Four clusters (1592–7, 1613–18, 1623–9, 1634–40) include almost all contiguous Sessional materials and the files for the Assizes in the adjacent years. Appendix 1 calendars the sample represented by these clusters. The sample includes all complaints of felony, trespass, or violation of statute brought before the courts. Except in Chapter 2, which contains an analysis of reported crimes, the standard unit of analysis is the case. The case represents business as a juror might hear it: one accusation against one person for one action. Juries considered each person in each indictment independently just as they heard multiple accusations against a single individual independently. The case, therefore, is not synonymous either with the crime or the indictment. Indictments, as the official records of the proceedings, provide the outline of criminal business, but because less formal documents such as recognizances, jail calendars and examinations have repeatedly proved to be more reliable than indictments, these documents also have been used extensively. In addition, parochial, manorial, ecclesiastical and other records have been used wherever possible to supplement the materials of the courts.[11]

Chapters 2 and 3 provide an introduction to the social environment of eastern Sussex, the crimes reported there, and the local relationship between the two major criminal tribunals. Among the shires of the Home Circuit (the only regular circuit for which extensive records from the Assizes and the Quarter Sessions in the early seventeenth century survive), Sussex was the least typical

---

[10] A more complete description of life in Sussex can be found in Chapter 2 below. On Essex, see Wrightson and Levine, *Poverty and Piety*; Hunt, *The Puritan Moment*; Sharpe, *Essex*; Samaha, *Law and Order*; A. D. J. Macfarlane, *Witchcraft in Tudor and Stuart England: A Regional and Comparative Study* (New York, 1970).

[11] On the difficulties of using indictments, see J. S. Cockburn, "Early Modern Assize Records as Historical Evidence," *Journal of the Society of Archivists* 5 (1975): 215–31; Alan Macfarlane, Review of J. S. Cockburn, ed., *Calendar of Assize Records: Essex Indictments Elizabeth I*, in *The American Journal of Legal History* 24 (1980): 171–8; J. M. Beattie, "Towards a Study of Crime in Eighteenth Century England: A Note on Indictments," in Paul Fritz and David Williams, eds., *The Triumph of Culture* (Toronto, 1972), pp. 299–314. On the sample used here, see Appendix 1 below.

of its region. It contained no major urban centers; it was only peripherally involved in trade with London; its gentry were primarily men of families long resident in the area. Sussex contained some of the earliest concentrations of Puritans as well as some of the most persistent concentrations of Catholics. The soil was too chalky and the forest too sandy for the county ever to be dubbed an "English Goshen" but the resources of the Weald, Downs and sea assured a modest prosperity. The patterns of both reported crime and juris-dictional divisions suggest some resistance to the innovations of the late sixteenth century. The courts spent more time on accusations of violence and less time on the reformation of manners than did the courts in shires such as Essex. And, although the Elizabethan and early Stuart governments tried repeatedly to rationalize the division of business between the Assizes and the Quarter Sessions, the quarterly court and its magistrates remained a viable forum for major criminal complaints.

Chapters 4 through 6 detail how the residents of eastern Sussex differen-tiated alleged crimes from forgivable errors. They trace the process of decision-making that turned grievances into accusations, accusations into indictments and indictments into crimes. In a world of common pastures, open windows, wandering peddlers, animals and servants, vulnerability to misdeeds (and especially to larceny) was pervasive. But not every misunder-standing became a formal accusation, and many cases that did reach court were dismissed as inappropriate for trial. Of the charges that received a full hearing, acquittals were almost as common as convictions. A loosely rep-resentative ideal is clear in the structure of participation; jurors served repeatedly but not continuously and different duties gravitated to different groups within the social structure. Discussing criminal investigation, the first step in the lengthy procedure of turning a grievance into a prosecution, Chap-ter 4 details the critical importance of victims in the investigation of alleged crimes. The work of detection rested primarily with those most intimately harmed by an alleged crime; the power of the law was peripheral until there was a suspect to arrest. Chapter 5 carries the story from complaint to indict-ment; Chapter 6 focuses upon the considerations that influenced acquittal or conviction. Both grand juries and petty juries tailored their decisions to suit the heinousness of particular crimes, the likelihood of particular punishments and the trustworthiness of particular defendants. As a rule neither the status of the defendant nor the victim was more important to jurors than solid evidence or the demeanor of the suspect.

Chapter 7 turns from criminal process to the nature of criminality. Here the criminal becomes central to the story, and so the analysis centers on individ-uals and their lives as well as on alleged crimes and cases. Chapters 4 through 6 analyze contemporary definitions of crime. Chapter 7 examines early modern ideas about the hardened criminal; this chapter particularly contrasts the treatment of recidivists, or repeat offenders, with the treatment of other convicts. Contemporary literature presented a clear picture of the typical English criminal as avaricious, devious and defiant. But the underworld portrayed so vividly in tracts and drama either touched eastern Sussex only rarely or it produced miscreants too clever to spend much time in local courtrooms. Felons who displayed clearly criminal characteristics were likely to be hanged, but most defendants (and almost all of the recidivists) seem to have been locals aiming at a more modest redistribution of income; relatively few of these men and women were sentenced to the gallows.

No one study can uncover the perceptions of crimes, criminals and justice in Tudor and Stuart England. Moreover, an approach that focuses on process carries within it the illusion of both consensus and rationality; by definition it silences the tensions of the courtroom and obscures the vagaries of collective decision-making. Conflict was probably routine to the legal process. Many decisions were undoubtedly reached in discord, many were simply compromises of frustration. As part of local life rather than a structure above it, criminal process also relied upon local men who were certainly not immune to pettiness. Many of their actions fell short of contemporary ideals of justice, many others would appall modern observers. But the tensions and caprices of the courtroom, producing no written evidence, are unrecoverable. Without denying the conflict and the whimsy often hidden within the legal process, this study illuminates the order within which the tensions were played out. The social history of the law will be reconstructed only with a foundation of innumerable building blocks, and the best size and composition for each piece are still uncertain. This work constitutes a bid for greater attention in that reconstruction to the legal process and its participants. It contributes to the literature on crime and to the literature on law, but its nature is that of a hybrid, revealing the important influences of legal ideals on social behavior as well as the important effects of social predispositions on the law. Like most hybrids, this one might be remembered more for what it is not than for what it is; it may seem too little a social history for some readers, too little a legal history for others. But, because it fits easily into neither category and, albeit awkwardly, into both, it is very much like the process that it seeks to record.

2

The setting

Life in any county reflects the advantages and shortcomings of the natural environment, but geographical setting has been particularly important in the history of Sussex. The physical location and geological configurations of the shire have decisively shaped social, political and economic life. Dismissed by Lord Chancellor Cowper in 1690 as "a sink of about fourteen miles broad," Sussex has long been notorious for its muddy setting. And contemporaries did not hesitate to extend their low judgment to the inhabitants of the county. A report submitted to the Privy Council in 1587 concluded that more justices should be allowed in Sussex than elsewhere because "it borders south on the sea and north on the wild: in which two places commonly the people be given much to rudeness and wilfullness."[1] A modern haven for retirees and writers, Sussex in the early modern era was famous for the inhospitality of both its highways and its inhabitants.

On the sea side, the border of the county is seventy-six miles of harbors and minor inlets that provided a ready haven for smugglers, wreckers, military invaders, and religious infiltrators. The vulnerability of such a coastline made Sussex a repeated target for the landing of invasions and probably inspired the administrative structure of the shire. To secure the most direct route between England and Normandy, William the Conqueror divided the ancient kingdom of the South Saxons into just five fiefdoms.[2] Each was equipped with a castle, a harbor and a market town, and each was entrusted to one of the Conqueror's close companions. These units, known as rapes, became the basis for local military, financial, and political obligations. In early modern Sussex, the rapes still provided the framework for almost all administrative subgroups within the county. Figure 2.1 outlines the rapes as well as the smaller subdivisions of hundreds as they were in the seventeenth century.

[1] Charles Thomas-Stanford, *Sussex in the Great Civil War and the Interregnum 1642–1660* (London, 1910), p. 6, for Cowper's comments; BL Lansdowne MS 53/164–5 for the report to the Privy Council.
[2] The original division combined the rapes of Chichester and Arundel into a single unit; *VCH*, 1: 351–4.

11

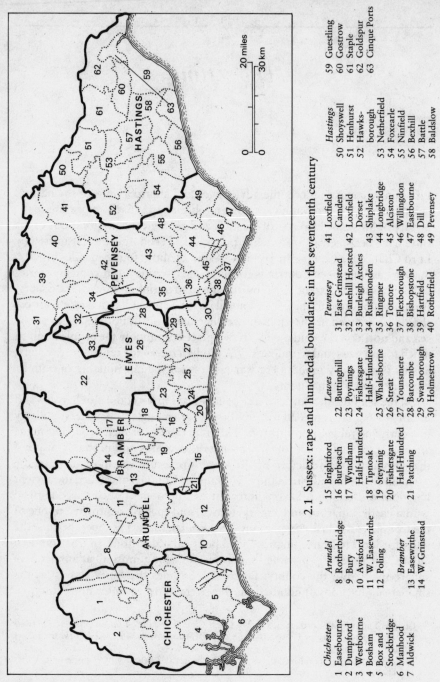

2.1 Sussex: rape and hundredal boundaries in the seventeenth century

Chichester
1 Easebourne
2 Dumpford
3 Westbourne
4 Bosham
5 Box and
 Stockbridge
6 Manhood
7 Aldwick

Arundel
8 Bury
9 Rotherbridge
10 Avisford
11 W. Easewrithe
12 Poling

Bramber
13 Easewrithe
14 W. Grinstead

15 Brightford
16 Burbeach
17 Wyndham
 Half-Hundred
18 Tipnoak
19 Steyning
20 Fishersgate
 Half-Hundred
21 Patching

Lewes
22 Buttinghill
23 Poynings
24 Fishersgate
 Half-Hundred
25 Whalesborne
26 Streat
27 Younsmere
28 Barcombe
29 Swanborough
30 Holmestrow

Pevensey
31 East Grinstead
32 Danehill Horsted
33 Burleigh Arches
34 Rushmonden
35 Ringmer
36 Totnore
37 Flexborough
38 Bishopstone
39 Hartfield
40 Rotherfield

41 Loxfield
 Camden
42 Loxfield
 Dorset
43 Shiplake
44 Longbridge
45 Alciston
46 Willingdon
47 Eastbourne
48 Dill
49 Pevensey

Hastings
50 Shoyswell
51 Henhurst
52 Hawks-
 borough
53 Netherfield
54 Foxearle
55 Ninfield
56 Bexhill
57 Battle
58 Baldslow

59 Guestling
60 Gostrow
61 Staple
62 Goldspur
63 Cinque Ports

Source: Fletcher, *Sussex*, p. 4.

12

Natural barriers also defined the northern perimeter of the shire. Dense forests almost completely covered the borders with Surrey and Kent. Although in the seventeenth century these woodlands were a mere reminder of the forests that William Camden claimed once covered the entire region, Sussex was still one of the most thickly wooded areas in the country. The heavy cover provided the protection that had once made Sussex a viable independent kingdom, but in the early modern era the governors of England considered the woods a serious impediment to the good governance of the shire. As the surveyor John Norden contended, "the people bred among woods are naturally more stubborn and uncivil than in the champion countries." The Sussex forest was "of so wild a character and bore such an evil reputation" that as late as the eighteenth century, travelers from London to Brighton planned their journeys to avoid the woodlands.[3] The growth of an iron industry within these forests added to the rough image. Although the industry created a demand for wood that somewhat thinned the denseness of the forests, the ironworks also attracted migrants anxious to find work. The government considered these new settlers to be potential troublemakers. The Privy Council and the local magistrates complained repeatedly about the instability of the northern border of the shire.

Between the natural frontiers provided by the sea and the woodland lay three distinct economic regions – the northern Weald, the southeastern marshlands and the southern Downs. The northern region of the county, known as the Weald or Wild, commenced with a wide belt of forest that rested upon sand and clay.[4] Wealden agriculture focused on the pasturing of livestock. Cattle provided beef and dairy products for home and export; sheep, pigs and poultry answered a more restricted regional demand. The wet, acidic soil of the Weald resisted arable farming, but local interest in agriculture persisted. In good years, the region produced most of its own corn and animal fodder. By the seventeenth century, wealden oats, hops and fruit were even being regularly exported. Most of the region had been enclosed into small fields long before the early modern era, and the configuration and

[3] William Camden, *Britannia: Surrey and Sussex*, ed. and ann. Gordon J. Copley (London, 1977), p. 29; John Norden, *The Surveyor's Dialogue* (1618), cited in Joan Thirsk, "The Farming Regions of England," in *The Agrarian History of England and Wales, IV, 1500–1640*, ed. Joan Thirsk (Cambridge, 1967), p. 111; *VCH*, 1: 305.

[4] Descriptions of the economic, social and geographical structure of Sussex below rely, except where noted, on Colin Brent, "Employment, Land Tenure and Population in Eastern Sussex 1540–1640" (Ph.D. dissertation, University of Sussex, 1973); Fletcher, *Sussex*, pp. 3–104; T. W. Horsfield, *The History, Antiquities and Topography of the County of Sussex*, 2 vols. (London, 1835); Arthur Young, *General View of the Agriculture of the County of Sussex* (London, 1808); Julian Cornwall, "The Agrarian History of Sussex, 1560–1640," (M.A. thesis, University of London, 1953); Thirsk, *Agrarian History*; *VCH*, 1–3; Joyce Mousley, "Sussex Country Gentry in the Reign of Elizabeth I" (Ph.D. dissertation, University of London, 1956).

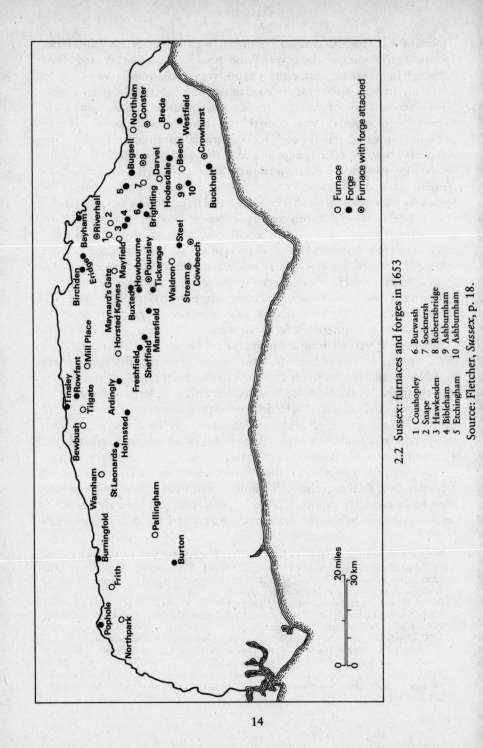

2.2 Sussex: furnaces and forges in 1653

1 Coushopley   6 Burwash
2 Snape   7 Socknersh
3 Hawkesden   8 Robertsbridge
4 Bibleham   9 Ashburnham
5 Etchingham   10 Ashburnham

○ Furnace
● Forge
◉ Furnace with forge attached

Source: Fletcher, *Sussex*, p. 18.

quality of the land discouraged further attempts to unify agricultural properties. Wealden holdings, while modest, were secure. Communal obligations were minimal and kept that way by the enormous size of most wealden parishes (up to twenty-three square miles) and by the dispersal of small settlements throughout the area. Economic organization centered on the smallholder, the cottager, and, by the sixteenth century, the small manufacturer.

Iron had been mined in the forests of Sussex since the days of the Romans and, in the sixteenth century, technical and organizational advances made the Weald one of the most important areas in England for producing iron. Camden's impression of the region was marked by the "incessant noise night and day [that] echoes all over the neighborhood." Forges and furnaces expanded both in number and capacity and estimates of the number of workers employed by the industry ran as high as 7,000 in the late sixteenth century. As shown in Fig. 2.2, the furnaces and forges were especially predominant in eastern Sussex. Although expansion stopped and, in the western Weald, even reversed after the first decade of the seventeenth century, Sussex remained a major source of products made from iron until coal replaced charcoal as the favored fuel for the industry and the northern Midlands became a more attractive site for exploitation.[5]

The Weald, like similar regions throughout England, supported a variety of local industries aside from ironworking. Inhabitants of the northern half of the country wove textiles, made bricks, tiles, glass, and gloves, tanned leather and crafted wood. None of these industries were pursued on a sizable scale or involved much capital, but their presence allowed local families to supplement incomes based on farming. Moreover, inhabitants combined not only farming with crafts but also crafts with other crafts. Few men matched the versatility of Thomas Upton, who was noted in his parish register as "ye Archimedes of Wadhurst... by trade a glover, a joiner, a carpenter, an instrument maker, a curious workman for jacks, clocks, pieces stoves and vices for glaciers," but many altered their occupations to suit immediate opportunities.[6]

Such possibilities invited immigration and between 1590 and 1640 the Weald increased in both wealth and population. The economy encouraged a mobile pool of laborers who sought economic advantages in taming the wildness of the forest. By 1640, despite its size, the Weald had more people per square mile than any other part of Sussex. Almost all of the citations brought to court against individuals for either erecting cottages or taking inmates illegally came from wealden parishes, and only one of the nine parishes

[5] Camden, *Britannia*, pp. 29–30 and 30 fn.; Ernest Straker, *Wealden Iron* (London, 1931).
[6] ESRO PAR 498/1/1/2/33, cited in Brent, "Employment," p. 175.

licensed to set up a poor house in these years was situated completely outside of the region. Although the Weald as a whole continued to grow after 1640, by that time some parishes, particularly those in the western part of the industrial district, seem to have reached a point of saturation. The pressure of population should not be exaggerated; even in 1640, the level of density was only forty-five persons per square mile. As its most recent historian has noted, the Weald was "not so much communities as sprawling federations of communities."[7] But the Weald was becoming more crowded and less profitable for some of its inhabitants. The relatively open-ended social structure of the sixteenth century was giving way to regional concentrations of the permanently poor.

The southeastern flank of the Weald melded into marshlands that followed the coastline from Westham in the south up to the Kentish border. The marshlands were the most valuable lands in Sussex, but they were also the most unhealthy. The region was given over to the fatting of cattle, sheep and horses. The steadiest employment was for "lookers" who watched the livestock. Since the area supported very little grain and few opportunities for non-agricultural labor, this handful of parishes had the lowest density of population (twenty-six people per square mile) in the county. Many parishes of marshland had more livestock than they had people. The high price of land restricted immigration and the danger of disease encouraged absenteeism among those who did hold property.

The most important contrast to the northern woodlands lay in the southern and southwestern regions of the county. Between the "wildness" and the sea rose the line of chalk hills known as the Downs, broad and desolate on the incline but capped with a short, sweet grass that supported some of the finest mutton in the country. On the seaward side, the Downs adjoined a fertile coastal plain. This land, only a narrow strip at Brighton, steadily widened to encompass almost half the breadth of the county on the western border. The soil was less acidic and less retentive than the northern clay, and farmers followed the patterns of sheep-corn husbandry as in other English counties. The parishes of the downlands, which usually combined sheepwalks with adjacent arable fields in the scarpfoot, were far smaller than those of the Weald both in acreage and in population. However, estates tended to be much larger (three hundred to four hundred acres was not uncommon) and holdings were usually leased *en bloc* or divided among only a handful of tenants.

The economy of the Downs relied on the export of grain, wool and mutton. The myriad opportunities for employment that played so prominent

---

[7]   Colin Brent, "Devastating Epidemic in the Countryside of Eastern Sussex between Harvest Years 1558 and 1640," *LPS* 14 (Spring, 1975): 45.

a part in wealden life were not available in the downlands. Although farming did not use labor intensively, the downlands lacked the raw materials to sustain most crafts. In addition, the geographical complexity of the region and the symbiotic balance of sheep–corn husbandry restricted the ability of farmers to expand the land under acreage. The economy of the downlands was not amenable to either cottagers or smallholders. When wool prices stagnated in the early seventeenth century, the security of small farmers rapidly degenerated. As economic pressures encouraged the consolidation of modest holdings, many individuals who had once farmed independently became laborers or servants or left the area entirely. By 1640, few small farms run by families survived and several parishes had been virtually depopulated.

The three farming regions of Sussex were not often broken by major urban areas. The shire contained numerous market towns, but most supported few inhabitants and served only their immediate vicinities. Since trade usually moved by water along the coast, the southern parishes, rather than the more heavily populated northern region, contained the largest towns. On the coast, towns such as Shoreham, Brighton, Rye and Hastings survived on the proceeds of trade and fishing, but even the biggest of these, Brighton, probably contained no more than a few thousand people. The diocesan seat, Chichester, was a regional trading center, but it lacked the general importance of ecclesiastical capitals in other shires. In contrast to Chichester, Lewes, the county town in the eastern rapes, dominated its surroundings. Lewes was situated not only at the junction of the Weald and the Downs, but also at the most viable crossing of the Ouse river. As a result the town enjoyed a natural advantage as a center for goods moving east–west and north–south. Consequently, the largest and most diversified group of local merchants in the county lived at Lewes, and local gentlemen from the eastern rapes built townhouses there as well. Lewes grew steadily throughout the early seventeenth century. Long the eastern focus of social, political and administrative life, by 1640 Lewes rivaled Brighton in both size and economic importance.[8]

Problems of travel exacerbated the regionalism of Sussex. Between the dangers and vulnerabilities of the woods and the coastline lay what many outsiders believed to be an endless sea of sand and mud. The folklore of the county is full of tall tales about the depth and gummy wetness of the roads. Every local administrative body tried and failed to control the annual destruction wrought by a rainy climate, porous soil and a stream of heavy wagons loaded with the products of the wealden iron industry. In the eighteenth cen-

[8] G. O. Cowley, "Sussex Market Towns 1550–1750" (M.A. thesis, University of London, 1965); John and Sue Farrant, "Brighton 1580–1820: From Tudor Town to Regency Resort," *SAC* 118 (1980): 331–50; Jeremy Goring, "The Fellowship of the Twelve in Elizabethan Lewes," *SAC* 119 (1981): 157–72.

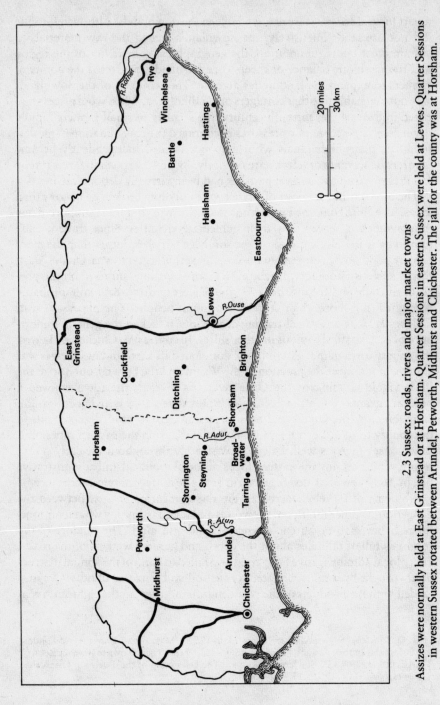

2.3 Sussex: roads, rivers and major market towns

Assizes were normally held at East Grinstead or at Horsham. Quarter Sessions in eastern Sussex were held at Lewes. Quarter Sessions in western Sussex rotated between Arundel, Petworth, Midhurst and Chichester. The jail for the county was at Horsham.

Source: Fletcher, *Sussex*, p. 6.

tury, coachmen who normally calculated their wages in distances, insisted that for Sussex they deserved "better pay for shorter ways." A trip in Sussex, they argued, was "better measured in days journey than by miles." Most byways were simply drovers' tracks or footpaths. The earliest known comprehensive map of Sussex, from 1675, listed only five major thoroughfares, and a cartographer of the 1720s dismissed these as mere open "horsetracks." The abysmal state of the roads in Sussex has been used to explain everything from local temperament to the shape of the calves of local women.[9]

Modern researchers have modified the quaintness of this picture, citing the navigable rivers running north–south through the county, the coastal highway running east–west, and the growing overland trade between Sussex and London. Figure 2.3 shows the major highways in eighteenth-century Sussex, as well as the navigable rivers and major markets. But, although it would be erroneous to equate bad roads with isolation, travel in Sussex was more difficult and more dangerous than in many other parts of England. The highway along the coastal plain served only a narrow strip in the eastern county. The rivers were useful for commerce, but too expensive and too localized for personal transportation. Overland trade never matched the business done by water in either volume or importance. Trade between Sussex and London was not as routine as business between the capital and the Home Counties. In good weather one could be in London within twenty-four hours of leaving eastern Sussex, but in the winter, or after the rains in the spring, many paths simply became impassable. Horsham, the site of the only authorized gaol in Sussex, was built on a vale of clay; after the rains, it could become completely inaccessible. Markets, elections, baptisms and even burials had on occasion to be altered because of problems over transportation. Moreover, as coaches and carriages became more common, mobility on good highways increased, but transportation on sinkable roads often grew even more difficult. A road in Sussex, an experienced traveler lamented in the eighteenth century, "is an almost insuperable evil."[10]

---

[9] *Magna Britannia*, cited in G. Joan Fuller, "A Geographical Study of the Development of Roads through the Surrey and Sussex Weald to the South Coast, during the period 1700–1900" (Ph.D. dissertation, University of London, 1950), p. 12. For other anecdotes on local travel, see Fuller, "Roads through Surrey," pp. 12–14, 143, 154; BL Additional MS 11,571/116–19; Daniel Defoe, *A Tour through the Whole Island of England and Wales, 1722* (London, 1927); Thomas-Stanford, *Sussex*, p. 210; Esther Meynell, *Sussex* (London, 1947).

[10] One does not want to press the notion of isolation too far; obviously many people with legitimate and not so legitimate motives traveled regularly in the shire. Nonetheless the evidence does suggest less movement both within and through the region than in many other places. For example, 77 destinations can be traced for vagrants escorted away through the region from Cuckfield and from villages in Hastings rape in the early seventeenth century; 25 percent were settled in other villages in Sussex and another 32 percent went no farther than Kent or Surrey; WSRO PAR 301/7/2/8 (vagrants whipped in Cuckfield 1618–38); PRO SP 16/320/17, 16/363/122, 16/393/85 (returns for Hastings rape 1635–8); cf. Sharpe, *Essex*,

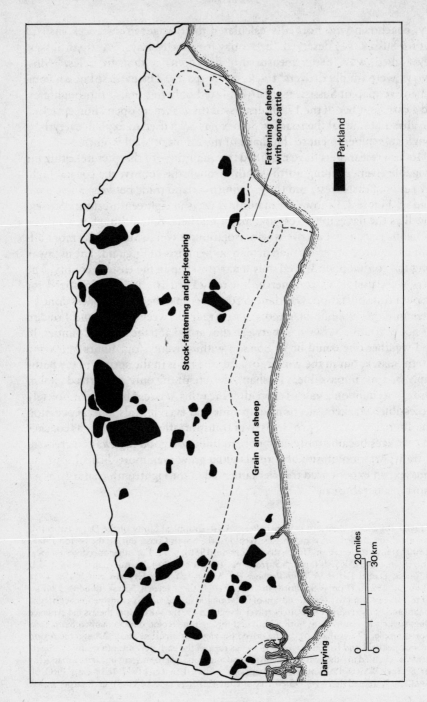

Fattening of sheep with some cattle

Parkland

Stock-fattening and pig-keeping

Grain and sheep

Dairying

20 miles
30 km

2.4 Sussex: the farming regions

The roads slowed, but certainly did not prevent, mobility within the shire. Self-sufficiency necessitated interaction. Although farmers in every rape but Hastings cultivated corn, most of the grain used locally came from the western rapes. Farming in the Weald demanded extended labor, but the timing of the wealden harvest freed laborers to move south and east to meet the need for workers in the downlands and the marshlands. Mobility, however, could not alter the fact that the economic needs of the two divisions of the county were diverging by the early modern era. Eastern Sussex was spared much of the suffering that periodic shortages of grain caused in other shires, but the growing demands of Londoners and of the navy tempted local entrepreneurs. In times of shortage, serious conflicts arose between the need for food in the eastern rapes and the desire of western exporters to use the eastern ports to ship grain abroad and to London.[11]

Despite the interdependence of the various regions of the shire, then, Sussex was too large and too diverse to operate effectively as a single unit. As a result, the county for practical purposes can be divided into two sections, East and West. As Figure 2.4 shows, downland best for grain and sheep lay mostly in western Sussex (the rapes of Arundel, Chichester and Bramber). The wealden and marshland regions, more suitable for pastoral activities, predominated in the eastern half of the shire (the rapes of Lewes, Pevensey and Hastings).[12] Western Sussex (and the southern sections of the East) exploited rich arable in a sheep–corn economy. The land was profitable, but had reached its peak of pre-industrial growth by the seventeenth century. The downlands supported the largest estates in the shire, and the fewest small farms. They supported the wealthiest individuals, and the largest number of live-in servants. The most populated villages, those concerned with trade and export along the seacoast, were in the flatlands, but so too were the least populated parishes in the county. The eastern region of Sussex (and the northern tip of the West) had a less naturally profitable, but more flexible, economy than did the western region. Residents in the eastern division lived

---

p. 165. More skeptical discussions of the condition of local roads can be found in Fuller as well as in the dissertations of Brent and Cowley, and J. A. Chartres, "Road Carrying in England in the Seventeenth Century: Myth and Reality," *EcHR*, 2nd series, 30 (1977): 73–94; 33 (1980): 92–9. On vagrancy see A. L. Beier, *Masterless Men: The Vagrancy Problem in England 1560–1640* (London, 1985); Paul Slack, "Vagrants and Vagrancy in England, 1598–1664," *EcHR*, 2nd series, 27 (1974): 379.

[11] Brent, "Devastating Epidemic," *passim*; E. A. Wrigley and R. S. Schofield, *The Population History of England 1541–1871: A Reconstruction* (Cambridge, Mass., 1981), pp. 671–84; F. J. Fisher, "The Development of the London Food Market 1540–1640," *EcHR* 5: 2 (April, 1935): 46–64; Fletcher, *Sussex*, pp. 147–51; *VCH*, 2: 194–5; *CSPD* 1637–8, pp. 278–9.

[12] The modern counties of East and West Sussex, divided on the basis of population rather than administrative history, fit these boundaries generally, but not exactly; cf. Local Government Act, 1972.

primarily from its cattle, its iron and its timber, but a variety of smaller industrial enterprises added to local opportunities. Social contrasts in eastern Sussex were often less marked than in the western part of the county, and economic life was often more secure. The difficulties of farming in the East discouraged estates large enough to support gentlemen and the possibilities intrinsic to the forest encouraged the immigration of cottagers and laborers. Settlements were fluid and scattered; trade was localized or carried overland. Although some parts of the region were beginning to show signs of over-population, the eastern rapes were easily the most productive and the most expansive area of Sussex in the seventeenth century.

The social structure of the upper classes in the eastern and western rapes paralleled the economic cleavage. Sixteenth-century Sussex was a land with more local nobles than "one shire can well bear," but most of the active ancient aristocracy resided in the West. Few genteel households in Sussex lacked a connection with recusancy, but the nobility of western Sussex was notorious for its Catholicism. By the late 1590s, the most adamant Catholics had retired from active politics rather than give up their faith. In contrast, eastern Sussex had one dominant aristocratic family, the Protestant Sackvilles, and they spent little time in the shire.[13] It was common for one lord lieutenant and one member of Parliament to be a Sackville, but the head of the family, the Marquis of Dorset, spent most of his time at Court, or, after 1607, at Knole in Kent. By the early seventeenth century, the most important members of the commissions of the peace in eastern Sussex were local gentlemen, many of whom were active Puritans. They were the backbone of the local administrative structure, in fact if not in title, and as deputy lieutenants and justices of the peace they tried to set the tone for local governance. Fiercely proud of their lineage, these men pursued ambitious marriages and styles of life, but they were solidly provincial. Many had been educated at the universities or the Inns of Court and some were drawn into national politics, but few spent much time outside of Sussex. Only a small number had townhouses in Lewes, far fewer in London. Most chose their spouses from within the county, many from within their own immediate geographical locale. Fortunes made by newcomers were welcomed and many older families profited from the boom in iron, but it was a rare parvenu who held an important local office before his family had been in Sussex for at least two generations. Despite its proximity to London, the landed classes in Sussex remained unquestionably rural; they acquired none of the suburban aura of

---

[13] PRO SP 12/165; Roger B. Manning, *Religion and Society in Elizabethan Sussex: A Study of the Enforcement of the Religious Settlement 1559–1603* (Leicester, 1969), pp. 151–65, 221–71. While the Gages, Dacres and Nevilles did maintain residences in eastern Sussex, none of them rivalled the Sackvilles in local influence.

their counterparts in Hertfordshire or Essex. An eighteenth-century traveler, in fact, despaired of the inhabitants, saying that "surely we cannot wonder if the rust, contracted in this muddy soil, should clog the energy of the mind itself . . . their greatest pride is to be thought a connoisseur of cattle."[14] By the late sixteenth century, the three eastern rapes were a region of livestock and ironworks dominated by independent farmers and Puritan gentry. The western rapes were more aristocratic, more conventionally agricultural, and more Catholic. Profoundly different from one another, the two divisions were united mostly by their common past and by their relative isolation from neighboring counties.

The government recognized early the difficulties of administering so diverse a shire as a single unit. A Henrician statute of 1504 created a system of alternating the sheriff's court between Chichester and Lewes. The traditional meeting of the court at Chichester had been a failure, the statute noted, because:

[Chichester being] in the extreme part of the same shire, the same shire being lxx miles in length, [by reason whereof] diverse and many of the King's subjects inhabiting that shire are sometimes outlawed and sometimes lose great sums of money in that court or before they have knowledge thereof to their utter undoing.[15]

The solution – dividing administrative responsibilities – was also followed informally in the nomination of members of Parliament and in the appointment of lords lieutenant and deputy lieutenants. By the 1590s, every administrative arrangement within local control respected the separation of the shire. Sussex had a single sheriff, one commission of the peace, one Assizes and one jail, but there were two full sets of Quarter Sessions. The Elizabethan Privy Council derided this arrangement as:

a thing so singular to yourselves, as but in your shire only we do not know of the like elsewhere . . . yet you see that within the county of Kent . . . never was such custom among them although the same shire be found both of more length and breadth than yours is.

They could find no justification for the peculiarity beyond the "private respect of a little ease to yourselves by saving travel . . . " However, the system

---

14 BL Additional MS 11,571/118–v; Clive Holmes, "The County Community in Stuart Historiography," *JBS* 19: 2 (Spring, 1980): 54–73, has cogently pointed out the error of classifying residents anywhere as truly parochial. The localism suggested here is relative, not absolute; cf. Holmes, *Seventeenth-Century Lincolnshire*, History of Lincolnshire, 7 (Lincoln, 1980); R. H. Silcock, "County Government in Worcestershire 1603–1660" (Ph.D. dissertation, University of London, 1974); Ann Laura Hughes, "Politics, Society and Civil War in Warwickshire 1620–1650" (Ph.D. dissertation, University of Liverpool, 1979); Keith Wrightson, *English Society 1580–1680* (London, 1982), pp. 39–65, 222–8.
15 19 Henry VII, c. 24; such complaints about Sussex were already longstanding by the early sixteenth century; see Robert C. Palmer, *The County Courts of Medieval England 1150–1350* (Princeton, 1982), pp. 7, 12–13.

did not arise simply from laziness. The Assizes, which visited briefly twice a year, usually convened at East Grinstead, the nearest town to the border of Surrey. Until 1487, the gaol at Guildford (Surrey) was used for prisoners from Sussex, and from the thirteenth century until 1636 (with a brief respite from 1566 to 1572), Surrey and Sussex shared one sheriff. The consensus was that Sussex lacked a natural center; most towns chosen for institutional meetings brought complaints of unfair distance from one corner or another. No single venue met the needs of such an extended and diverse county. Not only magisterial comfort, but also the logic of geography and social structure dictated the split between East and West.[16]

Sussex hosted seven, rather than the usual four, meetings of the Quarter Sessions. During the assigned Sessional weeks for Epiphany, Easter and Michaelmas, one court convened on Mondays and Tuesdays in the western section of the county, and another met on Thursdays and Fridays in the eastern section. The western meetings followed a set geographical rotation; the eastern Sessions were always held at Lewes. In the summer, when the Quarter Sessions normally convened immediately before the Assizes, one tribunal, held at either East Grinstead or Horsham, sufficed for the entire county. Quarter Sessions in the summer dealt primarily with matters involving both of the geographical divisions; most substantive complaints of crime waited for the Assizes or for the meetings of the divisional Sessions in the autumn. Although the single commission of the peace empowered local justices to preside at all meetings (regardless of East–West divisions), almost all magistrates attended only the tribunals closest to their homes. Crossovers in business were even more unusual.[17] By the reign of Elizabeth I, the Quarter Sessions of eastern and western Sussex were effectively independent, and the office of the clerk of the peace was the sole administrative link between the two.

The physical location of the courts in Sussex influenced business as well as personnel. Complaining that double sessions were slow, burdensome, and redundant, the Privy Council pleaded with the justices to work out some compromise:

. . . your resolutions sometimes growing different much time by messages and letters

---

[16] BL Harleian MS 703/16. Kent is not, in fact, longer than Sussex, nor was Sussex the only county unwilling to have a single venue for the Quarter Sessions. With the possible exception of Suffolk, however, no other shire seems to have had an identical system of split responsibility; see Sidney and Beatrice Webb, *The Parish and the County*, English Local Government, 1 (1906; reprint, London, 1963), pp. 425–33.

[17] Sixty-six justices of the peace attended the eastern Quarter Sessions between 1594 and 1640; of these, 56 had permanent homes in the area, 1 moved there later and 3 more were married to women from eastern Sussex. Of 1,442 cases presented to those Quarter Sessions sampled here, 28 list a site in western Sussex as the scene of an alleged crime; 21 defendants and 18 victims appear as residents of western Sussex.

is ofttimes spent before you can well accord . . . it cannot but advance the execution of justice within the shire, when the whole assembly of justices by their authority and presence shall much better both discern and judge of causes, than the one half of them may or can . . .

However, the convenience of local residents took precedence over the convenience of the Privy Council. The justices never attempted a unified scheme of meetings. When the Civil War disrupted the circuit of the Assizes, the county abandoned even its single general meeting in the summer. The Assizes resumed in 1646, but the semblance of unity between the Quarter Sessions did not. The eastern division held Quarter Sessions four times annually in Lewes, and the western justices changed to three yearly meetings rather than join their colleagues in eastern Sussex.[18]

The mud and clay of eastern Sussex, the charcoal burning and the iron-mongering, affected crime and the enforcement of the criminal law in the county. Despite its proximity to London, eastern Sussex was a land of small market towns, not major boroughs; of ancient gentry families, not glittering courtiers; of small-scale self-sufficiency, not large-scale agricultural commerce. It was, at bottom, a land of forest, chalk and marsh, a shire built of mud and iron.

Societies make laws, but individuals recreate those laws by applying or ignoring them. Before considering the decisions that resulted from criminal prosecutions in eastern Sussex, it is necessary to discover which actions regularly inspired prosecutions. What types of illegal behavior did local residents, reacting not only to the law but also to their particular economic and social circumstances, consider threatening enough to label as potentially criminal?

Although this question is basic, its answer can be only an educated speculation, and as such, should be treated skeptically. The dark figure of unreported crime haunts any attempt to measure criminality, but the specter has a particular importance for early modern England, a society without a professional police force, where unreported crime cannot be treated as an unspecified but an exceptional proportion of illegal actions that happened to elude the notice of legal officers.[19] In early modern England, responsibility for

[18] BL Harleian MS 703/16; *Quarter Sessions Order Book 1642–1649*, ed. B. C. Redwood, *SRS* 54 (Lewes, 1954).

[19] The criminological literature on this subject is vast. Some of the most useful recent discussions of the problem by historians are J. M. Beattie, "Judicial Records and the Measurement of Crime in Eighteenth-Century England," in Louis A. Knafla, ed., *Crime and Criminal Justice in Europe and Canada* (Calgary, 1981), pp. 127–45; V. A. C. Gatrell, "The Decline of Theft and Violence in Victorian and Edwardian England," in V. A. C. Gatrell, Bruce Lenman and Geoffrey Parker, eds., *Crime and the Law: The Social History of Crime in Western Europe since 1500* (London, 1980), pp. 238–370; Douglas Hay, "War, Dearth and Theft in the Eighteenth Century: The Record of the English Courts," *P & P* 95 (May 1982): 117–60.

prosecution in serious crime rested with the victim; if the accuser lost interest in prosecution, a conviction, even an indictment, was unlikely. Because the prosecution of alleged crimes was expensive, inconvenient and not particularly restitutive, some victims dropped their accusations well before the cases came to court. Because the formal categorizations of crimes and the punishments allotted to them were so harsh, some victims sought justice through extra-legal means. And, because the informal settlement of disputes was both acceptable and often mutually beneficial, many victims and suspects resolved their conflicts without any use of formal processes. As a result, the modern assumption that prosecutions reveal the outline, if not the extent, of illegal behavior, cannot be applied to the early modern era. In the sixteenth and seventeenth centuries, unreported acts – the ones that remained unsolved and the ones that found alternative resolutions – probably outnumbered reported acts in most categories of illegal behavior. Prosecuted cases may distort rather than reflect normal circumstances. An analysis of the business of the courts, therefore, must be presented cautiously, noting patterns within the evidence available, citing contrasts with other times and places, but never thoroughly equating numbers drawn from institutional records with reality.

The eighty-seven courts sampled for eastern Sussex between the years 1592 and 1640 include reports of 1,631 alleged crimes.[20] The rate of reported crime in the area was neither exceptionally high nor low; the accusations generally parallel patterns uncovered elsewhere.[21] Table 2.1 specifies the known complaints in eastern Sussex and shows that the most common problem brought to the courts was theft. Accusations of grand or petty larceny, as

[20] This includes both charges that later became indictments (1,429) and those later dismissed by grand juries (202); it is a reflection of allegations not of convictions and undoubtedly measures concerns about crime more than crime itself.

[21] The computation of rates of crime is inappropriate for two reasons. First, neither the demographic nor the judicial statistics are precise enough to make such measurements realistic. Secondly, the notion of a rate of crime suggests some level of crime universally identifiable as high or low, serious or manageable, when in fact such judgments cannot be divorced from their social context. In the early decades of the seventeenth century, about 40,000 people lived in eastern Sussex. The courts sampled here produced an average of 16 indictments per court between 1592 and 1618 and an average of 17 indictments per court between 1623 and 1640. This seems relatively high compared with Essex, which with a population of around 100,000 averaged 24 indictments per session between 1620 and 1639, but relatively low compared with Hertfordshire, where with a population of slightly more than 50,000 in 1603 the mean total of defendants indicted per year was 52 in the Assizes between 1583 and 1624, and 38 in the Quarter Sessions, 1591–1618. Brent, "Devastating Epidemic"; Lawson, pp. 16–20, 88–94, 214; Sharpe, *Essex*, pp. 13, 15, 183. The figures for Hertfordshire are inflated to some degree because Lawson has aggregated defendants rather than crimes. Using only indictments in the Assizes and working from dramatically different conclusions about population, Cockburn reveals a complementary pattern: see J. S. Cockburn, "The Nature and Incidence of Crime in England 1559–1625: A Preliminary Survey," in *Crime in England*, pp. 52–4. Cockburn's figures on population are derived from the Elizabethan muster returns and are uniformly lower than those cited here.

Table 2.1. *Reported crime in eastern Sussex*

Crimes		Complaints	% of total crimes
Theft		768	47
Grand larceny	361		
Petty larceny	251		
*Burglary	67		
*Horse theft	56		
†Breaking and entering	15		
*Highway robbery	10		
*Cutpursing	8		
Offenses against the communal peace		387	24
Unlicensed alehouses	62		
Unlicensed cottages	58		
Unapprenticed trading	57		
Neglect of roads, etc.	43		
Official negligence	43		
Defaulted taxes	24		
Illegal sales	19		
Encroaching	18		
††Other	63		
Disorderly offenses		375	23
Assault	226		
Riot, ill. assembly	47		
Trespass	43		
Hunting	37		
Forced entry	22		
Violent death		79	5
Felonious killing	33		
*Murder	31		
*Infanticide	15		
Miscellaneous felonies		22	1
*Witchcraft	10		
Bigamy	4		
*Rape	3		
*Buggery	2		
Coining	2		
*Arson	1		
Total		1,631	100

*Offenses for which benefit of clergy could *not* be pleaded
†After 1597, breaking and entering a dwelling house, day or night, and stealing goods valued at 5 shillings or more became a crime for which benefit of clergy could not be pleaded.
††Other includes less than ten complaints each of vagrancy, harboring recusants, shooting a gun in public, taking inmates, seditious words, leaving service, barratry, breach of contract, extortion, disorderly alehouse, fraud, perjury, desertion, drunkenness, professional negligence, forgery and rescue.

Table 2.2.* *Thefts, homicides and disorderly offenses:*
Essex, Hertfordshire and eastern Sussex

Crimes	Essex 1620–39 %	Hertfordshire 1591–1618 %	Eastern Sussex 1592–1640 %
Nonclergyable thefts	16	22	14
Other thefts	63	44	48
Violent deaths	5	3	7
Disorderly offenses	16	††31	31
Total	100	100	100
No.	†1,759 crimes	†1,381 defendants	†1,049 crimes

*Appendix 1, p. 207 below, is a summary of the courts sampled in eastern Sussex. For Essex, see Sharpe, *Essex*, p. 183 (Sharpe's table does not differentiate other forms of larceny), for Herfrodshire, see Lawson, ch. 7. Since each study uses different data and sampling techniques, all comparisons are approximations. The comparison between Sussex and Essex seems to hold also for the 1590s; see Samaha, *Law and Order*, pp. 19–20; see also Cockburn, "The Nature and Incidence of Crime," p. 55.
†The totals here exclude allegations rejected by grand juries as unindictable.
††This is a slight underestimate because Lawson provides a percentage but no exact numbers concerning poaching. His figure of 1.7 percent for such defendants fits the general pattern sketched above; the comparable percentages would be 1.6 in Essex and 3.5 in eastern Sussex.

well as more infrequent charges of burglary, breaking and entering or high-way robbery, accounted for almost half of all reported suspicions. Allegations of disorderly conduct and of offenses against the numerous statutes intended to regulate social and economic life dominated the remainder of the agendas. Complaints of homicides or other felonies were far less frequent, making up just slightly more than one in every twenty accusations.

But the allegations made in eastern Sussex are not identical to those made in other counties, and the deviations reflect the contemporary image of the area as both unruly and impenetrable. The allegations prosecuted before the courts suggest that the inhabitants of eastern Sussex may have been more violent, less concerned about moral reformation and less likely to report thefts than residents elsewhere in England. The pattern of accusations reveals a fairly prosperous region with less larceny than other prosperous regions, a parochial region with more commercial development than other parochial regions, and a puritanical region with less reforming zeal than other puritanical regions.

The accuracy of the Privy Councillors' concerns about the "rudeness and wilfulness" of the inhabitants of eastern Sussex seems to be confirmed by the relative prominence of violent crimes in the agendas of the Assizes and the Quarter Sessions. As Table 2.2 indicates, accusations of assault, trespass, riot and forced entry accounted for a larger proportion of the business of the courts in eastern Sussex than in Essex. And, although neither the demographic statistics nor the judicial records are full enough to allow the accurate computation of rates of homicide, the relative importance of violent deaths among the reported crimes is equally apparent. J. A. Sharpe's comparison of indictments from Sussex, Essex, Hertfordshire, Middlesex and Cheshire shows that in the seventeenth century only the courts in Cheshire spent significantly more time than the courts in eastern Sussex on allegations of violent deaths.[22] Reported homicides in eastern Sussex were more common than elsewhere, and also more brutal. Compared with seventeenth-century Essex, alleged killers in eastern Sussex were exceptionally fond of knives and blunt instruments. But such deaths were not more often visited upon kin; in eastern Sussex between 8 and 13 percent of all accusations of homicide involved a death within the family while in Essex between 13 and 25 percent of the known deaths were familial. J. S. Cockburn has suggested that in the late sixteenth and early seventeenth centuries, between 13 and 18 percent of the homicides in Essex, Hertfordshire and Sussex arose from disputes within families; by that measure, eastern Sussex clearly was atypical.[23]

This apparent propensity for violence is difficult to explain without invoking contemporary stereotypes, for certainly the economic and social changes occurring in eastern Sussex differed in degree rather than in kind from those happening elsewhere in the Southeast. Norden's observation that inhabitants of the forest were more uncivil than other people may have had some merit, but the pattern of accusations in eastern Sussex follows demographic and economic tensions as well as topography. Most charges of murder or felonious killing originated in the heavily populated Weald, but the parishes around the largest towns (Lewes, Brighton and the smaller centers of

---

[22] J. A. Sharpe, *Crime in Early Modern England*, p. 55. If the comparison is restricted to the period before 1640, Sussex shows a higher proportion of complaints of violent death than does Essex: Sharpe, *Essex*, p. 183.

[23] The higher figures include servants as members of the family; the lower figures exclude servants; J. A. Sharpe, "Domestic Homicide in Early Modern England," *HJ* 24 (1981): 34 (where the period under study is 1560 to 1659); cf. Sharpe, *Essex*, pp. 126–9; Cockburn, "Nature and Incidence of Crime," pp. 55–7. Cockburn also points out that, in contrast to Sussex, such deaths in Essex frequently involved killing children, step-children, or servants. See also Lawrence Stone, "Interpersonal Violence in English Society 1300–1980," *P & P* 101 (November, 1983): 27, where Stone estimates that, throughout England in the late sixteenth and early seventeenth centuries, between 15 and 20 percent of homicides originated within the biological family.

Battle and Eastbourne) also stand out as frequent sites of violent death.[24] The Weald and the urban areas were also prominent in allegations of less serious violence and disorder, but surprisingly several hundreds in the downlands or the marshlands appear frequently as well. In these less populated areas, competition over land, rather than close contact with other people, may have inspired complaints.[25] The strains of economic pressure show also in accusations of infanticide; two-thirds of these charges alleged crimes in or adjacent to one of the ten local parishes licensed to have a poor house.[26]

Despite the possible role of economic tensions in encouraging physical violence, the residents of eastern Sussex reported relatively fewer thefts than did their counterparts elsewhere. To be sure, crimes against property made up the bulk of judicial business, as they seem to have done throughout the country but, both as a group and in most specific categories, reports of theft were less prominent in eastern Sussex than elsewhere. Compared with Essex or Hertfordshire, neither the number of highway robberies reported in eastern Sussex nor the value of goods lost in such circumstances was impressive. Complaints of cutpursings were similarly rare. Even the number of complaints of breaking and burglary was relatively small in eastern Sussex. The residents of Lewes and Brighton reported only two break-ins and one burglary to the courts sampled between 1592 and 1640; 40 percent of the more rural hundreds in the region seem to have been entirely innocent of such intrusions. Among the crimes against property considered to be particularly heinous by the government, only the theft of horses seems to have been as much of a problem in eastern Sussex as it was elsewhere.[27]

[24] Of the 61 violent deaths of adults where a site of death is known, 57 percent occurred in rural wealden parishes, 10 percent in rural parishes in the downlands and the remainder in rural regions of mixed topography. Sixteen percent of the deaths took place in Lewes, Brighton, Battle or Eastbourne, although it is worth noting that in the local capital of Lewes, only a single death was judged deliberate.

[25] The scenes of 319 alleged disorders are known; 44 percent of the assaults and 54 percent of the trespasses, riots and forced entries occurred in the rural Weald; 17 percent of the assaults and 11 percent of the other disorders occurred in parishes with an urban center; 11 percent of the assaults and 5 percent of the other disorders occurred in rural parishes in the Downs; 1 percent of the assaults and 8 percent of the other disorders occurred in the two hundreds made up of marshland parishes. The remainder of the alleged disorders occurred in western Sussex, or in parishes of mixed topography. The rural hundreds of Longbridge and Holmestrow (in or near the Downs), and of Goldspur (in the marshlands) each accounted for more than 5 percent of the known disorders.

[26] The reported infanticides (with the parishes of the nearest poor houses following in parentheses) allegedly occurred in Wivelsfield (Chailey), Lindfield (2) (Chailey), Rottingdean (Iford), Barcombe (Chailey and Newick), Cliffe (Ringmer), Glynde (Ringmer), Ringmer (Ringmer), Mayfield (Waldron), Brightling (Penhurst), Bodiam (Sedlescombe). Infanticides were also reported from Eastbourne, Hailsham, Ticehurst and Hartfield, each more than one parish away from a licensed poor house. The poor houses are listed in Brent, "Employment," pp. 248–9.

[27] Among indicted thefts in eastern Sussex between 1592 and 1640, 9 percent were burglaries,

Since the bad roads could promise trouble for a thief who needed to dis-appear quickly with large amounts of property, geography may partly explain the relative freedom of eastern Sussex from aggravated thefts.[28] The relative infrequency of complaints of simple theft, however, is more puzzling. Perhaps such immunity simply meant that there was less to steal in the eastern rapes than in other places, or perhaps fewer persons in eastern Sussex needed to steal to meet their economic needs. But, although eastern Sussex was not famous for its affluence, the contributions of local residents to subsidies and other taxes belie any suggestion of generalized poverty.

The apparent infrequency of theft in eastern Sussex might indicate that the records themselves are deceptive, that eastern Sussex differed from other places less in its relative wealth or poverty than in the tenor of its social relations. The fact that the pattern of accusations follows the density of neither settlement nor wealth supports this notion.[29] So, too, does the rare-ness with which complaints associated with the tensions of inhospitality (arson, witchcraft, taking inmates and rioting over food) appeared on judicial agendas in eastern Sussex.[30] Thefts of small amounts of property valuable for

7 percent were horse thefts, 2 percent were breaking and entering, 1 percent were highway robberies and 1 percent were cutpursings. In Essex 1620–39 the comparable figures were 10 percent burglaries, 5 percent horse thefts, 3 percent breaking and entering, 1 percent each for highway robberies and cutpursings. In Hertfordshire, among persons indicted for thefts, there were 15 percent burglaries, 7 percent horse thefts, 7 percent highway robberies and 4 percent cutpursings. Lawson, pp. 257–75; Sharpe, *Essex*, pp. 91–114, 183; Sharpe, *Crime in Early Modern England*, p. 55; cf. Cockburn, "The Nature and Incidence of Crime," pp. 55, 64–6.

[28] Cockburn shows 9 highway robberies indicted and allegedly committed in Kent by men from eastern Sussex, but no highway robberies indicted in Sussex allegedly committed there by men from other southeastern counties. Although dates of crimes taken from indictments are not completely trustworthy, it is interesting that most of these robberies in Kent allegedly occurred between October and April while most of the robberies in Sussex by allegedly local residents seem to have occurred between May and September, when the roads were more passable: Cockburn, *Calendar: Kent, Elizabeth I*, entries 48, 409, 587, 661, 1359, 1440, 1469; *Calendar: Kent, James I*, entries 245, 414.

[29] In fact, most sorts of thefts were reported from a variety of regions in the eastern rapes. Accusations of the theft of any category of goods can be found in at least 40 percent of the hundreds in eastern Sussex and, since these figures exclude burglaries, the dispersal for items aside from livestock was in reality even higher. Only one hundred, Portslade, which probably had a population of less than 50 families, reported no larcenies or burglaries.

[30] Table 2.1 above, p. 27 (all of the complaints in these categories became indictments). Arson was also relatively uncommon in other counties. Prosecutions for witchcraft vary, but fewer cases were tried in Sussex than anywhere else on the southeastern circuit of the Assizes. On the social implications of these crimes, see Keith Thomas, *Religion and the Decline of Magic* (New York, 1971), pp. 502–69. On their frequency, Sharpe, *Crime in Early Modern England*, p. 55; Sharpe, *Essex*, pp. 159–67. Virtually all of the known riots in eastern Sussex concerned private arguments rather than protests over food; see Fletcher, *Sussex*, pp. 147–52; Brent, "Employment," pp. 277–9; *APC 1596*, pp. 202, 227; cf. John Walter and Keith Wrightson, "Dearth and the Social Order in Early Modern England," *P & P* 71 (May, 1976): 22–42; Peter Clark, "Popular Protest and Disturbance in Kent 1558–1640," *EcHR*, 2nd series, 29 (1976): 365–81.

use but probably not for resale were ubiquitous in the area. Most villages seem to have had not only local pilferers but also many residents who when necessary supplemented their incomes from the goods of their neighbors. But larceny, more than any other illegal activity, became a crime only if the victim chose to make it one. No external inquisitions were involved as in suspicions of homicides; no official negligence was risked as in offenses against the regulatory statutes. Suspicions of larceny could be settled without formal prosecution much more easily and satisfactorily than other sorts of crimes. In fact, such informal settlements could afford important opportunities for displays of noblesse oblige and deference.[31] It would be foolhardy to try to explain one negative phenomenon, the relative absence of prosecutions for thefts in eastern Sussex, with another negative phenomenon, the relative absence of economic polarization, but eastern Sussex does seem to have had a more stable economy than either Essex or Hertfordshire and one with gentler extremes of either wealth or poverty. Combined with a less transient genteel population than in these other counties, the economic situation may have encouraged a social structure headed by men who clung to ideals of communal responsibility and who felt that public prosecutions offered no advantage over private settlements.[32]

The single detailed local accusation concerning witchcraft in eastern Sussex reinforces the suggestion that economic tensions in the area differed from those in surrounding counties. David Fairman had only recently settled in the parish of Dallington when he accused three of his neighbors (John Rolfe, Richard Lowle and Alice Lowle) of using witchcraft to poison his animals. Rolfe and Fairman had fallen out in a dispute over the boundaries to their respective properties. Richard Lowle had argued with Fairman over a similar matter and Alice Lowle, Richard's wife, had accused Fairman first of overcharging the Lowles for the loan of a horse and later of deliberately letting his pigs trespass on their property. Fairman contended that the antagonism between the families was exacerbated by Lowle's envy that, despite their equal assessments for the subsidy, Fairman had more cattle. The hostile and competitive relationship between Fairman and his neighbors blossomed into accusations when his animals began to die without apparent cause. While Fairman's complaints are similar in many ways to the cases studied in Essex

---

[31] The fullest discussion of these possibilities is Douglas Hay, "Property, Authority and the Criminal Law," in Douglas Hay *et al.*, eds., *Albion's Fatal Tree*, pp. 17–63; see also Rhys Isaac, *The Transformation of Virginia* (Chapel Hill, 1982), "A Discourse on the Method," pp. 323–57.

[32] This suggestion is reinforced by the relative lack of prominence of the upper classes as victims of theft; gentry prosecuted less than one quarter of the alleged crimes in every sort of larceny where the status of the victim is known (668 crimes), and larcenies listing either gentry or yeomen as victims accounted for less than half of the accusations of thefts.

by Alan Macfarlane and Keith Thomas, the accusations are unusual because the accuser and accused were not exceptionally mismatched in terms of power. In eastern Sussex the rare accusations of witchcraft stand out because of the prominence of male defendants and because of the economic and social parity of the accused and the accuser. The charges seem to express ongoing competition rather than guilt or anger born of spurned hospitality, and, as such, they seem of a kind with accusations of trespass, unlicensed alehouses, or trading without an apprenticeship. Perhaps this explains why Rolfe, Lowle and Lowle were tried at the Quarter Sessions rather than at the Assizes, and why complaints of witchcraft in the shire so very rarely ended with convictions.[33]

The apparent combination of a relative reluctance to use the courts against the local poor with a relative willingness to use them against near equals shows up in complaints over offenses against the regulatory statutes as well as in more serious matters. Table 2.3 compares accusations for various offenses against the communal peace in eastern Sussex, Hertfordshire and Essex. The differences are striking. Eastern Sussex was home to many intensely religious men and women, but the agendas of the Assizes and Quarter Sessions reveal a smaller percentage of accusations of "immoral" behavior than in other places. The litany of offenses identified in other counties with upright conduct (e.g. complaints about drunkenness, disorderly alehouses, gaming, swearing and violations of the Sabbath) produced almost no prosecutions in eastern Sussex. In contrast not only to Essex and Hertfordshire, but also to Lancashire, Cheshire and Wiltshire, residents of eastern Sussex were noticeably unwilling to complain in court about such behaviors.[34] Table 2.3 also suggests that residents of eastern Sussex were

---

[33] ESRO Q/R/E 18/26–7, 28, 31, 59–60; 28/12. Ten years later Fairman accused Rolfe of trespass; the grand jury dismissed the charge as unfounded; cf. Thomas, *Religion*, pp. 502–69; Alan Macfarlane, *Witchcraft in Tudor and Stuart England*. For a provocative alternative explanation of witchcraft prosecutions, see Christina Larner, *Enemies of God: The Witchhunt in Scotland* (London, 1981). The sampled courts in eastern Sussex reveal accusations against 5 persons as witches, all of whom (2 men listed as husbandmen and 3 women listed as wives) were acquitted. The Assizes contain accusations against 2 more persons between 1590 and 1640 (a spinster, and a chandler). The chandler was acquitted; the spinster was convicted, but reprieved.

[34] The best discussion of the meaning of these offenses and their prosecution is Keith Wrightson, "The Puritan Reformation of Manners with Special Reference to the Counties of Lancashire and Essex 1640–1660" (Ph.D. dissertation, Cambridge University, 1974). While in eastern Sussex accusations of drunkenness, disorderly alehouses and other similar offenses against morality, excluding the unlicensed keeping of alehouses, never made up even 1 percent of known business, such accusations accounted for about 2 or 3 percent of known business in the Quarter Sessions in the other shires cited. The comparisons are not exact since the information available differs in different counties; Keith Wrightson, "Two Concepts of Order: Justices, Constables and Jurymen in Seventeenth-century England," in Brewer and Styles, eds., *Ungovernable People*, p. 300; M. J. Ingram, "Communities and Courts: Law and Dis-

Table 2.3.* *Offenses against the communal peace:*
Essex, Hertfordshire and eastern Sussex

Offenses	Essex 1620–39 %	Hertfordshire 1591–1618 %	Eastern Sussex 1592–1640 %
Drunkenness	4	5	1
Disorderly alehouses	6	42	1
Vagrancy	—	3	3
Unlicensed cottages	21	7	15
Taking inmates	7	†	1
Unlicensed alehouses	26	†	15
Illegal sales	6	10	5
Unapprenticed trading	8	†	13
Roads, bridges	9	28	12
††Other	13	5	34
Total	100	†100	100
No.	500 offenses	1,022 defendants	359 offenses

*Sharpe, *Essex*, pp. 39–56, 183; Lawson, pp. 220, 245–52.
†Lawson combines disorderly alehouses and unlicensed alehouses in a single category, unlicensed cottages and taking inmates in a single category, illegal sales and unapprenticed trading in a single category. He also combines prosecutions for the care of bridges and highways or for their obstruction with prosecutions for official misconduct.
††Other for Essex includes a category of community offenses (30) and of official misconduct (34). For eastern Sussex, it includes official negligence (40) plus the offenses listed as 'other' in Table 2.1 and not specified above. For Hertfordshire, it includes 47 defendants prosecuted for bastardy, bigamy, buggery, desertion, illegal gaming, swearing, or profaning the Sabbath.

relatively uninterested in formal action against vagrancy, the erection of unlicensed cottages, or the taking of inmates illegally. A concerted effort was made to suppress unlicensed alehouses, but the campaign lacked the intensity that accompanied it elsewhere. The regulatory offenses that produced business for the courts in eastern Sussex were those that directly concerned economic opportunity as well as morality. The battle over licenses for alehouses, for example, had economic as well as moral implications; fewer licenses reduced competition for those that had them. Economic jealousies

order in Early Seventeenth-Century Wiltshire," in *Crime in England*, p. 112; T. C. Curtis, "Some Aspects of the History of Crime in Seventeenth-Century England with Special Reference to Cheshire and Middlesex" (Ph.D. dissertation, Manchester University, 1973), pp. 56–70; Morrill, *Grand Jury*, pp. 27–9.

may also explain the high level of local complaints against persons for practicing a trade without apprenticeship; the percentage of indictments for such offenses in eastern Sussex was half as high again as it was in Essex. Conceivably, eastern Sussex simply had less immorality than other counties and more illegal economic activity, but more probably the divergence suggests differing priorities among the local populations. Regulatory enforcement in eastern Sussex focused on restricting economic competition, a goal reminiscent of the tensions that David Fairman imagined made him the target of sorcery. The disciplining of the poor, like their punishment before the courts for theft, seems to have been something considered better left to other forums.[35]

The pattern of reported accusations in eastern Sussex seems a mixture of features that scholars have usually associated with different regions of early modern England. In some ways, eastern Sussex resembles northern rural shires. As in Cheshire, complaints of violence played a prominent role in the business of the courts. As in both Lancashire and Cheshire, prosecutions linked to moral reformation took second place to mundane problems such as the passability of local roads.[36] These common features make sense: eastern Sussex, like Cheshire and Lancashire, was a rural county, relatively isolated from the capital by heavy woodlands and muddy roads. Moreover, each area boasted a relatively small, tightly knit hierarchy of landed gentry for whom loyalties of family and friendship were as important as the demands of politics and religion. However, eastern Sussex was not a northern county stranded on the southern coast. Like Essex and Hertfordshire, the local economy was influenced increasingly by the demands of London and European markets. Like the Home Counties, local fortunes grew by mixing the profits of agriculture and industry. And, as in all these counties, many residents found in puritanism an ideology well suited to both their self-righteousness and their insecurities. The reported crimes in eastern Sussex reveal a mix not simply of the geography, economy and social structure, but also of the idiosyncrasies that make the culture of any area its own.

Since eastern Sussex contained discrete economic and geographical regions, it is not surprising that the pattern of accusations differed by region within the shire. The level of reported complaints largely followed the density of population, but the type of charges generally mirrored local economic con-

---

[35] The relatively high number of complaints in eastern Sussex for official negligence in criminal matters (11 percent of the offenses against the communal peace compared with only 6 percent in Essex) further confirms this impression.

[36] Twelve percent of the indictments in the Lancashire Quarter Sessions 1626–40 concerned the state of the local roads; in Cheshire this accounted for 4 percent of indictments and recognizances before the court 1610–19, and concern over the problem continued into at least the middle years of the century; Wrightson, "Two Concepts of Order," p. 300; Curtis, "History of Crime," pp. 56–70; Morrill, *Grand Jury*, p. 27.

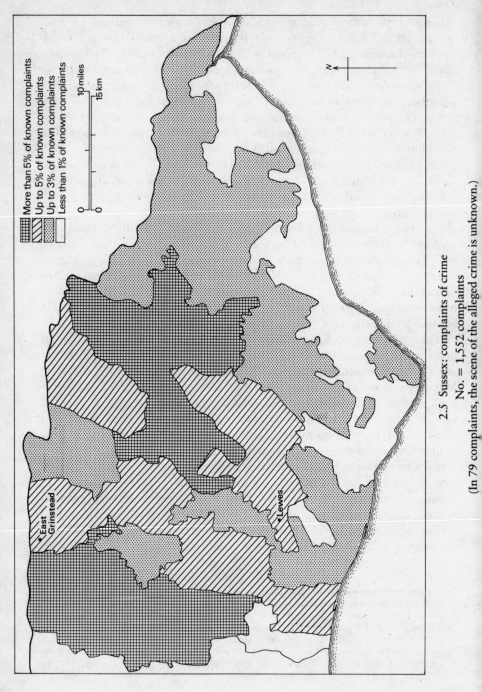

2.5 Sussex: complaints of crime
No. = 1,552 complaints
(In 79 complaints, the scene of the alleged crime is unknown.)

Legend:
- More than 5% of known complaints
- Up to 5% of known complaints
- Up to 3% of known complaints
- Less than 1% of known complaints

10 miles
15 km

East Grinstead
Lewes

N

Table 2.4.* *A comparison of reported accusations within eastern Sussex*

Category of crime	Ticehurst (Weald) %	Holmestrow (Downland) %	Bexhill (Marshland) %	Lewes (Urban) %
Violent death	5	—	9	6
Theft	52	7	73	28
Disorderly offenses	29	48	—	31
Anti-community offenses	9	17	—	6
†Economic offenses	5	28	18	27
Other	—	—	—	2
Total	100	100	100	100
No. of accusations	21	29	11	51
Area (sq. miles)	13	about 11	11	—
Approx. pop.	365 (in 1635)	365+ (in 1603)	374 (in 1603)	1,500–2,000 (in 1625)

*Because of the difficulty of finding a rural parish in the downlands with any significant number of accusations, a hundred roughly equal in area to the other parishes sampled was chosen. For Holmestrow and Bexhill population figures were computed from the 1603 ecclesiastical survey of adults, using a multiplier of 1.66. The Holmestrow figure is an underestimate since no contemporary statistics are available for the small parish of Southease or the port of Newhaven: "Ecclesiastical Returns for 81 Parishes in East Sussex made in 1603," ed. Walter C. Renshaw, *SRS* 4 (Lewes, 1905): 1–17. The population of Ticehurst relies upon figures published with a 1635 list of 135 householders: "Ticehurst Parishioners in 1635", *Sussex Genealogist and Family Historian* 4 (March 1983): 137–8. The Lewes figures rely on Fletcher, *Sussex*, p. 9, and Farrant and Farrant, "Brighton," p. 333. For the areas of parishes, see Brent, "Employment," pp. 63–6.
†Illegal practice of trades, illegal sales of grain or ale, unlicensed alehouses, breach of contract, and leaving a master's service. All other categories as in Table 2.1.

ditions as well. As Figure 2.5 shows, the parishes most frequently cited as scenes of alleged crimes were the most populous: those of the urban areas, the region between the downlands and the Weald and the Weald itself. Indeed, about half of the parishes in the less populated downlands and marshlands produced less than 1 percent each of the business of the courts. Table 2.4 adds further texture to these distinctions by contrasting the reported crimes in four areas representing the major economic regions of the shire. Although the sample undoubtedly simplifies the situation, the contrasts are clear. The wealden parish of Ticehurst, where the economy was fairly expansive, produced more complaints of theft than of violence and disorder while the southern parishes where the economic opportunities were more limited

(Holmestrow and Lewes) did just the opposite. The distinction holds in regulatory matters also; residents of Ticehurst provided the court with more complaints of anti-community offenses such as misuse of roads and commons while residents of Holmestrow and Lewes showed greater concern over economic offenses such as unlicensed alehouses and illegal trading. Despite the perennial sameness of crime, accusations did and do reflect specific social circumstances.

Criminal accusations were no more constant over time than over space; they fluctuated with changes in levels of crime, efficiency of enforcement, attitudes towards the law, economic circumstances and individual behavior. However, scholars have detected a national pattern in complaints of felony and petty larceny and eastern Sussex generally conforms to this model.[37] Historians agree that a variety of influences contribute to any change in criminal complaints but, not surprisingly, prosecutions for theft seem to have been particularly sensitive to fluctuations in the price of grain and to opportunities for employment. Consequently, the generally harsh years between 1590 and 1630 stand out as a period with high levels of prosecution. The 1590s and the 1620s, decades of high prices, unemployment and military demobilization, were particularly tense. It is less easily explicable, but a similar trend is apparent in alleged homicides. Although prosecutions in eastern Sussex for thefts and homicides fit the national pattern, since they range only from a high of twelve complaints per court in the 1590s to a low of nine complaints per court in the 1610s and 1630s, the shifts were fairly gentle. This relative stability may be an illusion caused by the small number of records extant for the region but, because the area was less vulnerable than others to vicissitudes in the prices of wheat and textiles, eastern Sussex may actually have been less likely to produce drastic highs and lows in prosecutions.

Figure 2.6 summarizes how the pattern of specific accusations in eastern Sussex shifted between the 1590s and the 1630s. The absence of extensive consecutive runs of records makes impossible any attempt to trace changes year to year or to estimate specifically the impact of prices or possibilities for employment. It is clear, however, that the business of the courts in eastern Sussex in the 1630s was very different from what it had been in the 1590s. The number of both thefts and homicides decreased; the number of disorderly offenses and violations of the regulatory statutes increased dramatically. The records suggest a shift away from prosecutions in long-established categories of crime and towards prosecutions in more recently determined areas of regulation. To some extent such changes were simply a

---

[37] Sharpe, *Crime in Early Modern England* is the most comprehensive survey, but see also Silcock, "Worcestershire," p. 112; Lawson, pp. 96–101, 179–87.

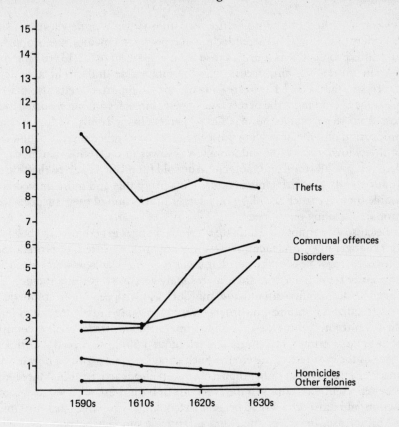

2.6 Eastern Sussex: average number of complaints per court meeting from 1590s to 1630s

response to external pressures. Even in eastern Sussex, the 1590s were years when bad harvests, high prices and unemployment encouraged both a rise in felonies and a rise in prosecutions. Complaints in the 1620s and the 1630s reflected not only local concerns but also those of Westminster; the governors in the capital encouraged, indeed demanded, that judicial officers give greater attention to regulatory matters. However, the shifts outline local as well as national priorities; they suggest tensions that seem to have made life in eastern Sussex increasingly disruptive.

Although these strains can be detected in the dramatic rise in prosecutions for offenses against the communal peace, they are clearest in categories of crime that received less attention from the central government. Reports of assaults, trespasses and land disputes rose sharply in the 1620s and 1630s, suggesting either a new intolerance for minor violence or new levels of such disorders. Despite the general decline in reported homicides, the proportion of deaths prosecuted as murders rose from 47 percent in the 1590s to 85 percent in the 1630s, and accusations for infanticide underwent a similarly impressive increase.[38] The decreasing number of reported thefts also masked a change of emphasis; the percentage of petty larcenies among reported thefts rose from 16 percent in the 1590s to 42 percent in the 1630s.[39] Moreover, the proportion of thefts involving food and tools was higher and the proportion of thefts involving cattle and money was lower in the 1630s than in earlier decades.[40] While food and tools could be sold for profit, reported thefts in the 1630s clearly favored items that were less profitable and more immediately usable than in earlier decades; some larger proportion of these suspects were probably stealing out of need.

Because we cannot discriminate between changes in actual illegal behavior and changes in enforcement, these shifts are open to several interpretations. However, regardless of the peculiar severity of the 1590s, it seems clear that accusations for behavior often associated with poverty (infanticide, food theft), with brutality (infanticide, murder) and with economic competitiveness (regulatory statutes, disorders) were increasing in the early decades of the seventeenth century. At the same time, behavior traditionally identified with serious criminality (burglary, felonious killing) occupied a shrinking place in the business of the courts. Such changes could signify a new intolerance of certain crimes rather than a change in illegal activity, but, more likely, they represent alterations in the behavior of both those who would become victims and those who would become defendants. Economic hardships might have increased levels of theft and infanticide among the poor as well as

[38] Infanticides as a proportion of violent deaths increased from 14 percent in the 1590s to 18 percent in the 1610s, 21 percent in the 1620s and 32 percent in the 1630s. Jacobean legislation increasing scrutiny of concealed births (21 James I, c. 27) may account for some of this change, but in that case one would expect also a lower conviction rate whereas the rate remained constant. More likely, an actual rise in infanticide accusations was part of the inspiration for the law. See Peter C. Hoffer and N. E. H. Hull, *Murdering Mothers: Infanticide in England and New England 1558–1803* (New York, 1981), *passim*; Keith Wrightson, "Infanticide in Earlier Seventeenth-Century England," *LPS* 15 (Autumn, 1975): 10–22.

[39] The rise in petty thefts was steady throughout the period and was matched by an equally steady decline in accusations for grand larceny. Reports of burglary and highway robbery, generally more professional crimes, were more irregular, accounting for 11 percent of thefts in the 1590s, 6 percent in the 1610s, 15 percent in the 1620s and 7 percent in the 1630s.

[40] The rise in thefts of food and tools and the decline in thefts of cattle were all steady throughout the period; trends in the theft of money were irregular, peaking in the 1620s along with burglaries. The decades with the highest proportions of accusations for different types of items stolen were as follows: clothing and cattle in the 1590s; household items, sheep and horses in the 1610s; money, finished cloth and miscellaneous items in the 1620s; food and small tools in the 1630s.

increasing prosecutions for disorder among the more established. The strains and polarization traced for these years in counties such as Essex seem muted in eastern Sussex, but present nonetheless.[41] Economic expansion in the area had certain natural limits, and by the middle decades of the seventeenth century these limits were being reached.

Similar tensions, however, do not always produce similar responses. The "rudeness and wilfulness" that so concerned the Privy Council in the 1580s was still apparent in the 1630s, but there is relatively little evidence of a generalized fear of the meaner sort or of a sustained enthusiasm for inculcating the poor with proper discipline. A distinctive combination of influences created the pattern of prosecutions in eastern Sussex and it also allowed a distinctive response to the pressures of political, social and economic change.

[41] See Wrightson and Levine, *Poverty and Piety in an English Village, passim*; Hunt, *The Puritan Moment, passim*.

3

Judicial power and cooperation in eastern Sussex

Since only what had to be preserved in writing can be used to reconstruct legal experiences in the past, the business of the courtroom shapes our perceptions of the application of the criminal law. The historian must grapple simultaneously with criminal allegations and with the priorities of those who recorded them. And, because the routines of the courtroom reinforced legal categories, the conventions of this central arena illuminate the more shadowy processes influencing definitions of law and crime.

In early modern England, the two basic forums for criminal, or crown, indictments were the Assizes and Quarter Sessions. The Assizes met semi-annually (during vacations between law terms at Lent and Summer) at the northern edge of the shire. Their brief appearances brought to Sussex the strength and influence of the central courts. The two judges of the Assizes were normally men who presided over the courts of common law in Westminster. These professionals, armed with commissions of *oyer et terminer* and gaol delivery, heard and tried all varieties of criminal complaints and were also authorized to hear litigation. During the period covered by their commissions, the judges on circuit could consider virtually any problem. Only these two men possessed the power to hear both crown and common pleas.[1]

The Quarter Sessions met four times annually (Epiphany, Easter, Trinity, and Michaelmas) at dates breaking the intervals between Assizes. The government chose local gentlemen annually to be justices of the peace, and these magistrates presided over the Quarter Sessions. Local standing, not legal expertise, qualified men as justices. Their charge was the maintenance of quiet rather than simply the punishment of criminals. The magistrates heard criminal complaints, but they also dealt with economic regulations and with many ill-defined, but pressing, problems of local life. Theoretically, the Sessions could punish any breach of the peace, but the Assizes heard the

---

[1] Cockburn, *Assizes* and Cockburn, *Introduction* are the best sources for the Assizes; the best sources for the Quarter Sessions are still Lambard, *Eirenarcha* and Dalton, *Countrey Justice*. See also *Quarter Sessions Order Book*, ed. Redwood, pp. vii–xxxiii.

prosecutions of most sorts of dangerous felony – murder, burglary, highway robbery – and the Sessions were a clearinghouse for the more minor troubles affecting daily life – trespasses, assaults, licenses for alehouses or cottages. Both courts shared jurisdiction over theft, the most ubiquitous criminal problem in the county.

Although other formal outlets for prosecuting crime were available, these two tribunals handled almost all of the criminal business in eastern Sussex. The ecclesiastical courts locally heard mostly complaints over tithes, absence from church, or various forms of sexual misbehavior.[2] Manorial and communal courts met regularly but most of their business involved minor debts, citations for brewing and the trespass of animals. The King's Bench, the court of common law at Westminster that specialized in pleas of the crown, seldom heard cases from eastern Sussex; only twelve cases from the area, and none for felony or petty larceny, appear in ten sampled indictment rolls from the King's Bench. The great courts outside the common law (Star Chamber, Requests and Chancery) and the *ad hoc* commissions occasionally empowered by the government were too distant, too long-winded and too expensive to be useful for ordinary complaints of crime.[3]

Despite the theoretical power of all these courts over violations of the

---

[2] For example, 20 instance causes (the rough equivalent of civil litigation) involving people living in the parish of Heathfield came before the court of the archdeaconry of Lewes between 1594 and 1640; the disputes concerned tithes (4 cases), the execution of wills (4), the payment of the clerk of the parish (1), the rebuilding of pews (2), the location of a missing surplice (1) and the sexual and religious propriety of local residents (8). Using the years 1593–5, 1616–18 and 1637–9 as a sample, one finds residents of the same parish involved in 13 detection causes (the rough equivalent of criminal prosecutions). Here the range of allegations is fairly narrow: 9 charges allege sexual misbehavior (adultery, bastardy, incontinence, bigamy, or living apart from one's spouse), 3 allege disrespectful behavior in church or absence from church and 1 alleges usury (WSRO Ep II/5/3–17; Ep II/9/7, 13, 14, 23). The scope of ecclesiastical jurisdiction was considerable, but its procedures and penalties limited its effectiveness. Much work remains to be done in local ecclesiastical records, however, before we fully understand the interaction of secular and ecclesiastical legal options in the seventeenth century. See M. J. Ingram, "Ecclesiastical Justice in Wiltshire 1600–1640 with Special Reference to Cases Concerning Sex and Marriage" (D.Phil. dissertation, Oxford University, 1976); R. A. Marchant, *The Church under the Law: Justice, Administration and Discipline in the Diocese of York, 1560–1640* (Cambridge, 1969); Christopher Hill, *Society and Puritanism in Pre-Revolutionary England*, 2nd ed. (New York, 1967), chs. 8–10.

[3] Examples of contemporary local court rolls for eastern Sussex can be found in ESRO ADA MSS 56; 73; 143; 157; SAS MSS 19F; RA/70–5; BL Additional MS 33,173–33,177. For the King's Bench: PRO KB 9/687–9; /720; /753–5; /778; /808; /812. For courts outside the common law and *ad hoc* commissions: *List and Index to the Proceedings in Star Chamber for the Reign of James I (1603–1625) in the Public Record Office*, comp. and ed. Thomas G. Barnes, 3 vols. (Chicago, 1975), vol. 3. The cases themselves can be found in PRO STAC 8. The massive Elizabethan files (STAC 5) are arranged only by the surname of the plaintiff. Virtually no Caroline files have survived. The records of the Courts of Chancery and Requests are also arranged only by the surname of the plaintiff. The few *ad hoc* commissions extant for eastern Sussex (PRO E 178/4653; /4654; /5675) all concern disputes over property.

peace, in practice the Assizes and the Quarter Sessions, the two tribunals least fully royal or fully local, were the most effective and the most efficient forums for prosecuting an injustice or protecting one's interests. Cases brought to the Assizes or Quarter Sessions were normally settled within a single meeting and while prosecutions routinely cost several shillings, compared to other courts there was a minimum of costly paperwork. No other local courts (aside from the special jurisdiction of the Cinque Ports) could invoke capital punishment; no other tribunals handled cases so cheaply, conveniently or quickly; no other forums were so communal in their involvement of local residents and in their determination to make decisions a public spectacle.

The qualifications of the Assizes and the Quarter Sessions to be major criminal courts were very different but, although the central government repeatedly tried to develop exclusive areas of authority for each court, the powers of the two tribunals overlapped considerably. The desire to separate the two jurisdictions arose from a lack of confidence in the justice dispensed at the quarterly courts. The Privy Council doubted the ability of local justices to reach dispassionate, rational decisions. The growing pressure in the late sixteenth century from local gentry to be appointed not only as justices of the peace but also as members of the quorum exacerbated this concern. The original purpose of the quorum had been to limit the authority of untrained magistrates by reserving special powers to men with legal educations. However, both the number of men who had spent some time at the Inns of Court and the social prestige of being a member of the quorum increased steadily in the last years of the sixteenth century. As the government capitulated to local demands and appointed both more magistrates and more members of the quorum, the distinctions among justices became almost meaningless. By 1604 in Sussex, 76 percent of the local justices, three times the proportion so distinguished in 1559, were members of the quorum. The rise was similar in other counties; the result was to allow more power to more men without formal legal credentials. The government hoped to offset this development by reserving serious legal questions for the professional judges at the Assizes.[4]

Four years before the date of the first extant file from a Quarter Sessions held in eastern Sussex (1594), the government had tried to give the Assizes a monopoly over serious crimes. The commission of 1590 instructed justices of

---

[4] BL Lansdowne MSS 53/164–5, 1218/29v–30v; Additional MS 38,139/159v–160v; Fletcher, *Sussex*, pp. 134, 356. Although at least four justices from eastern Sussex became sergeants at law or judges, in general the local commission included fewer men with legal training than in other shires. Cf. Lambard, *Eirenarcha*, pp. 47–8, 54; Lawson, pp. 128b, 206–7; Samaha, *Law and Order*, pp. 73–5; A. Hassell Smith, *County and Court: Government and Politics in Norfolk 1558–1603* (Oxford, 1974), pp. 51–60; Barnes, *Somerset*, p. 53; John H. Gleason, *The Justices of the Peace in England 1558–1640: A Later Eirenarcha* (Oxford, 1969), pp. 49–51, 86–7, 94–5; B. W. Quintrell, "The Government of the County of Essex 1603–42" (Ph.D. dissertation, University of London, 1965), pp. 40–5; Hughes, "Politics," pp. 101–4.

Table 3.1* *Cases indicted in the Assizes in eastern Sussex*

Category of crime	Percentage of category handled in Assizes	Total cases in Quarter Sessions and Assizes
Violent death	99	78
Nonclergyable theft	85	205
Miscellaneous felony	83	24
Clergyable larceny, petty larceny	55	669
Anti-community offenses	35	451
Disorderly offenses	13	601
Total	43	2,028

*On the difference between a case and a complaint, see above, p. x. The categories used here follow those in Table 2.1, p. 27 above. *Ignoramus* bills have been excluded from this and all comparative charts because of their uneven survival; see below, pp. 112–13.

the peace to refer all cases of "ambiguity and doubt" to the Assizes. The semi-annual court gained control over trials for treason, sedition, embezzlement and certain sorts of forgery, witchcraft and theft. While none of these crimes were among the routine business in eastern Sussex, the Assizes were also given preferential authority over more common serious felonies such as homicide and burglary. William Lambard, the Kentish magistrate and legal scholar, declared that these distinctions arose from suspicion that magistrates decided cases "upon the number of voices [rather] than upon the weight of reasons . . . "[5]

Table 3.1 shows that the Quarter Sessions and the Assizes in eastern Sussex generally respected this division of jurisdictions. The preponderance of serious felonies in the Assizes and the dominance of less serious, but no less bothersome, complaints in the Quarter Sessions is clear. The separation is even sharper in the list of complaints heard exclusively in one court or the other. The Assizes presided over all known indictments for infanticide, arson, bigamy, buggery, rape and the harboring of recusants. The Quarter Sessions handled all known accusations of perjury, shooting a gun in public, defaulting on taxes and illegally departing from a master's service. However, Table 3.1 also shows that most sorts of complaints appeared at least occasionally in both courts. Exclusivity was the exception, not the rule. The distribution of

[5] Lambard, *Eirenarcha*, p. 49; Dalton, *Countrey Justice*, pp. 19–20. The earlier Marian statutes on bond and examination (1 & 2 Philip & Mary, c. 13; 2 & 3 Philip & Mary, c. 10) suggest a similar concern.

Table 3.2. *Felonious thefts indicted in the Quarter Sessions*

Time period	Percentage of felonious thefts handled in the Quarter Sessions	Total cases in Quarter Sessions and Assizes
*Elizabethan	9	192
Jacobean	52	124
Transitional	35	93
Caroline	40	133
Total	31	542

*The specific courts representing these time periods here and throughout the book are detailed in Appendix 1 below.

Table 3.3. *Nonclergyable thefts* indicted in the Assizes*

Time period	Percentage of nonclergyable thefts handled in the Assizes	Total cases in Quarter Sessions and Assizes
Elizabethan	100	25
Jacobean	58	36
Transitional	53	15
Caroline	74	23
Total	72	99

*Horse theft, cutpursing, breaking.

Table 3.4. *Thefts of goods worth £5 or more indicted in the Assizes*

Time period	Percentage of thefts of goods allegedly worth at least £5 handled by the Assizes
Elizabethan	87
Jacobean	65
Transitional	89
Caroline	94
Total	83
No. of cases	82

business makes the normal purview for most crimes obvious, but the divisions were not invariable. And well into the seventeenth century the regular business of the quarterly court in eastern Sussex continued to include the trial of felonies.

Complaints of larceny were the most common accusations made to the courts in eastern Sussex and, not surprisingly, larceny was the felony most frequently heard in the Quarter Sessions. Table 3.2 illustrates the importance of the Quarter Sessions in the prosecution of felonious thefts in eastern Sussex. Except in the 1590s, the quarterly court always handled at least one third of these prosecutions. Moreover, this proportion actually underestimates the Quarter Sessions as a forum for trying complaints of felonious theft because it excludes those cases where, after an undervaluing of the stolen property, felonies were indicted as petty thefts.[6]

The division between grand and petty larceny (whether the stated value of the stolen property was twelve pence or more) had gone unchanged since the medieval era, so by the sixteenth and seventeenth centuries it failed to reflect accurately the true gravity of offenses. Tables 3.3 and 3.4 illustrate two alternative measures of the predominance of the Assizes in the trial of serious larcenies. Nevertheless, whether one isolates thefts by the value of property allegedly stolen or by their legal categorization, the Quarter Sessions emerge as an important, albeit a secondary, arena for complaints. Moreover, victims seem to have interpreted the greater majesty of the Assizes in financial rather than in legal terms; they preferred the Assizes most regularly not for heinous crimes but for those where the alleged value of the stolen property was the greatest. Absence of legal grandeur did not persuade victims to exclude the Quarter Sessions as an arena for the trial of felonies.

The viability of the quarterly court in eastern Sussex as an alternative for judicial business is also clear in the local interpretation of legal policies. In theory, the judges of the Assizes enjoyed several prerogatives unavailable to the magistrates of the Quarter Sessions. These advantages reinforced the logic of reserving serious felonies to the semi-annual court, but, as with the division of business, regulation and reality did not always mesh. Since the coroners, who reported directly to the Assizes, had investigative powers equal to those exercised by the local justices, the Assizes did monopolize prosecutions for violent death.[7] Since only the judges could convene juries of matrons to

---

[6] Such devaluations seem everywhere to have been the most widespread form of plea bargaining and mitigation; the number of indictments concerning goods valued at ten or eleven pence (just under the level of felony) is enormous. For especially blatant examples in eastern Sussex, ESRO Q/R/E 20/60, 72; 25/35, 67; 43/9, 29, 58; see also Babington, pp. 55–6; Cockburn, *Introduction*, pp. 66–9; Samaha, "Hanging for Felony," p. 781; Sharpe, *Essex*, pp. 92, 146.

[7] Smith, pp. 84–5; Cockburn, *Introduction*, pp. 32–3. A list of the coroners from eastern Sussex in this period can be found in Herrup, diss., p. 415.

determine whether condemned felons were pregnant, the Assizes also monopolized the most routine strategy for delaying the execution of a female felon.[8] But in matters that did not depend so heavily on other personnel, the superiority of the judges was less apparent. In theory only they could alter death sentences through benefit of clergy. In theory only they could dismiss unsupported accusations of felony without a formal hearing. In practice, magistrates often ignored both of these restrictions.

The most common mitigation of capital punishment in early modern England was benefit of clergy. The rules for granting the plea of benefit of clergy, as developed in the twelfth century, provided clerics with virtual immunity from the royal courts. The only medieval exceptions to clerical rights were in convictions for treason, highway robbery or willful arson. The Tudor monarchs, however, restricted both the scope and the extent of clerical exemptions. By 1590, benefit of clergy could be claimed only for a first conviction (ensured by branding the felonious cleric's thumb), and the privilege was eliminated entirely from convictions for petty treason, murder, piracy, horse theft, cutpursing, rape, burglary and certain types of breaking and entering.[9] Although benefit of clergy had outgrown its original purpose by the sixteenth century, it remained in use because it provided a means for punishing first offenders (whether clerical or lay) without executing them. Benefit of clergy might involve a painful branding, but it was a far cry from the severity of the alternative.

Because by the sixteenth and seventeenth centuries, clerics could not be identified by dress or tonsure, the decision to grant benefit of clergy in early modern courts rested upon the convict's ability to read a neck verse (so called because the proof of literacy saved one's neck) from the Scripture. The judges controlled this test, although in theory an ecclesiastical officer, not lay officials, determined its outcome.[10] The Bishop's Ordinary, who attended the

---

[8] Cockburn, *Introduction*, pp. 121–3; Herrup, diss., p. 338, n. 20; James Oldham, "On Pleading the Belly: A History of the Jury of Matrons," *Criminal Justice History*, 6 (1985): 1–64, but cf. *Worcester County Records, Calendar of the Quarter Sessions Papers 1591–1643*, ed. J. W. Willis Bund, 2 vols., Worcestershire County Records, 11 and 12 (Worcester, 1899–1900), pp. xcv–xcviii. Women could not plead benefit of clergy at all until 1624; 21 James I, c. 6, allowed women convicted of larcenies concerning goods valued at no more than 10 shillings to plead clergy; 3 William & Mary, c. 9, granted women eligibility equal to men's in 1691.

[9] Branding and the single offense restriction were ordered under 4 Henry VII, c. 13. The statutes excluding specific crimes from benefit of clergy were: petty treason (12 Henry VII, c. 7); murder (4 Henry VIII, c. 2); piracy (28 Henry VIII, c. 15); horse theft (1 Edward VI, c. 12, 31 Elizabeth I, c. 12); cutpursing (8 Elizabeth I, c. 4); rape and burglary (18 Elizabeth I, c. 7); burglary or breaking (1 Edward VI, c. 12, 39 Elizabeth I, c. 15); abduction of a woman (39 Elizabeth I, c. 9); stabbing (1 James I, c. 8).

[10] The outcome probably had little to do with actual literacy; on the procedure, see Cockburn, *Introduction*, pp. 117–21; Leona C. Gabel, *Benefit of Clergy in England in the Later Middle Ages*, in S. B. Fay and H. U. Faulkner, eds., Smith College Studies in History 14 (1928–9): 71–2; Thomas A. Green, *Verdict According to Conscience: Perspectives on the English*

Table 3.5. *Grants of benefit of clergy: Assizes and Quarter Sessions*

Time period	Assizes		Quarter Sessions	
	Convictions and confessions of clergyable felonies	Benefits of clergy granted (% of convictions and confessions of clergyable felonies)	Convictions and confessions of clergyable felonies	Benefits of clergy granted (% of convictions and confessions of clergyable felonies)
Elizabethan	87	80	2	100
Jacobean	26	85	17	88
Transitional	37	68	13	39
Caroline	29	59	13	54
Total	179	75	45	64

Assizes for this purpose, was not regularly summoned to the Quarter Sessions. Lambard believed that if the Ordinary happened to be at the quarterly court, benefit of clergy could be provided, but that without clerical advice magistrates could only execute or reprieve convicted felons. Clearly, the Ordinary did come to the Sessions in person or by deputy, or simply in theory because, as shown in Table 3.5, the justices in Quarter Sessions routinely granted benefit of clergy. Since it is highly unlikely that the Ordinary attended all meetings of the Quarter Sessions, it seems that the magistrates, on their own discretion or with the help of local churchmen, administered benefit of clergy.[11] This frequent recourse to clerical privilege is especially interesting because, since most felonies heard at the Quarter Sessions were grand larcenies, executions could have been avoided simply by manipulating the value of the stolen goods. However, from the viewpoint of the justices, benefit of clergy might have been preferred to the devaluation of property for several reasons. The branding that accompanied benefit of clergy theoretically allowed magistrates to isolate repeating felons if they appeared again before the courts; whipping, which was the penalty in petty thefts, was not similarly distinctive.[12] Justices had more control over the use

---

Criminal Trial Jury, 1200–1800 (Chicago, 1985), pp. 116–23. Peers did not have to read (1 Edward VI, c. 12) and, although benefit of clergy was not abolished until 1827, the reading requirement was dropped in the early eighteenth century (6 Anne, c. 9).

[11] Staunford believed that benefit of clergy could be given without the Ordinary, but Lambard preferred his own reading; Lambard, *Eirenarcha*, p. 554. Although some justices of eastern Sussex were also Doctors of Theology, no relationship exists between their attendance at the Sessions and the granting of benefit of clergy.

[12] Some contemporaries complained that brands were not effective either: see Edward Hext, "To Burghley on the Increase of Rogues and Vagabonds," in *Tudor Economic Documents*, eds. R. H. Tawney and Eileen Power, 3 (London, 1924), p. 341; Hawarde, p. 38.

of benefit of clergy than they did over decreasing charges of grand larceny to charges of petty larceny; for the latter task, they needed the cooperation of victims and/or jurymen. Moreover, clerical privilege, granted only after a confession or conviction, had a psychological impact that mitigations invoked at earlier stages in prosecutions lacked. Benefit of clergy combined mercy, punishment and suspense in a public and dramatic way. As long as the justices of the peace regularly exercised their jurisdiction over felonies, it was probably inevitable that they would also grant benefit of clergy.

The justices were similarly assertive about discharging suspects despite the formal restriction of this right to the judges at the Assizes. Magistrates were not supposed to free any suspects accused of felony without retaining a bond for a future appearance in court. The job of the justices was to investigate and transfer all serious accusations regardless of the strength of the evidence, to the Assizes. If a case was too weak to be heard even by a grand jury, the judges at the Assizes could then free a suspect by proclamation. However, before the Assizes convened, an accused person could spend months in jail. The interval between meetings presented a serious dilemma; even legal authorities who trusted the superiority of the Assizes acknowledged the unfairness and the danger of leaving accused men to linger untried in prison. As Sir David Williams, a judge at the Assizes in Cambridge, argued, "It [is] not meet to keep poor prisoners in the gaol for small matters or felonies, from one Assize till another . . . " The magistrates in eastern Sussex agreed with Williams. The records show fifteen cases in which magistrates held defendants in jail to await the Assizes, but at least nine other instances where the justices dismissed alleged felons without any formal action. Not surprisingly, most of the suspects held for the semi-annual court faced charges of serious felonies, while most of those dismissed had been accused only of simple grand larceny. Only in crimes of particular heinousness did the technical superiority of the Assizes outweigh the limitations of its infrequent meetings.[13]

Obviously, the real division of responsibilities between the Assizes and the Quarter Sessions in eastern Sussex differed significantly from the ideal. The sustained vitality of the Quarter Sessions was not unique, but many of the other jurisdictions where it is most apparent (Essex, Somerset, Kent) had notoriously large agendas of criminal business. Cockburn has suggested that judges at the Assizes in such places used the Sessions as a sort of adjunct court to ease the press of business. Conceivably, a similar partnership existed in eastern Sussex. The agendas of criminal business in the region were unexcep-

[13] Williams is cited in Dalton, *Countrey Justice*, p. 50. See also Lambard, *Eirenarcha*, pp. 8, 11, 374, 552. A survey of recognizances certified into the Quarter Sessions and then excused confirms this pattern. Lists of those discharged by proclamation at the Assizes can be found in PRO ASSI 35.

tional, but the judges might have preferred a viable Quarter Sessions at Lewes to traveling through the interior of the shire themselves. Whether because of large agendas, local roads or local pride, the overlap between the Assizes and the Quarter Sessions remained considerable. Pragmatism set limits on all early modern administrative schemes and the reform of criminal enforcement was no exception. Rules from Westminster were modified to fit the practicalities of life in the countryside.[14]

Both the Assizes and the Quarter Sessions also performed important non-judicial functions. As in most societies, the job of legal officers was administrative and pedagogical as well as judicial. The authority of the Assizes reached far beyond its powers over crimes but these other powers also affected the enforcement of the criminal law. The judges on circuit embodied the majesty of the sovereign, the rituals of the courtroom reinforced the power of the judges, the justices and the crown. Formalities in the court emphasized the awesome, almost magical, authority of the law. The fact that the judges arrived, presided, and then immediately departed lent an air of mystery and finality to the Assizes that the resident justices of the peace found impossible to imitate. In eastern Sussex, the judges were outsiders without strong connections in local society. They were professional lawyers, not gentlemen who accepted legal duties as part of the obligations of gentility. Most important, the judges were barristers, and many officers of the Assizes were attorneys. The Quarter Sessions operated with a modicum of legal regulation set against a background of longstanding intimacy. The Assizes ideally reduced considerations of individual demands to a minimum and dealt in the universality of legal principles.[15]

The political functions of the Assizes were as vital as their judicial mandate. The semi-annual meeting of judges and magistrates was an occasion for general exchange between the ruling voices of Westminster and the countryside. Because of the functional division of Sussex into two shires, the Assizes were also one of the few occasions for a unified assembly of men from the

---

[14] Cockburn, *Introduction*, pp. 22–5; Barnes, *Somerset*, pp. 50–6; Quintrell, "Essex," pp. 70–9, 83–6; Silcock, "Worcestershire," pp. 187–9. In Hertfordshire, the only county on the Home Circuit with dockets smaller than Sussex, the magistrates do not seem to have sustained their interest in trying felonies or even petty larcenies, see Lawson, pp. 55–60.

[15] Cockburn, *Assizes*, pp. 49–59, 65–85; judges were legally barred from serving in their counties of residence without special permission. Such grants were not uncommon, but no judge on the Home Circuit in this period had a residence in Sussex. For an example of the ceremonials used in Sussex, see William Albery, *A Millennium of Facts in the History of Horsham and Sussex 947–1947* (Horsham, 1947), pp. 217–19, and on the importance of such rituals generally, see Kai Erikson, *Wayward Puritans: A Study in the Sociology of Deviance* (New York, 1966), p. 16; Ivan Illich, *Deschooling Society* (Harmondsworth, 1971), pp. 55–6; Isaac, *Virginia*, pp. 88–98.

eastern and the western rapes, providing an arena in which to arbitrate disputes that spanned geographical boundaries. The judges also advised magistrates on difficult questions of criminal law or administrative policy. They heard complaints about the inefficiency of royal government. They listened to the woes of the local governors and, in turn, lectured the gentry on the desires of the central administrators. The judges acted as ombudsmen for the shires and they provided a needed source of information for the monarch. Sir Francis Bacon said, "the judges in their circuits are sent *a latere regis* to feel the pulse of the subject and to cure his disease." Bacon's successor at the Chancery, Thomas Coventry, called the judges on circuit the "eyes of the kingdom" and claimed that it was "fitter that they should instruct the king than the king them." Judges back from circuit advised the privy councillors on a variety of issues and suggested candidates for local offices. As one Lord Chancellor noted, the judges visited the counties "not for justice alone, but for the peaceable government of the country."[16]

The judges also served as supervisors and mediators in the administrative network that bound Sussex to London. In the 1630s, after the suspension of Parliament, the other major source for information about the localities, this role became particularly important. From 1631 on, the Book of Orders required justices to meet monthly to improve their enforcement of regulatory statutes and made the judges of Assizes overseers of these monthly, or petty, sessions. The Book of Orders commended the past "care and diligence" of the judges, but suggested that informal efforts to obtain accurate information from local magistrates had failed. The magistrates, therefore, were henceforth to present the judges with formal reports of the business done at their monthly meetings. These certificates supplemented the plentiful stream of documents already flowing from the magistrates to the Assizes (including examinations of suspects and reports on recusants). Despite the limited success of this arrangement, the goal set for the Assizes was to lay open the entire apparatus of local government and report on it to Westminster.[17]

The Assizes, moreover, were important forums of publicity for the govern-

[16] *The Letters and the Life of Francis Bacon*, comp. James Spedding, 6 vols. (London, 1872), 6: 303; PRO SP 16/232/42; Quintrell, "Essex," p. 79. For examples of the myriad uses of the Assizes, see Fletcher, *Sussex*, p. 137; BL Additional MSS 12,496/274; 23,007/40v; Lansdowne MS 72/41; Bodleian Tanner MS 288/18/266–71; Barnes, *Somerset*, pp. 85–96; Cockburn, *Assizes*, pp. 153–261; Holmes, "The County Community," pp. 64–5; Thomas G. Barnes and Alan Hassell Smith, "Justices of the Peace from 1558 to 1668: A Revised List of Sources," *BIHR* 32 (1959): 227–8. This role is further implied by the frequent use of the Assizes to publicize punishments imposed from the Star Chamber; Hawarde, *passim*.

[17] BL Additional MS 12,496/269–84; Fletcher, *Sussex*, pp. 224–6; Barnes, *Somerset*, pp. 172–202; Paul Slack, "Books of Orders: The Making of English Social Policy 1577–1631," *TRHS*, 5th series, 30 (1980), pp. 1–22; B. W. Quintrell, "The Making of Charles I's Book of Orders," *EHR* 95 (1980): 553–72. A list of the monthly certificates returned from eastern Sussex and the business of those sessions can be found in Herrup, diss., pp. 422–5.

ment. In their formal speeches, the judges reaffirmed the priorities of the monarch and reassured citizens of the king's good intentions. For example, Sir Edward Coke's speech at the Assizes in Norwich in 1606 addressed all the major concerns of the day, including the new king's title to the throne, the recent peace with Spain, religious extremism, and economic abuses. Coke devoted most of his remarks (twenty-seven out of thirty-nine printed pages) to a history of recusancy in England. Every plot, every threat, every papal decree from 1569 to 1604 was recounted in lurid detail. The drama reached high pitch when Sir Edward retold the early events of the current king's reign. James, he reminded his listeners, was England's heir by "most royal and lineal descent." He had made peace with Spain, successfully eliminating one accomplice to the Roman menace. The king could not afford to tolerate Catholics, Coke explained, and he would never do so. Toleration would not bring peace, only foreign domination, the replacement of "Eden" with "herds of blood desiring wolves." The recent plot by Guy Fawkes showed not only the need for constant vigilance, but also the importance of convincing the less dangerous dissenters, the Puritans, that no ceremonial dispute justified destroying the unity of the church. Closing with a pledge of attention to economic grievances, Coke charged the grand jury to investigate abuses in the use of monopolies and purveyance. The role of the Assizes as apologist for the government was even clearer in the crisis of 1642. Before the circuit began in the summer of that year, the Lord Keeper instructed the judges to let people know that Charles I would hear any petition that they presented "in a humble and fitting way." The judges were to assure their listeners that the king was "resolved to maintain the laws of this our kingdom and by and according to them to govern our subjects and not by any arbitrary power . . . "[18]

If the Assizes linked capital and countryside, the Quarter Sessions and the local justices of the peace completed the chain. The Quarter Sessions connected the middling sort, whose interests were defined by the boundaries of hundred, town, or parish, with the royal representatives whose concerns were more sweeping. The Quarter Sessions in the sixteenth and seventeenth centuries were regional social occasions, combining a criminal court with an administrative coordinator, a licensing agent, and an investigative pipeline for the Assizes. Any decline in the judicial powers of the Quarter Sessions after the new commission of 1590 was more than offset by the growing

---

[18] Coke, *The Lord Coke, his Speech and Charge*; the 1642 speech is cited in *Somerset Assize Orders 1640–1659*, ed. J. S. Cockburn, Somerset Record Society, 72 (London, 1971), pp. 51–2. For other examples of charges as given either at Assizes or in the Star Chamber to the assembled judges as a guide for their own speeches, see BL Lansdowne MS 160/81–2v, 331–2; Bodleian Rawlinson MS D720/51; PRO SP 16/232/42, 16/491/52; *Bacon*, 6: 211–14, 302–6, 315; *The Harleian Miscellany*, ed. W. Oldys, 12 vols. (London, 1808–11), 6: 105–28; Hawarde, pp. 20–1, 57–8, 102, 106, 159–60, 162, 186–92, 263–4.

responsibility for regulatory statutes. Already in the late sixteenth century, Lambard had complained of the "stacks of statutes" left to the magistrates; by 1618, Michael Dalton claimed in his handbook for justices that such matters monopolized the magistrates' attention.[19] Although Lambard and Dalton exaggerated the burden considerably, justices were called upon regularly to cope with statutory business even before the Book of Orders formally created petty sessions. Special sessions considered riots and trespasses, and licensing sessions controlled local alehouses. After 1631, petty sessions oversaw the control of alehouses, apprenticeships, the settlement of vagrants, and other social problems. All of these meetings were reminders of judicial vigilance over the well-ordered commonwealth.[20]

In addition to these meetings out of sessions, justices were expected to arbitrate local disputes before they escalated into business for the courts. Magistrates examined, admonished, bonded, and committed people who seemed to threaten the local peace. They tried to settle disagreements without resort to litigation or indictment. As local gentlemen, justices were natural arbitrators in the community. Lambard placed great emphasis on this obligation, saying that a justice should "step in betwixt those that be at variance, as (by reason of his learning, wisdom, authority and wealth) he is like to prevail more, by his mediation and entreaty than is another man." This was part of the meaning of the word gentleman.[21]

The justice of the peace was not only accessible, but also highly visible. The

---

[19]   Lambard, *Eirenarcha*, p. 37; Dalton, *Countrey Justice*, pp. 19ff; BL Additional MS 12,496/262–91; Barnes, *Somerset*, pp. 56–60, 85–96. Most magistrates' notes suggest a task made oppressive by its variety, repetitiveness and constancy rather than by its size; "Ephemeris," in *William Lambarde and Local Government*, pp. 15–52; "Notebook of a Surrey Justice," ed. Granville Leveson-Gower, *Surrey Archaeological Collections* 9 (London, 1888): 161–232; KAO U522/04; *The Official Papers of Sir Nathaniel Bacon of Stiffkey, Norfolk, as Justice of the Peace 1580–1620*, ed. H. W. Saunders, Camden Society, 3rd series, 26 (London, 1915); but cf. Quintrell, "Essex," p. 68.

[20]   Special sessions were held before two or three justices and specially impaneled local juries. Eleven special sessions held in eastern Sussex and 11 more held in western Sussex have been identified. Individual justices, justices meeting in special brewsters' sessions or the full commission at the Quarter Sessions could grant licenses to alehousekeepers; the extant records, clearly incomplete, show 484 licenses granted in brewsters' sessions, which often convened immediately before the Quarter Sessions, and 75 licenses given at the quarterly courts themselves. ESRO Q/R/E, *passim*; ESRO QI/EW1; Herrup, diss., pp. 426–8, for a listing of these meetings and their business.

[21]   Lambard, *Eirenarcha*, p. 11; both prescriptive and practical examples of this obligation are numerous; see for example, Eaton Hall, Grosvenor MSS Commonplace Book/51–4 (I am indebted to Richard Cust for photocopies of these MSS); "Notebook of a Surrey Justice," *passim*; "Diary of Robert Beake," *passim*; Stephen K. Roberts, *Recovery and Restoration in an English County: Devon Local Administration 1646–1670* (Exeter, 1985), p. 2; Hawarde, pp. 23–5, 153. This was not, of course, a duty restricted only to gentlemen; ministers and respected neighbors regularly acted in similar capacities; see *Diary of Ralph Josselin, passim*; Adam Eyre, "Diurnall," *passim*; *The Life of Adam Martindale, passim*; Ingram, "Wiltshire," pp. 93–4, 280–1, 301; Seaver, *Wallington's World*, pp. 130, 146.

magistrate at the Quarter Sessions was also the gentleman who sat in the front
pew on Sunday, who commanded the local muster, who assessed and collected many taxes, and who held land and rents throughout the area. It was
the prestige of the gentleman turned justice that lent stature to the quarterly
court, not its royal commission. Although the Quarter Sessions, like the
Assizes, met only briefly, the men who presided there did so by virtue of their
permanence in the county. The formal court was temporary, but the individual justice and his authority endured throughout the seasons. Most
justices of eastern Sussex resided in the county and belonged to families
known locally for generations. As elsewhere in early modern England,
appointment to the commission of the peace was a badge of accomplishment
and a means of integration for newcomers, but the hallmark of the bench in
eastern Sussex was its stability. Twenty-four of the thirty families represented
in the Caroline commission of 1635, for example, had been in the shire for at
least a century; fifteen of the thirty had been among the local ruling classes
in 1570. Local stature and maturity did not necessarily translate into
enthusiasm for office, but no justice of the peace in eastern Sussex seems to
have shared the dilemma of Sir John Oglander who, having been put into the
commission at age 22, "was ashamed to sit on the Bench as not having then
any hair on my face and less wit."[22]

The crown hoped that, by appointing justices who lived in various sections
of a shire, a regional system of enforcement could be created that would
operate continually despite the infrequent meetings of the courts. Dalton said
that the very presence of a magistrate, "daily to administer justice and to
execute their office at home," drastically reduced problems severe enough for
prosecutions. A comparison of judicial residences and business in the courts
in eastern Sussex suggests some truth in Dalton's statement. The Privy
Council never attained its ideal of one magistrate every six or seven miles, but
the commission of the peace covered eastern Sussex more effectively in 1640
than it had done earlier. Most residents did have access to at least one
justice.[23]

Both the judges of the Assizes and the justices of the Quarter Sessions, however, were passive officials. They needed accurate information from others

---

[22] *A Royalist's Notebook: The Commonplace Book of Sir John Oglander, Kt of Nunwell*, ed.
Francis Bamford (London, 1936), p. xiv; on the commission in Sussex, Fletcher, *Sussex*, pp.
27, 42–4, 128, 133–4, 348–57; Mousley, "Sussex Country Gentry," pp. 11–12, 17–19, 30,
287–96; Jeremy Goring, "The Expansion of the Sussex Gentry 1525–1600," *Sussex Family
Historian 5* (September, 1982): 76–86. Cf. Hughes, "Warwickshire," pp. 101–5; Samaha,
Law and Order, p. 76.

[23] Dalton, *Countrey Justice*, p. 19; Fletcher, *Sussex*, pp. 130–1, 137–9; Herrup, diss., pp. 68–
70. See also Lawson, p. 130; *Diary of Ralph Josselin*, pp. 160–1, but cf. Peter Clark, *English
Provincial Society from the Reformation to the Revolution: Religion, Politics and Society in
Kent 1500–1640* (Rutherford, NJ, 1977), p. 145; Quintrell, "Essex," pp. 40–5.

before they could enforce local peace and quiet. The courts were part of a delicate mechanism rooted in the early medieval tradition of the jury of inquest that continuously sought more and better facts on local conditions and local attitudes. The Privy Council relied on the judges; the judges relied on the justices; and the justices waited upon the constables who served as grand jurors and upon the men who served as petty jurors. The consensus among the governors was that, if a lack of good order ensued, it was because accurate information failed to reach administrators. The system was rooted in the belief that since evil – social, economic, and political – stemmed from individuals, not society, it was possible with enough facts to discover and punish all evil doers. However, a basic contradiction undermined the foundations of this informational network. The officials of the Assizes and Quarter Sessions who received reports about local life not only transmitted their findings to their own superiors, but also judged, administered, and supervised the men who were their informants. An open relationship between central and local representatives was both necessary and impossible.[24]

The Assizes were particularly restricted in their ability to obtain full information because, despite almost limitless authority, the inescapable fact about the Assizes was their transiency. Almost everything connected with the court was temporary, migratory, and consequently often makeshift. The powers of the Assizes rested on commissions granted at the beginning of each circuit and rescinded at the end of each circuit. The judges chose their assignments only a few weeks before the courts met and the appointments were reworked every season. Even the locations of the courts inside each county were impermanent. Some towns, especially those with working jails, were traditional sites for meetings, but at least twenty-one different places within the Home Circuit hosted the Assizes between 1558 and 1714. For the session of the summer of 1636, the undersheriff and his men in Surrey had to build an entire courtroom in Dorking complete with hangings, cloth, and boards brought down from London to provide "convenient places for the Assize judges to sit."[25]

The Assizes lasted only two or three days in a county and judges left town directly after finishing their business. The circuit was a splendid way to bring the king's good order to the people, but the lasting impact of the Assizes depended upon the persistence of local officials after the deliberations of the court had ended. The Assizes were like any other grand visitation; their auth-

---

[24] Social explanations for crime in early modern England were unusual, but not non-existent; see Sir Thomas More, *Utopia*, in Complete Works, eds. Edward Surtz, SJ, and J. H. Hexter (New Haven, 1964), 4: 61–3; William Bullein, "A Dialogue against the Pestilence," in *Everyone a Witness: The Tudor Age*, comp. A. F. Scott (New York, 1977), pp. 189–90; William Harrison, *The Description of England*, ed. George Edelen (Ithaca, 1968), p. 192.

[25] PRO E 368/642; the bill was about £15.

ority was momentous and their grandeur was awesome, but their real power
rested ultimately on far less educated and far less eminent officials than the
judges. If the judges were the eyes of the kingdom, they were eyes restricted
by blinkers, confined to the sights and sounds of a two-day visit in one town
in every shire. Bacon's description of the circuits as "rivers in Paradise" is particularly apt. Like rivers they visited many areas, but also like rivers they ran
through the kingdom, permanently impermanent, leaving a silt of orders and
commands and moving on before the deposit had fully settled.[26]

The Assizes in Sussex were peculiarly hampered by such limitations. The
Home Circuit, which included Sussex, Essex, Surrey, Hertfordshire and Kent,
was the least desirable of the six judicial progresses. No single set of priorities
dictated judicial assignments but, by several criteria, the southeastern
counties were disagreeable. The *per diem* was one of the smallest; the dockets
were the largest; the terrain was generally familiar, unexciting and poor for
hunting. Nearness to London did not guarantee cleaner quarters, safer surroundings, or more congenial inhabitants. Since the assignments were chosen
in order of judicial seniority, it is not surprising that only two Chief Justices
served the Home Circuit between 1590 and 1640 with only brief tenures.
Sergeants at law, who presided when full judges were not available,
accounted for eleven of the thirty men who sat in the Southeast, a percentage
of the judiciary higher than in any other circuit. The Home Circuit also had a
higher judicial turnover than did other locations. The relatively frequent fluctuation of judges on the Home Circuit added mystery and distance to royal
justice, but it must also have made it especially difficult to establish reliable
networks for information. When, as in Sussex, an ever-changing Bench faced
a relatively stable and inbred commission of the peace, many magisterial
shortcomings and dilemmas probably remained secret. The pace imposed by
a schedule that squeezed five meetings of the Assizes in a circuit of one
hundred and seventy miles into seventeen days undoubtedly also restricted
the ability of judges to engage in meaningful exchanges of information.[27]

The institutional peculiarities of Sussex presented further problems. In
many counties, the Assizes met in the town or towns with an ancient, but

---

[26] BL Lansdowne MS 160/331, 81v; *Bacon*, 6: 303.

[27] Chief Justices Henry Hobart and Thomas Richardson rode the Home Circuit for 3 sittings
and 2 sittings respectively. Cockburn says that in Elizabeth's reign, one judge serving on the
same circuit for 15 years was not unusual, but under James and Charles assignments more
commonly lasted between 1 and 4 years. The average tenure on the Home Circuit between
1590 and 1640 was 3 years. However, the contrast between impermanence and stability
should not be stretched too far; 30 judges rode the Home Circuit for more than 5 years each
and the clerks of Assize (and some members of their staffs) had tenures that lasted for
decades. How familiar such repetition made outsiders with local men cannot be determined
with any real certainty; Cockburn, *Assizes*, pp. 24–7, 50–7, 70–85, 262–93, 314; *Introduction*, pp. 3–10.

usable, gaol. Sussex had no ancient gaol and no accepted center. Horsham, the site of the gaol since 1487, was neither conveniently located nor the major local metropolis. The primitive state of the roads complicated the problem of finding an acceptable location for the court. The judges were hardly immune to considerations such as the ease of travel. When an entire circuit lasted only seventeen days, precious time could not be wasted stuck in the mud of Sussex. Consequently, in the winter, the Assizes always met at East Grinstead, the closest town to London and to the other counties in the circuit (see Figure 2.3), but eighteen miles from the local gaol and a ride of two or three days from the local centers of population. In the summer, the Assizes occasionally convened at Horsham or Lewes, but East Grinstead was the standard venue until 1799. Even when the Sessions House literally collapsed around the judges in 1684, they returned to East Grinstead rather than move into the heart of the shire.[28]

The choice of a town on the border of the shire as a site for the Assizes obviously affected the influence the court had on the county. The southern and eastern parishes of eastern Sussex reported far fewer cases to the Assizes than did the northern and western parishes. Money, leisure, or spitefulness was necessary if one was to travel the length or breadth of the eastern rapes to bring a complaint to trial at the Assizes. Daily life was full of technically criminal occurrences – thefts, assaults, communal irresponsibilities – but it was time-consuming and expensive to carry such grievances to the Assizes. The number of cases presented to the court decreased broadly in inverse proportion to the distance of a parish from East Grinstead, as Figure 3.1 indicates. The direct information available to the judges about these areas probably paralleled their modest participation in criminal business.[29]

The Assizes were a potent symbol, a legal backdrop. Since most persons never attended the court, the authority it represented relied on the beliefs of local individuals. The Assizes lacked the time, the personnel and the local knowledge to deal adequately and flexibly with all of the problems within their purview. The majesty of royal justice as the Assizes was most effective when used sparingly. The objectivity of the Assizes was their great advantage as well as one of their most severe limitations.

---

[28] ESRO Accession 2189; ESRO QCP/EW4; ESRO Q/R/E 34/1; KAO Sackville MS U269/C118/2; M. J. Leppard, "Replies, East Grinstead Assizes III," *Sussex Notes and Queries* 17 (1969): 130–1.

[29] A day's ride in Sussex at a moderate to slow pace was usually between 12 and 18 miles; PRO E 368/657 provides some examples of traveling time between major towns. Most fees for prosecution (apart from costs for travel or witnesses) ran to between 5 and 12 shillings. Other expenses obviously varied with one's tastes; Thomas Pelham, the leader of the justices in eastern Sussex, spent £1 3s 6d on writing expenses alone at one Assizes (BL Additional MS 33,145/50).

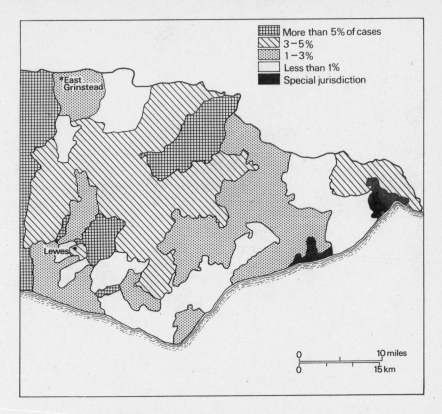

More than 5% of cases
3–5%
1–3%
Less than 1%
Special jurisdiction

East
Grinstead

Lewes

0 _____ 10 miles
0 _____ 15 km

3.1 Eastern Sussex: indictments in the Assizes 1592–1640

In contrast, the justices who lived in Sussex were much better equipped than were the judges of the Assizes to gather local information, and their tribunals were more frequent and more accessible as well. As shown in Figure 3.2, the greater convenience of the Quarter Sessions allowed substantial participation from most sections of the eastern division. The convenience undoubtedly affected not only the agenda but also the collection of facts about local conditions.

William Lambard maintained that, if the monarch was England's "good physician" in matters of justice, and the magistrates were the healer's "mouth," then the grand jurors who served the Sessions were the mender's "eyes." "But how shall we that be the mouth speak unless you the eyes will first show and tell us whereof?" he lamented. The constables and the grand jurors who were the minor officials of the Quarter Sessions were also expected to be the agents of their local areas. Collectively, they knew the

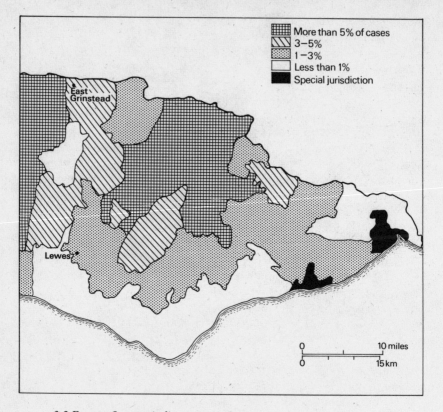

More than 5% of cases
3–5%
1–3%
Less than 1%
Special jurisdiction

East
Grinstead

Lewes

0   10 miles
0   15 km

3.2 Eastern Sussex: indictments in the Quarter Sessions 1592–1640

parishes and hundreds of eastern Sussex intimately. The constables of the
hundreds, acting as grand jurors, had a special responsibility to seek out and
report disorder. Lambard repeatedly admonished the Kentish grand jurors
for their lack of initiative. "Depend not altogether upon that which others
shall bring to you, but examine your own knowledges . . . " he told them.
Lambard's charges to the Elizabethan juries at the Quarter Sessions in Kent
returned often to this theme, and it was echoed by magistrates in other
shires.[30]

The job of the magistrates in relation to lesser legal officials paralleled the
position of the judges of the Assizes toward the justices themselves. The

[30] *William Lambarde and Local Government*, pp. 69, 80 and *passim*; see also
Eaton Hall Grosvenor MSS, Quarter Sessions charges; BL Harleian MS 1603/24v–5;
Larminie, *The Godly Magistrate*, pp. 16–17.

general reputation of constables and jurors was not high, but their notoriety is somewhat misleading. Ignorant and corrupt officials existed at all levels of law enforcement, but lesser officials did not outdo their betters in this regard. Since the Assizes and Privy Council repeatedly upbraided justices for their soft-heartedness toward troublemakers, it is hardly surprising to find that the magistrates, in turn, complained bitterly of their own inferiors. As surely as information passed from juror to justice to judge, admonishments about negligence and "foolish and fond pity" passed down along the same route.[31]

Whether the Assizes and Quarter Sessions were collecting information, judging criminal cases, or dealing with other problems, the central administrator in the system was the magistrate. He was the only member of the complex legal network who regularly participated in both criminal courts. Judges did not attend the Quarter Sessions, and the minor officials of the Sessions rarely went to the Assizes. But the justices of the peace were trapped in a conflict of obligation and position. Regardless of the limitations imposed by the participatory structure of law enforcement, for most of the year and in most of the county, the magistrate could claim to be the key to justice – he arbitrated, licensed, bonded, tried, and punished. At the Assizes, however, the justice's role was subordinate; he came to inform and to listen rather than to judge. He came to learn rather than to lecture. By his attendance, the magistrate provided others with an example of deference to higher authority. In an age that believed examples to be the most effective tools of teaching, the justice's participation at the Assizes, although personally humbling, was socially important. Not surprisingly, justices were not always eager to attend the semi-annual tribunal. Attendance was higher in Sussex than in the other counties of the Home Circuit (helped probably by the extra importance of a joint meeting between the two divisions), but commonly only about half of the working members of the commission of the peace were present.[32]

The legal activities of a justice at the Assizes are less clear than his social and political functions. Unlike justices in some counties, magistrates in Sussex did not serve as grand jurors at the Assizes. Nor do they seem to have acted regularly as prosecutors.[33] Magistrates who had investigated pending cases

---

[31] Eaton Hall Grosvenor MSS, Quarter Sessions charges; Wrightson, "Two Concepts of Order," pp. 21–46; Samaha, *Law and Order*, pp. 84–8; Hext, "To Burghley," p. 340; J. A. Sharpe, "Crime and Delinquency in an Essex Parish 1600–1640," in *Crime in England*, pp. 94–7; Hawarde, *passim*; Joan Kent, "The English Village Constable 1580–1642: The Nature and Dilemmas of the Office," *JBS* 20: 2 (Spring 1981): 26–49; but cf. Cockburn, *Introduction*, chs. 5–6, 8; Roberts, *Recovery and Restoration*, chs. 4–5.

[32] Magisterial attendance ranged from a low of 25 percent (Winter, 1595) to a high of 80 percent (Winter, 1596); the average attendance of the active commission was 51 percent: see Cockburn, *Introduction*, p. 31. Holmes, *Lincolnshire*, p. 85, provides an example of magisterial resentment towards the judges in Lincoln.

[33] *Quarter Sessions Order Book*, ed. Redwood, p. xxiii is mistaken about Sussex; for other counties, see Morrill, *Grand Jury*, p. 41; PRO SP 14/190/43–4; Cockburn, *Introduction*,

attended the Assizes more regularly than other justices and, if absent, they were more likely to have sent formal excuses, but logically the men most likely to attend were also the men most likely to be active outside the courtroom. Even in eastern Sussex a quarter of the prosecutions where the committing magistrate can be identified proceeded in the absence of that justice. The specific assistance that justices in eastern Sussex provided when they did appear remains obscure; the fact that they were more energetic in the name of victims outside of the ruling classes than they were in the name of social equals or near-equals suggests that at least some magistrates were anxious to offset any confusion caused by strange surroundings and procedures.[34] But the presence or absence of the committing magistrate had no discernible impact on the outcome of a complaint; roughly 60 percent of the cases ended with guilty verdicts whether the committing magistrate was present or absent. The minimal procedural role of magistrates at the Assizes, however, did not negate their importance in non-legal matters. The gentry discussed local, inter-divisional and national issues of importance during the Assizes; they assisted the judges with certificates, information and opinions; and they brought back to their local areas the ideas presented to them by the representatives of Westminster.

The relationship between the Assizes and the Quarter Sessions, of course, was never static. If the need to rely upon unpaid local amateurs as officials meant that the formal distinction between the criminal courts was fluid, it also meant that the success of the courts relied more upon men than upon mechanisms; distaste for policy could easily transform itself into the passive resistance of lax enforcement. Whether one looks at business, personnel or procedure, it is apparent that the relationship between the two tribunals in the early seventeenth century was under increasing strain.

In the 1630s, prosecutions in eastern Sussex focused more heavily on dis-

---

p. 48; Clark, *English Provincial Society*, p. 115. Interest in the notion of the magistrate as prosecutor has been revived by John H. Langbein, *Prosecuting Crime in the Renaissance: England, Germany, France* (Cambridge, Mass., 1974), especially pp. 34–43. More recently Cockburn has suggested instead that prosecutorial duties at the Assizes belonged to the clerks of the Assize: *Introduction*, pp. 100–3.

[34] The justices responsible for individual cases can be identified in 479 prosecutions; in 16 percent more of the cases the magistrate had sent a formal excuse (and probably the pertinent written examinations) to the Assizes, cf. Cockburn, *Introduction*, p. 101. Justices appeared in 83 percent of the cases where the victim was identified as a husbandman or laborer compared with appearances in 77 percent of the cases involving yeomen or gentlemen, 74 percent of the cases involving women and 54 percent of the cases involving men outside the agricultural community. If one includes magistrates who sent excuses to the court, the priorities remain the same with male victims, but women were supported more regularly than any male group. Statistically the status of the victim is one of the few variables that seems to have had a significant relationship to magisterial behavior (Significance = .0024, Cramer's V = .30102); see Herrup, diss., p. 346, n. 70.

orders and less heavily on felonies than in earlier decades. Since the Quarter Sessions traditionally handled most nonfelonious accusations, as early as 1614 the quarterly court had outpaced its more majestic counterpart in terms of business. As complaints of disorder increased and complaints of felony declined, the size of the dockets in each court diverged accordingly.[35] The different specialities of the courts explain some of this divergence, but looking at grand larcenies, the most flexible type of prosecution, a more complex interrelationship emerges. Although nonfelonious business in the Quarter Sessions increased steadily, the Assizes in the 1630s did not handle significantly more thefts or even a larger percentage of felonious thefts than it had done earlier (see Table 3.2). Referrals between the courts also suggest a change. The records for the 1630s show fewer cases passed by the magistrates to the judges than in any earlier period and, for the first time, cases being referred in the opposite direction.[36]

Such changes reflect attitudes toward enforcement. The judges at the Assizes sentenced more people to be executed in the 1630s than in either the 1590s or the 1620s. They rejected almost one in every five pleas for benefit of clergy. And they revived a practice common twenty years earlier – adding to convictions for lesser crimes and even to acquittals disciplinary penalties such as time in the House of Correction.[37]

However, not everyone concurred about the need for such severity. Fewer men were willing to serve as grand jurors in the Assizes in eastern Sussex and grand juries altered more charges there in the 1630s than in earlier years. Petty juries at the Assizes were also more likely than in earlier years to find defendants only partially guilty.[38] The picture suggested by the records of the

---

[35] See Chapter 2 above, p. 39. Some of the decline in business at the Assizes may have resulted from an increasing concern with litigation. This would parallel the increased disruptiveness suggested by the records of the local Sessions; Cockburn found a decisive rise in litigation in the Assizes of the Western circuit in the 1630s; *Somerset Assize Orders*, ed. Cockburn, p. 1, fn.

[36] Although it is difficult to assess the completeness of these figures, the number of cases referred from the justices to the judges was 17 in the 1590s (7 percent of business), 10 in the 1610s (6 percent of business), 14 in the 1620s (4 percent of business) and 7 in the 1630s (1 percent of business).

[37] The percentage of convicted felonies that resulted in sentences of execution from the judges at Assizes was 36 percent in the 1590s, 48 percent in the 1610s, 31 percent in the 1620s and 46 percent in the 1630s. The judges rejected no pleas for benefit of clergy in cases from eastern Sussex in the 1590s, but 2 in the 1610s (8 percent of all requests), 2 in the 1620s (6 percent of all requests) and 7 in the 1630s (21 percent of all requests). Similar changes may have occurred elsewhere, see Silcock, "Worcestershire," p. 112; Quintrell, "The Making of Charles I's Book of Orders," p. 567, fn. 2, but cf. Sharpe, *Essex*, pp. 143–5.

[38] Thirty-six obvious manipulations by trial juries are extant in the files of the Assizes; 5 date from the 1590s, 6 from the 1610s, 11 from the 1620s and 14 from the 1630s when trial business was the smallest. On personnel, see below, pp. 163–4. Ten of the 13 known cases where grand juried reduced accusations occurred after 1625, but only 3 date from the late 1630s.

Quarter Sessions is very different. No drop in attendance by either potential grand jurors or petty jurors can be traced, and the Sessions as a whole show signs of growing leniency that contrast with the severity of the Assizes. In the 1630s, the justices allowed more charges of grand larceny to be reduced to petty larceny than in earlier decades and they allowed more grants of benefit of clergy. In 1638 and 1639 the Quarter Sessions and the Assizes diverged from established custom by holding their summer meetings in separate locations. While the Assizes met in East Grinstead, the Quarter Sessions convened in Lewes. Such a separation occurred only two times between 1592 and 1640: 1627–9 and 1638–9, both periods of political crisis. The Quarter Sessions in the summers of 1638 and 1639 tried an exceptional number of felonious larcenies and granted an exceptional number of benefits of clergy. In contrast to 1627–9, moreover, the Sessions handled very little western business. The Assizes in the summers of 1638 and 1639 heard only minimal business from the East. Who controlled the venue of the Quarter Sessions or why it was changed is unclear; 1638 and 1639 were years of high local mortality as well as years of political tension. Since the magistrates did not shun the Assizes, however, the relocation of the Sessions may have had more to do with the justice likely in East Grinstead than with the dangers of disease.[39]

The severity of the judges in dealing with thefts is not surprising, but it is surprising that the Quarter Sessions in eastern Sussex in the 1630s exhibited a pattern so different from the Assizes. In the 1630s, while the judges responded to theft with renewed harshness, the justices met complaints with renewed tolerance. The greater familiarity of the justices with the region may have made them more aware than the judges of gradual economic deterioration and more tolerant of its repercussions, but political disillusionment probably also explains their response. Because the Assizes were a political as well as a legal forum, most changes in their business had political and legal origins and repercussions. Dealing with the decade before the Civil War, an almost unavoidable temptation exists to perceive patterns where in fact there may be only lines and dots, but the disparate shifts in personnel, business and

[39] The summer Quarter Sessions of 1636 and 1637, at East Grinstead, tried only 4 cases, 3 for petty larcenies. The 1638 and 1639 Lewes meetings heard 10 trials, 9 for grand larceny. The reunited 1640 Sessions had no trial business. Of the 11 pleas of benefit of clergy heard by the Quarter Sessions between 1636 and 1640, 36 percent were administered in the summer meetings of 1638 and 1639. The Summer Assizes for 1638 heard only 4 larcenies from eastern Sussex, 3 for horse theft; the 1639 Assizes file for the summer circuit does not survive. ESRO Q/R/E 35; 42; 46; 50; WSRO Q/R/WE 31; PRO ASSI 35/80/9; Fletcher, *Sussex*, pp. 242–3. On the high mortality in these years, which seems to have arisen from a widespread epidemic of influenza, see Brent, "Devastating Epidemic," p. 47; Brent, "Employment," pp. 52, 267–8, 276, 279; Wrigley and Schofield, *Population History*, pp. 333–4, 671–84. Two-thirds of the active magistracy attended the Assizes in the summer of 1638.

venue suggest that the largely Puritan bench in eastern Sussex increasingly preferred to enforce the law as autonomously as possible; they were dissatisfied with the definition of justice shown in the Assizes, if not with the government *per se*. Although the governors of eastern Sussex needed the real and symbolic powers of the Assizes and they were themselves needed for information and assistance, the partnership between the Assizes and the Quarter Sessions grew increasingly uneasy in the 1630s. The tension was not unique to the decade before the Civil War nor can it firmly be tied to later events, but although it was not causally linked to the later struggle, the strain probably colored responses once the struggle had been joined.[40]

Since the Assizes and the Quarter Sessions shared the burden of maintaining good order, there were serious limits to any desire for disassociation. The Assizes still embodied abstract legal wisdom and, as such, were still the most appropriate forum for mediations and for the trial of major crimes. The judges still served as a conduit between Westminster and Sussex, shuttling opinions and information between the capital and the countryside. The Assizes, as the most important institution associating the two divisions of the shire, still provided the only regular unified social congregation of the local gentry. The Quarter Sessions, moreover, still provided local knowledge to which its grander judicial partner had no other access. The magistrated allowed the judges to avoid entanglement in the daily annoyances of local life. By 1640, the always delicate relationship between the two courts in eastern Sussex seems to have been strained, but neither could function well without the other. Only together could the Assizes and the Quarter Sessions embody an ideal of justice that was accessible yet distant; intimate, yet disinterested; hierarchical, yet participatory.

No administrative structure in the early modern era functioned independently of the men and women who used it. No case came to court without the coordinated decisions of many individuals. Victims had to complain of an alleged crime; neighbors had to investigate it; constables had to present cases to local magistrates. Prosecution depended upon choices made by victims, magistrates, sureties for bail, witnesses and jailers. Without the concurrence of all of these persons, not to mention two separate juries, conviction was impossible. The criminal law, as the inheritance of the community, was above all else the responsibility of local residents. The road from action through

---

[40] Between 1616 and 1618, the judges of the Assizes also routinely added disciplines to sentences, rejected pleas for benefit of clergy and condemned an exceptional number of convicts. In these years, too, local magistrates heard a large number of cases of felony, but in 1616–18, unlike in the 1630s, the response of the justices generally paralleled that of the judges; Cockburn, *Introduction*, pp. 115, 121; above, pp. 38–41, Cockburn, "The Nature and Incidence of Crime," in *Crime in England*, p. 70. On the political persuasion of the eastern Bench, PRO SP 16/442/137; *VCH*, 2: 32; Fletcher, *Sussex, passim*. This refines some of the views elaborated in Herrup, "The Counties and the Country."

prosecution to conviction ran as if dotted with a hundred independently-owned tollbooths – each keeper's assent opened up the road, but only for the short distance to the next obstacle. Each keeper had the potential to block the road and make the entire journey futile. It is this road, from the complaint of a wrong to its legal resolution, that the next chapters will examine.

4

From crime to criminal accusation

The body of Agnes Cheesman's child is found dead, bruised and bloodied; George Wenham's best hog is missing from its pen; John Hooke gets angry and tells Justice Pelham about some suspicious tools that Hooke's master purchased recently. How did incidents like these come to the notice of the law? How were potential suspects singled out? How was evidence assembled to support suspicions? These matters are crucial to our understanding of early modern notions of criminality and order, but because pre-trial depositions were not formally acceptable as evidence, scholars interested in trial procedures have not systematically exploited them. And, because almost no depositions taken in accusations of serious felonies have survived for the early seventeenth century, scholars interested in crime have been similarly cautious.[1] Although the evidence is essentially restricted to thefts tried before the Quarter Sessions, the information in these documents, confused, rambling and one-sided as it may be, allows us to reconstruct the detection of suspects in the countryside of early modern England. In turn, this reconstruction tells us important things about contemporary ideals of behavior, official duty and communal responsibility.[2]

[1] After the enactments of 1 & 2 Philip & Mary, c. 13 and 2 & 3 Philip & Mary, c. 10, depositions should have been taken in all accusations of felony, but their survival into the twentieth century is largely fortuitous since, as informal documents, they had no clear use after the pertinent session of a court. Only a handful of depositions from the Assizes in the early seventeenth century has survived, almost all from the North of England: PRO ASSI 45/1/1. For printed examples of depositions, see *Depositions from the Castle of York Relating to Offences Committed in the Northern Counties in the Seventeenth Century*, ed. James Raine, Jr, Surtees Society 40 (1861) for the Assizes. On the use of depositions for trial, see Dalton, *Countrey Justice*, pp. 295–302; Cockburn, *Introduction*, pp. 98–100. While the anecdotal uses of these documents have long been realized, there have been few serious studies of depositions. See, however, John Styles, "An Eighteenth Century Magistrate as Detective: Samuel Lister of Little Horton," *The Bradford Antiquary*, new series, 47 (1982): 98–117.

[2] Of the 266 examinations extant from eastern Sussex, all are from the Quarter Sessions and 225 concern simple larceny. Contemporary pamphlets and interrogations taken in the Court of Star Chamber provide additional, but much more casual, information about investigations. All of these documents, of course, detail successful rather than unsuccessful detec-

The initial response to alleged crimes in early modern England combined communal and official participation. Since by the seventeenth century private complaints in criminal matters (appeals) had been virtually replaced by public accusations (indictments), public officials should have been in charge of investigations. However, while some part in detection was played by constables, observing, investigating and accusing suspects seem to have remained as much a private concern as a governmental duty. The initiative in identifying and prosecuting misbehavior was shared between the formal representatives of the law – constables, coroners, magistrates – and ordinary people. At least in routine felonies, practical considerations ensured that the victim was almost always the principal investigator; communal cooperation was a necessary concession in a world of rural theft and part-time officialdom. The direct participation of aggrieved parties added determination to the detective process, although it also gave rein to social prejudice and private malice. Such motives did lay the groundwork for some criminal charges, but a rudimentary notion of probable cause seems to have restrained the effect of such wayward enthusiasm. Grand juries repeatedly showed their preference for cases based on solid, witnessed detection over those built from circumstantial inference.

At the base of the structure of officials responsible for enforcement was the constableship, an office which was amateur and communal in both its qualifications and duties. The inhabitants of eastern Sussex relied upon one officer, the headboro (or petty constable), for immediate help if they were victims of a crime. One or two headboros served each parish annually; they, in turn, were supervised by one or two constables responsible for each hundred. Traditionally both sorts of officials were elected at the spring meeting of the court leets, but by the early seventeenth century, when many leets had become inactive, other methods of designation were used also. In Wiltshire and parts of Lancashire, for example, the office of headboro rotated among the freeholders or the householders; in Essex juries at the leet still elected headboros but, as in Wiltshire and Norfolk, justices of the peace appointed the head constables; in Kent both offices seem to have been elective. No single pattern of selection predominated in eastern Sussex. In rural Heathfield, officials were elected at the court leets as they had traditionally been; in the more urban setting of Brighton, the governing council chose officials from men

tions; modern studies of investigation suggest that failed prosecutions have very different histories from those that succeed. Because of the communal and commonsensical nature of local investigation in the seventeenth century, the peculiarities of successful investigations were probably much less striking; however, the distinction is an important one of which to be aware; see David Steer, *Uncovering Crime: The Police Role*, Royal Commission on Criminal Procedure Research Study 7 (London, 1980).

nominated at the leet; in the county town of Lewes, the ruling oligarchy controlled appointments.[3]

Regardless of these differences, constables everywhere were expected to be jacks of all trades. These few men were responsible for controlling any disturbance within their communities. Headboros enforced regulations against suspicious strangers and organized local responses to hues and cries. They made monthly searches for illegal residents and supervised the enforcement of most local economic, social, and military obligations (especially control over brewing and gambling). They were also general deputies for nearby magistrates, executing judicial orders for searches, arrests, and committals to jail. Hundred constables not only oversaw the collection of local rates, the maintenance of roads and bridges, and the work of lesser parochial officers; they also were expected to attend the meetings of the Quarter Sessions and to serve there periodically as grand jurors.

The constableship, like the magistracy, was a position without formal training. Several handbooks for constables existed by the late sixteenth century, but how regularly they were used is unclear. Written manuals of instruction, no doubt, were relatively expensive and it required a fair degree of literacy to absorb them. Although some constables were probably capable of using such guides, the time and expense of reading official handbooks was a substantial commitment for a job that was occasional, temporary, and unpopular.[4]

The impermanence of local office reinforced the need for communal participation in law enforcement. Because the job was temporary, the distinction between official public authority and unofficial private power was somewhat

---

[3] For general discussions of these offices, the following are particularly useful: Smith, p. 86; Lambard, *Constables*; H. Simpson, "The Office of Constable," *EHR* 40 (1895): 625–41; Kent, "The English Village Constable". On Sussex: BL Additional MS 33,174/B4/119–275v; /B8/409–442v; ESRO ADA MSS 56; 143; *The Book of John Rowe*, ed. W. H. Godfrey, SRS 34 (Lewes, 1928); Farrant and Farrant, "Brighton 1580–1820," p. 339; Goring, "The Fellowship of the Twelve," pp. 158–9. Other shires: Joel Hurstfield, "County Government: Wiltshire c.1530–c.1660," reprinted in Hurstfield, *Freedom, Corruption and Government in Elizabethan England* (Cambridge, Mass., 1973), pp. 282–3 (Wiltshire); Walter J. King, "Prosecution of Illegal Behavior in Seventeenth Century England with Emphasis on Lancashire," (Ph.D. dissertation, University of Michigan, 1977), pp. 39–40; Silcock, "Worcestershire," pp. 62–4; Quintrell, "Essex," pp. 195–200; Hassell Smith, *County and Court*, pp. 94–5, 112 (Norfolk); Clark, *English Provincial Society*, p. 116 (Kent); Roberts, *Recovery and Restoration*, pp. 103, 114–17 (Devon).

[4] The problem of retaining men of proper status for these offices was endemic in early modern England. Some constables in eastern Sussex were well off enough to be assessed in the subsidy, could sign their names, and left wills bequeathing property: Herrup, diss., pp. 457–65; but cf. PRO ASSI 35/55/7/5 where in 1613 a justice complains that local officials in Sussex were "honest men but of mean estate and few of them know what belongs to their office." For examples both positive and negative from other counties, see Wrightson, "Two Concepts of Order," pp. 26–9, where the author also notes that constables in Sussex were neither outstandingly able nor ignorant in terms of literacy.

arbitrary. The difference between a yeoman or husbandman and a constable was often simply a matter of who carried the white staff of office and its attendant burdens. Both the staff and its aura of expertise would, within a few months, be transferred into new hands. Just as the line between the gentleman and the justice of the peace was fluid, the division between a constable and a yeoman or husbandman constantly shifted. The stature of a magistrate ensured him a minimum of deference from most local residents, but at best the headboro or the constable was an equal among equals; that meant that he was likely to be directly resisted at times by other people and that he could not counter that resistance easily without popular support.

As a consequence of this situation, the basic level of the policing system demanded not only communal participation for its staffing, but also the assistance of non-officials for its operation. Because headboros and constables were rarely members of the gentry, legal office was part-time. Since miscreants did not restrict themselves to hours convenient for headboros, fast action in a crisis might well preclude the presence of a legal officer. Bailiffs and deputies lent assistance in special circumstances, but without the help of able-bodied individuals, even a minimum of daily peace might have been impossible. The nature of crime and the criminal law made vigilance a communal obligation; the administrative realities of life in Tudor–Stuart England ensured that it stayed communal.

By the seventeenth century, the ancient method for apprehending criminals, the hue and cry, seems to have been only marginally important in eastern Sussex. A written warrant sworn before a justice of the peace and issued to a constable was replacing the traditional verbal alarm. This written hue and cry served to redefine what had once been a communal responsibility into an official duty. In the early middle ages, the verbal alarm (at least in theory) had alerted the full community; criminals were hunted down by all male adults. If a suspect escaped, the entire hundred paid compensation to the victim. As Sir Thomas Smith wrote in the sixteenth century, "every English man is a Sergeant to take the thief," but by the 1590s local legal officers, not their communities, were accepting the blame when a thief was left untaken. The headboro was expected to ensure local participation in a hue and cry and to pass along the alarm to the next parish if that was necessary. Although the community could, theoretically, still be assessed if a felon escaped, the files of eastern Sussex record no such payments. Instead, the new warrant for the hue and cry was a step toward defining the culpability of legal officers; several officers in eastern Sussex were fined for negligently allowing criminals to escape.[5]

---

[5] Smith, pp. 83–4; Lambard, *Constables*, pp. 19–23, 37; Pollock & Maitland, 2: 587; an

The limitation of a communal responsibility to an official duty coincided with a lessening in the importance of the hue and cry in apprehending criminals. Although a handful of cases in eastern Sussex mention the hue and cry as though it was commonplace (without specifying written or verbal versions), no defendants in larceny were actually captured through the process. Several local residents were highly critical of its inefficiency; their doubts were echoed by contemporary authors. William Harrison complained that public spirit had declined so drastically in England that, despite the hue and cry, felons wandered freely through the countryside. Robert Green made his fictional cutpurse, Ned Brown, a master of deception who claimed, "I little cared for hues and cries, but straight with disguising myself would outslip them all." Some legal experts, Sir Edward Coke among them, doubted the validity of warrants initiating hues and cries since neither a magistrate nor a constable had an immediate interest in the arrest of unindicted suspects. Sir Francis Bacon did not question the legal propriety of such documents, but he claimed that the replacement of the verbal hue and cry with the written version was directly responsible for a rise in thefts in the early seventeenth century. Bacon noted that "now hues and cries are of no consequence, only a little paper is sent up and down with a soft pace, whereas they should be prosecuted with horse and foot and hunted as a thief."[6]

Contemporary evidence from outside of eastern Sussex supports such pessimism. The most extensive constables' accounts published for the seventeenth century, those of Manchester, list an average of twelve precepts per year for hues and cries between 1612 and 1631. Covering a wide range of crimes, the entries suggest a relatively rapid response by officials to suspicions and show how alarms passed between shires as well as within local areas. Although many precepts name specific individuals as suspects, none contains any notation of a successful conclusion to an investigation and most indicate that notice had been passed along to another constable. Moreover, many precepts include only a cursory description of either suspects or stolen

example of a hue-and-cry warrant can be found in BL Lansdowne MS 569/52v. For examples of negligent escapes, ESRO Q/R/E/13/118v; 19/20; 27/23–4; 39/113v; 40/9; 42/42. It is unclear if officials were fined in lieu of, or in addition to, local communities. On hues and cries in Sussex: PRO ASSI 35/55/7/4; 35/77/6/19, 58; ESRO Q/R/E 12/16, 106, 123; 16/8, 62–3; 25/35, 67; 39/9, 95; PRO STAC 8/28/17; 8/90/12; on the use of hues and cries elsewhere: PRO SP 12/252/93; *CSPD*, Addenda 1580–1625, p. 532; *CSPD*, 1601–3, and Addenda 1547–65, p. 309; *Western Circuit Assize Orders 1629–1648: A Calendar*, ed. J. S. Cockburn, Camden Society, 4th series, 17 (London, 1976), p. 198; Hawarde, pp. 23–4; "Notebook of a Surrey Justice," pp. 178–9; "Diary of Robert Beake," p. 125; *Diary of Ralph Josselin*, p. 161; *Beverley Borough Records 1575–1821*, ed. J. Dennett, Yorkshire Archaeological Society Record Series 84 (1933), p. 186; Cockburn, *Introduction*, pp. 89–90.

6 Harrison, *Description of England*, p. 194; Green, "The Black Book's Messenger," in *The Elizabethan Underworld*, p. 255; *Bacon*, 6: 306; according to Spedding, the original manuscript says haunted as a thief.

property; some simply warn of suspicious persons. In the 1650s the villagers of Monkton near Houton (Devon) complained bitterly about the frequency with which hues and cries were pursued through their villages; well into the eighteenth century, constables were asking reimbursement for raising hues and cries. Obviously in some places, the hue and cry retained its vigor, but it is impossible to generalize about the behavior behind the complaints and the paperwork. In eastern Sussex, individuals were willing to apply both horse and foot to hunting suspects, but usually only when an alleged crime touched their families or their neighbors. In some hearts the ideal of responsibility for the full community endured, but generally it was superseded by a more restricted definition of obligation. Ironically, a full acceptance of officials as public representatives did not accompany this contraction.[7]

Legal officials and private individuals also shared the responsibility for detection in circumstances where the victim believed that the suspect might be in the immediate area. The division of labor depended on how a crime came to notice. Usually the discovery happened in one of three ways: a victim realized his misfortune, suspicious behavior suggested that a crime had been committed, or the results of a crime (a body or stolen property) were found and traced back to illegal activity. In the first two circumstances, the aggrieved individual usually took immediate action to find the alleged criminal. Either the victim, or the victim's relatives or neighbors, organized the detective work to identify the proper suspect. Relatives and neighbors rather than legal officers assisted with the investigation; they also served later as witnesses. Of 182 witnesses who can be identified from the Quarter Sessions, only twenty-five seem to have been legal officials. In the parish of Heathfield, for example, only two of the twenty-three men known to have served as headboros or hundred constables between 1594 and 1640 were called as witnesses during their tenures in office. Only in the third type of discovery, where the results of a crime initiated investigation, did the job of detection belong clearly to legal officials. As long as theft was the predominant criminal accusation, familiarity with local property was an important asset for the investigators. As long as alleged criminals were routinely no more dangerous than angered victims, familiarity with local inhabitants was helpful in identifying suspects. As long as private individuals were willing to participate in the process of detection, the arrangement was both reasonable and, within limits, reasonably effective.

Since criminal investigations usually began when the victim discovered a

---

7   *The Constables' Accounts of the Manor of Manchester 1612–1647 and 1743–1796*, ed. J. P. Earwaker, 2 vols. vol. 1 (Manchester, 1891–2); Roberts, *Recovery and Restoration*, p. 39; *The Wigginton Constable's Book 1691–1836*, ed. F. D. Price, Banbury Historical Society, 11 (Chichester, 1971).

loss of property, in thefts such revelations were often rapid. Many larcenies simply involved a sharp eye and a fast hand – linens were taken off hedges, tools from hanging hooks, food from open windows. Although few persons encountered their adversaries face-to-face, some thieves did not disguise the fact of their invasion. Several suspects claimed merely to have taken advantage of holes or cracks in the walls of houses, but a few admitted to using axes or other tools to gain entry. One case heard at the Quarter Sessions in January 1627 outlined how two boys dug a hole in the foundations of William Homewood's house, entered, stole some clothing, and then exited without covering the hole up again. Other break-ins were immediately apparent because of broken locks. Richard Avington, arriving one morning in 1627 at the warehouse in Laughton where he stored shoes, found that the lock had been jimmied. His abuser was subtle, however, compared to the man who allegedly robbed Goddard Longley. Longley maintained that his wife Mary latched their door and went to fetch water from a spring about two hundred yards away. When she returned, the entry was open, and the lock and doorpost had been completely broken off. Even without violent entry, the theft of goods was usually obvious because most victims had too few material possessions for even a small loss to go long unnoticed. In most cases, some investigation was begun within a few days of the alleged theft.[8]

If a crime were discovered quickly enough, the malefactor might be immediately apprehended. If someone were taken with stolen goods near the scene of a crime, protestations of innocence were fairly useless. This encouraged victims to begin searching for a suspect without taking the time even to call a legal officer. Stephen Copping and some of his friends captured Robert Leigh and William Woodyer in the nearby woods as the two thieves divided up the clothing and cash that they had just taken from Copping's home. Samuel Cornford was seen by a maidservant as he lifted a sheet from the hedge near the home of Robert Jarrett. Jarrett heard his servant's cries and ran to capture Cornford, who drooped not only his loot but also one shoe in his efforts to escape. Jarrett pursued him by following his unique footprints in the mud. He discovered Cornford hiding beneath a hedge, nursing a tender and bloody bare foot. Both of these confrontations ended with indictments, trials, and convictions. In the face of such clear evidence, a suspect often

---

[8] Neither confrontation nor violence seems to have been routinely connected with theft in early modern England; only 35 cases in eastern Sussex mention any interaction between the victim and a thief. The records may not be complete in this matter, but similar evidence appears in other counties, see Sharpe, *Essex*, p. 104; on gaining entry: ESRO Q/R/E 10/26, 59, 77a; 20/48, 51; 25/4, 42, 45–6, 68–9, 71–2; 35/38, 81, 87; 37/32, 70; 43/29, 58–9; on the initiation of investigations: ESRO Q/R/E 25/35, 67; 26/26, 53; 15/43, 66, 86; although indictment crime dates are not absolutely reliable, examination evidence bears this out. Of the cases studied here, 26 percent (197 out of 763) produced a suspect before a justice of the peace within five days of the alleged crime; 40 percent did so within two weeks.

confessed to the pursuer. The victim might accept the return of the stolen property as adequate compensation, but he could also insist that the suspect repeat the confession before a justice of the peace. William Smith, a laborer of Bexhill, confessed to two crimes at once. Smith, who was the apprentice of a local gentleman, stole a small amount of food from John Boorner's house one Sunday in 1637. He tried a second break-in on the following Tuesday, but Boorner caught him red-handed; Smith admitted both escapades. He was whipped for his sticky fingers, and his master, Thomas Delve, broke Smith's indenture of apprenticeship, telling the magistrates at the Quarter Sessions that Smith was "so lewd and disorderly that he is utterly unfit to be continued in his service."[9]

In such spontaneous pursuits and captures, the constable had no particular responsibility. Even if a suspect was nowhere nearby, however, victims often preferred to follow a line of clues immediately rather than passing the information on to a legal officer. James Payne's servant cleverly began his hunt by "taking the foot of the party" (i.e. footprints), which he and his master followed to the culprit's home. John Weller and his servants, upon discovering the loss of several linens, found that two "rogues" had been seen leaving the area. After a chase that lasted for five hours, they caught up with the men, who not only still had the stolen goods, but also were willing to confess their crime.[10]

The role of a legal official was even peripheral in what was perhaps the most common type of extended investigation, the search of houses for stolen property. Because most suspects were not captured near the scene of the crime with ill-gotten goods, a formal search was usually needed to link a suspect to misbehavior. Organized searches rather than immediate pursuits produced most arrests in eastern Sussex. At least three persons together – the complainant, the headboro, and a servant or neighbor who acted as a witness – normally conducted these investigations. The headboro's role was less investigatory than coercive and observational. The onus of the investigation remained with the victim, but when an arrest was imminent, common sense dictated that the headboro accompany the aggrieved party. If stolen goods were found on search, the officer could witness the challenge of ownership. He could also confiscate the questioned items and ensure the swift transportation of the accused to the nearest justice of the peace for formal interrogation. If a suspect confessed, the headboro again was a solid witness.

[9]　ESRO Q/R/E 27/61 (Leigh and Woodyer); 26/25, 52 (Jarrett); 37/32, 70, 102v (Smith); see also ESRO Q/R/E 10/13, 74; 14/17, 39, 41; 16/13, 72–3; 21/48, 110; 26/25, 52; 27/61; 34/57, 96; 37/102v; 44/31, 60; WSRO Q/R/WE 16/12, 39.
[10]　WSRO Q/R/WE 16/19, 44; 16/12, 39; see also ESRO Q/R/E 2/10; 3/37; 13/35, 93; 16/13, 72–3; 20/25, 34, 56, 61; 26/25, 52; 37/15, 66; 49/18, 77; Lambard, *Eirenarcha*, p. 214; Dalton, *Countrey Justice*, p. 302; *Diary of Ralph Josselin*, pp. 550–1.

If a culprit, once accused, grew violent or tried to escape, the officer had the power to commandeer local passersby for assistance. Since warrants were neither required nor universally used, the headboro's presence also provided a semi-official authorization for the search and a formal reminder of the power of the law.[11]

Most of the complainants who used searches had chosen their likely suspect before they ever called in a headboro or constable. A search normally began at the residence of this primary suspect. Many initial accusations were merely hunches, but others were based on detection. George Wenham of Penhurst, for example, discovered one morning that a hog had been taken from his close. He had few clues to aid him until about a half mile from his home, he discovered a site used recently for slaughtering. The animal's paunch was cast over a hedge, blood covered the ground, and horses' hoof-prints led clearly both to and from the area. Wenham followed the prints and drops of blood, but stopped his search when night fell. Because the trail ended within two miles of the home of John Markwick, Wenham asked the constable to search Markwick's residence. When two flitches of bacon were found, Wenham accused Markwick, even though nothing clearly linked the bacon and Wenham's hog. A trial jury acquitted the accused, but later evidence suggested that he might have been the receiver, if not the actual taker, of the stolen animal. Wenham's investigation is typical of the initiative taken by victims or their servants. The time to call the headboro was when his authority and punitive powers could inspire cooperation from those under suspicion. The legwork of discovering the suspect belonged to the injured party.[12]

Many of the clues used to identify primary suspects were even less solid than those put forward by George Wenham. Some persons were suspected on general reputation; John Rice was confronted, for example, because he was known to be "lewd, discordant and suspicious." Some were accused because they had been seen in the vicinity of a crime, because they were enemies of the victim, or because a third party had reported them. Sometimes indiscreet behavior – ostentatiousness, bragging, or simply a new ability to put meat upon the table – drew attention to particular individuals. In other cases, suspicion fell on alehousekeepers, itinerants or strangers. When no specific

---

[11] Lambard, *Constables*, pp. 14–18; search warrants are rarely mentioned specifically, but see ESRO Q/R/E 34/38, 91; 44/28–9, 59; Bodleian Rawlinson MS B431/8v; Hawarde, p. 87; "Diary of Robert Beake," *passim*. The physical presence of a legal officer undoubtedly compensated for the fact that most persons (and some officials) could not read a search warrant. See David Cressy, *Literacy and the Social Order: Reading and Writing in Tudor and Stuart England* (Cambridge, 1980); Wrightson, "Two Concepts of Order," pp. 26–9. Constables could put uncooperative residents into the local stocks and they were not above reminding individuals of this fact; see ESRO Q/R/E 10/26, 59, 77a; 34/59, 100.

[12] ESRO Q/R/E 12/30; 13/35, 93.

evidence could be discovered, "the butler did it" was always considered a plausible explanation; servants, lodgers or laborers commonly became defendants. Given the social tensions intrinsic to a hierarchical, under-employed society, charges founded on social prejudice or malice are no revelation; what is striking is the clear preference of grand juries for charges supported with careful investigative work.[13]

If there was no indication of a probable culprit in a larceny, searchers went from house to house throughout an area until they found something that brought the case into focus. Investigators hoped that a search would establish both that stolen items were in the possession of a suspect and that the goods had been deliberately taken. Because the most common types of property were those stolen the most frequently, proving that the discovered items actually belonged to the victim was an important and often difficult task. To prevent accusations from degenerating into contests of one person's word against another's, investigators put great stress on the recovery of physical evidence linking a suspect to a crime.

Very little detailed information survives from which to reconstruct how searches were conducted. Little is known about the popular response to such intrusions, but extant complaints suggest a fear of searches as well as occasional anger at the invasion of one's home. Most of the hostility was verbal, but sometimes an officer was assaulted or an accuser faced with a counter-accusation. Some suspects attempted to hide evidence; others bolted away when they heard searchers approaching. One widow, who later said that she had found an allegedly stolen sheep while out nutting, panicked when investigators came to her son's house for the lost animal. Unable to find the key to her locked portion of the residence, she, "being fearful," broke her own wall down, and threw the remains of the mutton out of a window. Her actions hindered more than they helped. The victim alerted his companions and recovered the mutton from a nearby bush. The widow was convicted and whipped for the theft. Neither direct opposition nor indirect attempts to avoid scrutiny were effective means of escaping suspicion once it was aroused. If anything, such actions suggested that a suspect was hiding something.[14]

---

13   ESRO Q/R/E 10/13, 74; on general suspiciousness: see also ESRO Q/R/E 10/68–9; 13/24, 94–6; 20/28, 53, 75–6, 109; 22/53, 121, 161v; 22/34, 104, 113–15; 23/33, 97; 25/2, 64–5, 73; 29/22, 65–6; 29/33, 68, 70; 37/15, 66; 39/8, 49, 98; 40/32–3, 64; 45/37, 73; 49/20, 78; WSRO Q/R/WE 16/13, 39; PRO STAC 8/242/5; on accusations against servants, lodgers and laborers: ESRO Q/R/E 10/16, 75; 10/11, 70; 13/33,91; 16/12, 65; 22/32, 124–5, 24/23, 71–3; 25/1, 30, 74–5; 25/36, 79; 29/28, 61–2; 34/57, 96; 34/40, 88; 38/57, 105–6; WSRO Q/R/WE 16/19, 44; for similar cases elsewhere: "Notebook of a Surrey Justice," pp. 193, 199, 202, 208, 212. On the relationship between servants and masters generally: Ann Kussmaul, *Servants in Husbandry in Early Modern England* (Cambridge, 1981).
14   ESRO Q/R/E 36/50, 104–5; see also ESRO Q/R/E 35/31; 36/102v; 37/31, 62, 65; 41/46, 83;

Investigators on search kept a sharp look out not only for specific stolen items and specific suspects, but also for anything out of the ordinary. Search warrants identified particular goods reported missing, but investigations were not limited to these objects. For example, when John Longley of Mayfield lost two geese, he and the headboro searched house by house for evidence. They stopped at the home of William Pankhurst to get a candle for light, but at their arrival, Pankhurst's wife ran up the stairs and threw something inside one of the beds. This strange behavior alerted Longley and the headboro, so they insisted, over the woman's protests, on searching the chambers on the second floor. In the bedstraw of one of the rooms, they found half of a goose with Longley's markings. Francis Pankhurst of Heathfield (no known relation to the Pankhursts of Mayfield) was even more unfortunate. After John Ellis found some familiar looking grain at the local miller's, he went to Pankhurst to ask about its origins. Ellis accused Pankhurst of theft, and began to search the house. He found no grain, but discovered a half of a goose that he claimed resembled one missing from his father's property. Although this second accusation was eventually dismissed, Pankhurst arrived at court accused of two thefts, rather than just one.[15]

Victims and officials alike were often willing to make repeated visits to a suspect if his answers were unsatisfactory. Such repeated intrusions constituted harassment, but they often produced confessions. The interrogation of Robert Walcott, suspected of stealing a lamb from Christopher Deering, is a good example of the efficacy of repeated visitations. Deering and the headboro began their investigation with a thorough search of local residences. They found animal broth on the stove in the Walcotts' home, but Walcott and his wife denied slaughtering any animals. A week later, Deering and the officer returned and again they found meat broth at the Walcotts', but again no flesh. Walcott's wife still denied that any meat had been recently boiled in the household. Unconvinced, Deering and the headboro found Walcott at his work, and asked him what meat he had brought for his dinner. When he insisted that he had none, they searched his bag and found a boiled loin of lamb. At least in part because of his earlier denials, Walcott's claim that he discovered the lamb starving on the local common was disregarded. Under questioning by the local magistrate, Walcott admitted to having taken Deering's animal. It was rare for a constable to be so persistent an

---

WSRO Q/R/WE 16/18, 43; and for instances of more direct resistance ESRO Q/R/E 34/37, 94–5; 34/55, 89, 93; 35/21; 51/24; 52/149v. In Sussex no instances are recorded of searchers being denied entry to a dwelling; but cf. Samaha, "Hanging for Felony," p. 775.

[15] ESRO Q/R/E 22/58, 76, 96–7, 111 (W. Pankhurst); 39/8, 49, 98 (F. Pankhurst); see ESRO Q/R/E 46/45, 56, but also the Essex case of George Dibney, cited in Samaha, "Hanging for Felony," p. 775.

investigator, but in several cases, victims methodically and painstakingly followed a suspect's story to its logical end.[16]

Because of the type of goods taken in all but the largest thefts, searching was a logical, but troublesome, investigative tool for solving early modern larcenies. Many of the goods stolen were not readily identifiable as out of place in a modest home. House or farm goods could easily be added to a thief's personal inventory. Food or small livestock could be eaten. Only major livestock, money, plate, and luxuries had to be hidden or sold to avoid immediate discovery. The ubiquity of the goods routinely stolen meant that the knowledge of the searchers about the property was often crucial to identifying stolen goods. A constable or headboro alone could make little progress trying to find items as common as sheep or grain, particularly if the recoverable evidence was no longer in its original form, but had been transformed into a leg of mutton or a loaf of bread. The handful of examinations that discuss searches without mentioning the presence of the complainant deal either with dated crimes or with investigations conducted over several parishes. Even in these cases, victims had initiated the searches and they, not just the constables, were examined by the magistrates.[17]

The problem of recognizing stolen goods, of course, varied with the items taken. Sheep, cattle and horses were often marked with brands, slits, or dye. If an animal had not already been killed and quartered, such practices made identification fairly simple, but not foolproof. When William Scrase had a sheep stolen, he thought that the distinctive red he used to mark the ears of his animals would make his property immediately recognizable. William Pearse, a shepherd in the area, had sheep with such coloring and Scrase confronted him, but Pearse claimed that the marking was also his peculiar brand. The grand jury that heard the case at the Quarter Sessions could not sort out the confusion; they dismissed Scrase's charges as insubstantial.[18]

Goods such as grain or timber could be positively identified by comparison with the original stock, but this was possible only if the goods were recovered in their original condition. When James Turner challenged a former employee for the theft of lumber, his evidence was the bits of furniture that he claimed

---

[16] ESRO Q/R/E 46/45, 56; see also ESRO Q/R/E 12/45, 102v; 21/54, 74, 111–12; 22/54, 129; 34/55, 89, 93; WSRO Q/R/WE 16/19, 44.

[17] The theft of expensive property comprised only 24 percent of the indicted cases of larceny and 22 percent of the known larceny accusations in eastern Sussex; the absence of investigative information from the Assizes is particularly unfortunate since that court dominated the trial of such accusations. For examples of the difficulty of identifying common types of property: ESRO Q/R/E 14/20, 42; 15/20, 85; 22/58, 76, 96–7, 111; 24/9, 76; 25/30–1, 74–5; 25/36, 79; 28/16, 72; 29/31, 69; 34/61, 101; 34/55, 89, 93; 35/42, 93; 37/31, 62, 65; 39/10, 99; 45/72; 46/30, WSRO Q/R/WE 16/8, 41. For searches with no mention of the victim's presence: ESRO Q/R/E 23/62, 93–4, 98; 25/30, 74; 29/31, 69; 34/55, 89, 91; 45/44, 103; 45/12, 71; WSRO Q/R/WE 16/8, 41.

[18] ESRO Q/R/E 27/101–3; see also ESRO Q/R/E 21/54, 74, 111–12; 29/22, 65–6.

had been constructed from the stolen wood. The jury was unsympathetic and acquitted the defendant. Linens and iron were similarly malleable, and few accusations about the original identity of new clothes or remolded iron were given credence. Particular imperfections sometimes marked household items, tools, or money, but the process was very haphazard. Few victims mention deliberately branding small goods as they might do with sheep or cattle. Personalized property, such as old clothing, was relatively easy to recognize, especially if it was worn unaltered. Not surprisingly, many suspects caught with clothing were nowhere to be found by the next meeting of the court. The identification of stolen articles was a persistent problem. The most successful prosecutions for converted stolen items were those in which defendants incriminated themselves by telling blatant lies about the origins of disputed property or those in which suspects panicked and were taken while trying to hide evidence.[19]

A formal search was not the only way to identify a suspect.[20] In a case without specific clues or involving easily hidden items, a search might be impracticable or ineffective. One alternative to a formal search was a stakeout. Victims either waited for a suspect to reveal his guilt, or they set a trap for a suspected culprit. The local headboro occasionally was consulted about strategy in a stakeout, but no depositions show legal officers acting as principals in this type of investigation. Stakeouts, like other types of early modern detection, depended on a minimum of manpower and a maximum of common sense for their success. They worked best for thefts of goods that could be clearly recognized once recovered, and they had the added advantage of implicating the suspect on the basis of behavior as well as possession of stolen property.

Richard Avington, the shoemaker whose warehouse lock was jimmied, successfully employed the passive stakeout. Avington, on discovering that seventeen shoes were missing from his stock, decided that silence was the best way to smoke out the thief. He waited for someone to appear in shoes that

[19]   ESRO Q/R/E 15/20, 85; see also ESRO Q/R/E 12/6, 46, 104–4v; 22/33, 120; 34/48, 91; on linens and iron: ESRO Q/R/E 29/31, 69; 35/42, 93; on household items: ESRO Q/R/E 18/34, 56–7, 62–3; 28/14, 69, 74; 29/28, 61–2; 36/45, 98; on clothing: ESRO Q/R/E 25/35, 67; 27/61; 38/25, 99; and for similar difficulties elsewhere, see *A Royalist's Notebook*, p. 150; Mildred Campbell, *The English Yeoman under Elizabeth and the Early Stuarts*, reprint (New York, 1968), pp. 200–1. For examples of self-incrimination: ESRO Q/R/E 36/50, 104–5; 37/17, 69; 44/28–9, 59; 46/45, 56; see also ESRO Q/R/E 14/20, 42; 15/20, 85; 22/58, 76, 96–7, 111; 24/9, 76; 25/30–1, 74–5; 25/36, 79; 28/16, 72; 29/31, 69; 34/61, 101; 34/55, 89, 93; 35/42, 93; 37/31, 62, 65; 39/10, 99; 45/72; 46/30; WSRO Q/R/WE 16/8, 41.

[20]   Although no depositions from eastern Sussex record similar habits, evidence from elsewhere suggests that cunning men and astrologers were used not only by victims looking for suspects but also by suspects hoping to avoid detection; see Thomas, *Religion*, pp. 211–12, 307–8, 345–6, 442–3; King, "Prosecution of Illegal Behavior," p. 43; "The Bloudy Vision of John Farley," cited in Christopher Hill, *The World Turned Upside Down: Radical Ideas during the English Revolution* (New York, 1975), p. 70.

resembled the stolen footwear. Within a few days, one Edward Page appeared shod in suspicious gear. Page at first said that he had bought the shoes at a nearby fair, but later he decided that he had purchased them from Avington several weeks earlier. The petty jurors did not believe Page's story, but they limited their conviction to the single recovered pair of shoes and valued these just under the level defining grand larceny. Edward Hider of Rotherfield used a similar approach to find the thief of a piece of gold worth eleven shillings that was taken from his home at Christmas, 1625. Hider suspected that one of the Bartons who had dined with him over the holidays had pilfered the coin, but he took no action against them or anyone else to recover his property. When he heard that the Bartons' daughter, Agnes, had gone into a local shop and exchanged a piece of gold for "white money," he questioned the young woman and obtained a confession.

Some victims used more active techniques to implicate their suspects. Perhaps the most elaborate recorded scheme was that of John Tyler, a founder from Buxted. Tyler had several items, including a fleece, taken from his home before New Year, 1628. When he looked for his lost property, he found the fleece hidden under several inches of hay stored in his barn. He asked advice from Nicholas French, the local headboro, who suggested that Tyler mark the fleece, return it to its hiding place, and set up a watch for the thief's inevitable return. Tyler snipped a piece of leather from his apron, and inserted it inside the skin. He recruited two local men to help with the stake-out. For several nights, the three watched and waited, but to no avail. On the fourth evening, however, the wife of a local carpenter visited Tyler and acted, according to Tyler, very oddly. He checked the barn and found that the fleece was missing. With a warrant obtained by Nicholas French, Tyler (accompanied by French and the two neighbors) searched the home of the suspected thief and discovered the marked fleece in a bedchamber. The carpenter, William White, claimed that he had unexpectedly found the fleece while feeding Tyler's horses. The petty jurors felt that if the discovery was innocent White's possession of the goods was not. He was convicted and whipped. Once again, the division of responsibility between officials and victims is clear. French's task as headboro was basically advisory and his participation was less important than that of the immediate complainant and his neighbors. French became vital to the investigation only after others identified the suspect. In situations where the aggrieved party discovered his own misfortune, then, the obligation for criminal detection rested on the wronged individual, his neighbors and his family. The formal authority of the legal officer was used essentially to confirm a suspicion and to confront a suspect.[21]

[21] ESRO Q/R/E 26/26, 53 (Page); 20/4, 54, 69–70 (Barton); 29/30, 63–4 (White); see also ESRO Q/R/E 13/30, 98; 21/57, 102–5, 111, 146; 28/14, 69, 74; 34/61, 101; 36/45, 98, 101; 36/97; 39/8, 49, 98.

Although most investigations began with a complaint by the victim, some defendants drew suspicion to themselves by their behavior. In such cases, private persons and local officers together looked into the possibility that eccentricity hid criminal activity. Although individuals normally did not conduct such investigations independently, neither did they invariably report odd conduct to legal officers and consider their involvement finished. If a person saw someone commit a crime, he was justified in making an immediate arrest. A felony discovered anywhere in a parish entitled inhabitants to take into custody persons who acted suspiciously. Even when no crime was known to have occurred, everyone was expected to watch for odd behavior and to report it to the closest headboro.[22]

The definition of suspiciousness, of course, was discretionary. Certain sorts of individuals endured more than their share of interrogations for behavior that in other people would have passed unnoticed, but few of the accusations recognizably based on social prejudices alone ended in convictions. The rationale for suspicion is often obvious from the deposition. Regardless of governmental expectations, few persons in early modern England probably willingly involved themselves when they could avoid doing so; those few, however, often made the difference between the capture and the escape of an alleged criminal. For example, Mary Worgar, a fisherman's wife from Brighton, was shopping at the fair in Lewes in the summer of 1614 when Richard Plawe, a tailor from Uckfield and a stranger to Worgar, suddenly told her to check for her purse. The bag was missing. Plawe rushed after a man who was hurriedly leaving the site of the fair and grabbed him by the shoulders. The thief, John Davis, returned Worgar's goods and begged her forgiveness (although he also denied having stolen anything). Richard Amherst, the examining magistrate, checked Davis's claim that he was a respectable shoemaker from London. Amherst found no record of the man, his alleged mistress, or the shop in Smithfield in which he said he worked. Amherst concluded his report to the justices at Quarter Sessions with the comment that Davis was probably an "old crafty cutpurse." The petty jurors agreed and convicted him of grand larceny. But for Richard Plawe's quickness, Davis would have escaped.

Francis Pellat, a yeoman of Hartfield, played an equally important role in arresting another suspect. One summer's day in 1628, Pellat noticed John Burt walking near Cowden Furnace. Burt was "meanly dressed" and carried a pig on his back beneath his jerkin. Pellat grew suspicious when he realized that the pig was dripping enough blood to soak through the waist of Burt's breeches. Burt claimed that he had paid fourteen pence for the animal at the fair in Lewes. Pellat was not satisfied by this response, and he grew even more

[22] Sir James F. Stephen, *A History of the Criminal Law of England*, 3 vols. (London, 1883), 1: 193.

uneasy when he saw that the pig's head had been crushed in (a hasty technique for slaughtering that indicated the pig was probably stolen). Pellat forced Burt to accompany him to the nearest headboro, from whom, it turned out, the unlucky man had just escaped. Between this confrontation and his questioning by a magistrate in late October, Pellat observed Burt several more times. He reported that Burt strutted around in fine clothing and showed off new pieces of gold. Burt insisted that he was innocent, claiming that his new wealth was the legacy of an aunt in Somerset. By the meeting of the court in January, however, Burt had disappeared, and the accusation was never tested. Since this was probably the same John Burt who had been indicted, convicted and granted benefit of clergy in 1627 for a theft, his disappearance is not too surprising, but his success in evading justice was no fault of Francis Pellat, whose behavior fitted the ideal set out for every dutiful subject of the crown.[23]

Direct observation was not the only way to become aware of a suspect. Careless boasting could also initiate an inquiry. Thomas Brown and Walter Russell, for example, were drinking in an alehouse in Lindfield when Edward Tab joined them and bragged of his prowess as a small-time thief. The men warned Tab "to hold his peace or else he would be troubled." Tab replied that "he cared not, he would answer it well enough." Brown and Russell reported Tab to the local headboro and he soon found himself indicted for a recent larceny.[24]

Even people spared contact with suspicious behavior or idle bragging had a responsibility to be on the alert for potential criminals. Consumers were expected to account for the origin of any goods they purchased. The common law divided criminal responsibility equally between a thief and his receivers; the convicted accomplice could hang along with the principal. Moreover, since the law did not allow the trial of an accomplice before the conviction of a principal, if the primary suspect was at large, a receiver might face indictment as the active criminal. These dangers made cautious buying common sense. Not every buyer cared about such matters, but many depositions suggest at least a cursory interrogation when strangers wanted to make a sale. In the turnover of a major piece of property, such as a horse, customers might protect themselves with sureties for the salesman's ownership, witnesses to the actual exchange of goods, and payments stretched out over time. Concern to ensure a safe bargain was undoubtedly a more powerful

---

[23] ESRO Q/R/E 11/13, 49, 52 (Davis); 28/43; 29/22, 65–6 (Burt); see also ESRO Q/R/E 10/11, 70; 15/62, 80, 83–4; 15/73, 81; 20/15, 59, 65, 74; 20/28, 53, 75–6, 109; 21/48, 110; 22/34, 104, 113–15; 23/33, 91; 27/5, 60; 29/33, 68; 35/31; 36/40; 36/58, 102–3; 37/15, 66; 39/91; 39/92–3; 40/18; 45/37, 73; 40/20, 78, cf. Hill, *World Turned Upside Down*, p. 216.
[24] ESRO Q/R/E 45/37, 73; see also 35/91; 36/40.

impetus to investigate unknown vendors than altruism, but indictments against negligent receivers seem to have been relatively rare.[25]

If people hesitated to lose a bargain by exercising their communal responsibilities, they were understandably even more reluctant to report crimes committed by members of their families. Wives were excused from any obligation to reveal their husband's activities. The assumption that they had little choice but to obey their spouses limited their culpability. No wives in eastern Sussex testified against their husbands, but in at least one case, a falling out between spouses encouraged a woman to alert a headboro to her husband's suspicious behavior. Children were not so privileged as wives, and occasionally in criminal matters, juveniles did testify against their parents. Neither victims nor legal officers were reluctant to exploit childish fears or naïveté. Children who did not report the errors of their elders, however, were not considered to be accomplices.[26]

The duty of male heads of households was more ambiguous. Legally a wife could become a felon without her husband's knowledge, but in many instances husbands were assumed to have control over everything that went on within their families. A man might be indicted with his wife, or even in her stead, regardless of his actual participation in a crime. Children were technically more autonomous than wives, but parents commonly tried to conceal the illegal activities of their offspring. If a parent clearly profited from a child's misbehavior, the adult as well as the child was held responsible. The exact culpability of a master for a servant or a servant for a master is uncertain. Masters accepted no particular obligation for employees who were indicted at the Quarter Sessions, and there is no indication that the court expected such responsibility. In many cases, the master's compliance in theft was not in question because the master was himself the victim. When servants had accessories, the accomplices usually came from outside the household. Most employers probably preferred to discipline privately servants suspected of thieving. Masters, in fact, seem rarely to have reported crimes by members of their own households unless the master himself had been the victim.[27]

[25] On accomplices, see Stephen, *History of the Criminal Law*, 2: 229–36, 238; J. S. Cockburn, "Trial by the Book," pp. 66–7; ESRO Q/R/E 13/30, 98; 13/29, 41, 43; 15/21, 26, 82; 16/17, 28, 38, 60; 16/19, 70; 17/32; 25/1, 30, 74–5; 26/24, 41, 50–1; 35/42, 93; 36/46–8, 99; 40/28, 32–4; 41/43–5, 54, 64; 44/21, 58; 45/34, 111v; 48/27, 61; WSRO Q/R/WE 16/6, 22, 26; PRO ASSI 35/76/9/29, 77. On sureties for sales: ESRO Q/R/E 12/52, 99, 105; 16/8, 62v–3; 17/6, 8–9, 34–8; and elsewhere, Eyre, "Diurnall," pp. 16, 76. For receivers who testified against larceny principals: ESRO Q/R/E 21/37, 102–5, 113, 146v; 22/50, 68, 110; 22/53, 78, 123; 23/62, 93–4, 98; 27/5, 26, 59–60; 28/14, 69, 74; 36/45, 98, 101; 36/97; 47/10–15, 51.

[26] Dalton, *Countrey Justice*, pp. 296–7; T. E., *The Law's Resolution of Women's Rights* (London, 1632), pp. 206–7; on spouses: ESRO Q/R/E 35/31, 36/102–3; 12/6, 46, 104v; 21/13–14; on children: ESRO Q/R/E 5/64–7; 10/26, 59, 77a; 20/4, 54, 67–9.

[27] On spouses: ESRO Q/R/E 13/29, 41; 16/13, 72v–3; 21/13–14; 25/4, 42, 45–6, 68–9, 71–2;

Servants were less hesitant to report their employers, no doubt in part because silence might implicate them in matters that could cost them their lives. It took considerable spite, courage, or fear to turn to a headboro against one's master, but there are a few recorded instances of such complaints. Thomas Love's servant accused him of "incontinence and unhonest behavior." John Hooke, a blacksmith's apprentice, grew tired of being sent to buy scrap iron from a laborer in Heathfield who did business only outside under cover of darkness. Hooke complained to his grandfather, then to his guardian, and finally to the local justice of the peace, who sent the headboro to begin an investigation. Madeline Carnoll, the housemaid of John Wicker of Worth, found herself in a situation similar to Hooke's. Carnoll observed that Wicker always sent his wife and servant early to church on Sunday and never accompanied them. She noticed mutton boiling in the house and parts of sheep discarded nearby. Her master had a private chamber upstairs where Carnoll thought that he butchered animals. Carnoll told Wicker's wife that seeing "these doings" she could stay no longer in the residence. The wife, siding with the servant, called in the headboro who uncovered a full slaughterhouse in Wicker's chamber. Wicker was indicted for stealing sheep. When a servant or a wife reported on a male head of the household, the participation of the local officer was vital to the successful conclusion of the case. Without his help, no capture or accusation was likely. The headboro was the muscle behind a discovery and capture, but the private complainant still initiated the investigation.[28]

Only a handful of cases survive where neither the victim's distress nor the odd behavior of a suspect alerted the community to a mishap. In these few instances, the appearance of evidence set off an investigation. Because the victim was initially unknown, the legal officer himself traced the origins of mysterious goods. The injured party was notified of the investigation after the headboro made a report to the justice of the peace. The 266 examinations analyzed in this sample include only two such instances and the fact that

29/31, 69; 36/50, 101–5; 49/42, 63, 86; on children ESRO Q/R/E 12/45, 102v; 13/24, 36, 94–6, 114; 34/37, 94–5; 36/93–5; 41/46, 83; 42/134v; 43/42, 88v; WSRO Q/R/WE 16/56–57v; on masters and servants: for cases in which the victim was the defendant's master, PRO ASSI 35/57/5/22; 35/57/5/35–7; ESRO Q/R/E 15/21, 82; 16/19, 51, 70, 17/6, 8–9, 15, 42, 51, 53–4, 56; 20/3, 30, 55, 71; 21/57, 102–5, 113, 146v; 21/56, 72–3, 114–15; 23/32, 124–5; 34/40, 88; 38/44, 113; 48/27, 61. See also ESRO Q/R/E 13/33, 91; 16/12, 34, 65; 22/30, 135; 24/23, 71–3; 25/35, 67; 25/30, 74; 28/14, 69, 74; 29/28, 61–2; 29/30, 63–4; 38/57, 105–6 where victims are referred to as the temporary employers of defendants; PRO STAC 8/90/12, and for examples from elsewhere, Eyre, "Diurnall," pp. 71, 116; "Notebook of a Surrey Justice," pp. 193, 199, 202, 208, 212; *A Royalist's Notebook*, pp. 55–6; Kussmaul, *Servants*, pp. 44–8.
28   ESRO Q/R/E 12/17 (Love); 22/53, 121, 123 (Hooke); 35/31, 36/103 (Wicker); see also ESRO Q/R/E 11/47; 14/20, 42; 22/53, 121, 161v; 34/37, 95; 35/31; 36/2; Stephen, *History of the Criminal Law*, 3: 139–40.

neither accusation resulted in a conviction reinforces the argument that early participation by the victim was a vital part of successful prosecutions.[29]

Identifying a specific suspect, of course, was only the first step towards an indictment. The next task was to detain the questionable goods and to bring both suspect and accuser before a magistrate for formal interrogation. Private individuals had some authority to make arrests, but restraining and transporting suspects was basically the job of the headboro. Because arrests could be violently resisted, relying upon someone with formal authority was both logical and necessary. Indictments for the illegal rescue of suspects from official custody confirm the need for forcefulness. Most captures, no doubt, were peaceful, but several constables were assaulted in the line of duty and one messenger from Westminster found himself "struck many blows," called "base rogue and rascal," and frightened badly enough to ask the Privy Council for relief. Moreover, the longer the journey to a magistrate took, the greater the chance that the accused would assault his captor, be rescued, or find some way to escape. Suspects were often handcuffed on the way to prison, but restraints were rare *en route* to examination by a justice. Constables had some discretion as to which magistrate they brought the accused before, but geography normally dictated the choice. Suspects could solicit allies to serve as sureties for recognizances, but Lambard warned that officers who allowed themselves to "dance up and down after the party" while sureties were sought, simply tempted suspects to try for freedom. His concern was understandable, for some captives certainly did escape custody in the brief time before an officer brought them to a justice.[30]

Most of those arrested, however, did end up before a local magistrate. After questioning the accuser, the accused, and any pertinent witnesses, the job of the justice was to restore the local peace. Normally he employed one of three options to this end. If it was possible to arbitrate a dispute without formal charges, the justice sued out bonds for keeping the peace and sent both parties home. If a complaint seemed to warrant indictment, but the suspect was not dangerous, the magistrate used recognizances to ensure quiet until the next

[29] ESRO Q/R/E 29/33, 68, 70; 36/45, 98, 101; these cases are not the same as those where the victim was still unknown at the time of prosecution.

[30] *CSPD*, 1637, p. 11; records for eastern Sussex include 50 cases where locals rescued compatriots from official custody (it should be noted, however, that most of these rescues related to charges in actions pending at Westminster rather than to criminal accusations); Lambard, *Constables*, p. 21; Stephen, *History of the Criminal Law*, 1: 193; on arrest violence: ESRO Q/R/E 10/3–4; 13/1, 18; 13/11, 20; 19/13–14; 21/13–14; 22/36; 34/42; 35/31; 36/102v; 37/15, 66; 47/4, 29; 49/18, 77; 51/24; PRO STAC 8/228/11; ASSI 35/35/8; for inhabitants unwilling to assist officers in trouble: ESRO Q/R/E 19/13, 14; PRO STAC 8/244/15; for escapes *en route* to examination: ESRO Q/R/E 13/11; 15/56; 21/30; 24/12; 29/22, 65–6; 36/36; PRO STAC 8/90/12; ASSI 35/76/9/12, 35; 35/77/9/18.

meeting of the court as well as to ensure appearances at that session. Finally, if a problem was serious enough to necessitate not only a future appearance but also some immediate constraint, the magistrate ordered the prisoner conveyed to the gaol in Horsham to await the next court. The justice was supposed to record the basis of the future case for the crown, to assess the danger to the local peace, and to guarantee the later appearances of both suspect and victim. Despite the prominence of victims in discovery and investigation, magistrates controlled the binding over or gaoling of suspects. The earlier distribution of responsibility was here reversed; now it was the private individual whose power was secondary. Because recognizances needed the guarantee of sureties, successful conveyances needed vigilant guards, and prosecutions needed the testimonies of private witnesses, local inhabitants retained peripheral authority over prosecutions, but that control was limited. Without official status, residents could activate the machinery of legal administration, but they could neither move beyond it nor drop accusations once made, without the help of a magistrate.

Because most justices were essentially stay-at-home interrogators, their opinions relied heavily on information received by examining those directly involved in an alleged crime. The thoroughness of such discussions varied with each magistrate, but it was not unknown in an accusation of larceny for a justice to question the accuser, the prisoner, the supporting witnesses, and then submit the accused to further examination. Justices tried to acquire ancillary evidence from landlords, employers, servants, and persons who had done business with the suspects, and eyewitnesses to the crime or to the discovery of the evidence. Hearsay obtained from eyewitnesses was acceptable, but most extant depositions record only the immediate knowledge of the informant. Suspects who traded confessions for mercy were also legitimate sources.[31]

Magistrates used examinations to assess the character of a suspect. Justices were to determine the reliability of the accused and the risk involved in allowing the suspect to remain free before his trial.[32] Both Lambard and Dalton

---

[31] Dalton, *Countrey Justice*, pp. 295–300; Lambard, *Eirenarcha*, p. 213; Smith, pp. 83–4; Langbein, *Prosecuting Crime*, pp. 11–13. Forty-four percent of the cases with examinations surviving (118 of 266) used 3 or more separate testimonies as evidence; for particularly complete examples, see ESRO Q/R/E 34/37, 94–5; 35/31, 36/58, 102–3; 36/50, 104–5; in cases of particular interest to a magistrate, he might be more active; such instances were exceptional, however, and even here, magisterial involvement was limited; Cockburn, *Introduction*, pp. 97–100; Lawson, p. 125a; "Notebook of a Surrey Justice," pp. 175–8, 183, 214–15; and, for later examples, Styles, "Eighteenth Century Magistrate," pp. 101–4; Alan Macfarlane, *The Justice and the Mare's Ale: Law and Disorder in Seventeenth-Century England* (Cambridge, 1981).

[32] The following discussion relies on Dalton, *Countrey Justice*, pp. 301–2; Lambard, *Eirenarcha*, pp. 211–14; Smith, 83–4. Conrad Russell has pointed out to me the equal importance of "common fame" in seventeenth-century impeachment proceedings; see Colin

gave extensive attention in their handbooks for magistrates to the difficulty of measuring the trustworthiness of an accused person. The authors were confident that a suspect's reputation and life before his accusation, his demeanor at the scene of the crime and his behavior after the illegal incident would reveal his character. Careful justices investigated the accused's childhood and current life thoroughly – were his parents "wicked"? Did he spend his youth in work, or "brawling, quarrelous, lightfingered or bloody-handed"? Dalton in particular counseled close attention to the prisoner's reputation and company: "for if a man lives idly or vagrant, it is a good cause to arrest him upon suspicion, if there have been any felony committed." Persons who spent their time with ruffians or who had earlier been suspects in crimes were worthy of careful observation. The likeliest defendant, Dalton believed, was often the one whose past marked him as unreliable.

Even persons with bad reputations were relatively safe if no one linked them specifically to the crime. The experts insisted on an investigation into a suspect's story – was he arrested near the crime, or in a suspicious area? Was he well placed to have done the deed easily? Had he the wit and the capacity to do it? Did others have a similar opportunity? Did the alleged defendant have much to gain from a crime, and was there reasonable expectation that success was possible? Did he have a specific motive and, if so, was it deliberate or spontaneous, malicious or circumstantial?

The prisoner's behavior after accusation could confirm or alter a magistrate's conclusions about a suspect's character. The common fame and voice about an accusation was an important influence on a magistrate's opinion, as were the local witnesses who accused or supported an individual in trouble. Commonsense clues also helped – did the accused have stolen property in his possession? Were his clothes torn and bloody? Psychological signs were equally damning. A defendant who tried to silence the gossip of neighbors, to avoid arrest, or to make a private settlement with the aggrieved party increased the likelihood of his own indictment. The suspect who was "doubtful or inconstant" in answering questions, or who blushed and trembled, was similarly unreliable. With a logic reminiscent of the theory behind medieval oathtaking, early modern experts were certain that both the innocent and the guilty would show their true selves by their behavior.

Contemporaries maintained this belief although they also were aware that men could be bullied into unfair confessions; the problem of intimidation by the splendor of a gentleman's residence or by the awesomeness of the law was acknowledged but not formally taken into account. The gentlest questioning could be frightening if one believed that one's life hung in the balance, and not

G. C. Tite, *Impeachment and Parliamentary Judicature in Early Stuart England* (London, 1974), pp. 13–14, 102, 152.

all magistrates were gentle. Although some justices showed little respect for
the suspects brought before them, others did try not to be overbearing.
Lambard counseled that a suspect's guilt "was not to be wrung out of himself,
but rather to be discovered by other means and men." Sir Richard Grosvenor,
a justice in Cheshire, was more explicit, writing:

When poor men shall be brought before you to examine . . . neither triumph over
them, nor trample upon the misery of such for that is to add misery to affliction. And
in the examination labour to discover the truth, but entrap not poor simple men in
their own words. Let them thoroughly understand themselves before you record their
examinations.

As a further precaution in this direction, depositions were normally read
aloud and signed or marked by both magistrate and informants.[33]

Having heard the available evidence, the magistrate decided how to handle
each complaint. Grosvenor encouraged justices to use informal means
whenever it was possible. "Be a chancellor rather than a justice among your
neighbors," he said; "persuade and move them to a reconciliation." A recognizance through which an individual swore to keep the peace of the community helped to enforce this type of agreement. The bond worked like a
sword of Damocles over troublesome inhabitants – it held no penalty as long
as they behaved, but disruptiveness meant a fine and possible indictment. As
a further check on unruliness, sureties guaranteed the bonds. Most of the
recognizances entered at the Quarter Sessions were discharged without
further action. The power of a bond reflected only a suspect's fear of the law,
the fine and the disapproval of his sureties, but such fears were not necessarily
negligible. But at least one individual, John Vincent of Rotherfield, declared
that a recognizance so constrained him that "he could not strike a dog."[34]

The magistrate's freedom to mediate disputes did not extend to accusations
of felony, although in simple thefts it would be surprising if this limitation
was never breached. The expectation of formal prosecution in all felonies
arose because such prosecutions in effect had two complainants, the
immediate victim and the monarch. The magistrate had to ensure the
presence at trial not only of the alleged defendant but also of the victim; juries

[33] Lambard, *Eirenarcha*, p. 213; Eaton Hall Grosvenor MSS Commonplace Book/52–3; ESRO
Q/R/E 10/26, 59, 77a; 34/59, 100; PRO STAC 8/29/23; 8/111/104; BL Harleian MS
1603/9; "Notebook of a Surrey Justice," pp. 214–15; Hawarde, pp. 23–4, 234–5; *The Life
of Adam Martindale*, pp. 147–53. Thirty-two informants signed, rather than marked,
their examinations; only five, however, were connected with the defendant's side of the
allegations.

[34] Eaton Hall Grosvenor MSS Commonplace Book/47–51, 53; ESRO Q/R/E 36/2; see also
Lambard, *Eirenarcha*, p. 11; ESRO Q/R/E 12/17; 20/66; 21/5, 7, 146v; 21/76, 106–7; 24/1,
31; 38/138, 139v; PRO STAC 8/294/23; 8/172/12; Lawson, pp. 125–6; only 20 peace bonds
sampled here were noted as defaulted, but for the misuse of such devices see Eaton Hall
Grosvenor MSS Commonplace Book/53; PRO STAC 8/111/04; 8/229/8; 8/172/02.

were reluctant either to indict or to convict suspects whose accusers were not present. Going to court took time and money, and many victims willing to cast aspersions on the honesty of a suspect were not willing to put him on trial for his life. Moreover, the interval common between accusation and the meeting of a court allowed plenty of time for victims to be dissuaded from prosecution by money, by threats, or simply by the cooling of passions between the parties. Since if a victim decided that the trial of a suspect was undesirable, the affront to royal authority and the public peace also went unpunished, magistrates routinely bound victims and their witnesses to appear before the court. In counties such as Elizabethan Essex, the default of victims who had initiated prosecutions was a common problem; for reasons that are not immediately apparent, in eastern Sussex such failures were relatively rare.[35]

A more universal problem was ensuring the appearance of suspects; whether to grant bail to the suspect using two sureties to guarantee compliance or to send the accused to gaol for safekeeping was important not only for the local peace, but also for the fate of the alleged offender. Misplaced trust could allow a troublemaker to evade retribution. A trip to gaol, however, was humiliating for the captive as well as potentially dangerous for those assigned to accompany him. Gaols were notorious as centers of disease, abuse, extortion, and encouragement to lives of crime.[36]

Magistrates granted bail or ordered committals according to regulations that counseled attention to the suspected crime, the accused individual and the gathered evidence. Persons charged with felonies and anyone of "bad reputation" could expect to await trial from gaol; confinement was also to be

---

[35] ESRO Q/R/E 10/27–9, 53; 27/59–60; 28/16, 72; 36/50, 97, 107; 37/42; 36/93–5; 38/24, 64, 107; 45/70, 74–5; 46/53–4, 57; 48/38, 62; even if every accusation listed in the Assizes as discharged by proclamation was dropped because the victim had defaulted (a clear exaggeration), the proportion of such cases would be only 15 percent of all those reported to the Assizes; among persons accused of felony in Elizabethan Essex, Samaha found that a full third were released because the victim had defaulted: Samaha, *Law and Order*, pp. 47–8. Conceivably in a region such as eastern Sussex, where prosecutions for thefts were relatively unusual, victims who initiated prosecutions were particularly determined to see them through. On the reluctance of victims elsewhere, Dalton, *Countrey Justice*, p. 300; Hext, "To Burghley," pp. 340–1, "Notebook of a Surrey Justice," pp. 179, 198–9; Wrightson, "Two Concepts of Order," pp. 30–2.

[36] On the mechanics of conveying prisoners to gaol in eastern Sussex: ESRO Q/R/E 15/114v; 15/43, 66, 86; 19/13–14; 25/53, 121, 123, 161v; PRO ASSI 35/39/7/35, 52, 56; 35/67/8/67, 69; 35/76/9/12, 35; STAC 8/224/1; 8/111/104; E 101/633/4; E 368/583, 630, 646, 653, 657; inquests taken on all prisoners who died in gaol between 1592 and 1625 include 51 prisoners from the gaol at Horsham in Sussex (including those from both the eastern and western divisions of the shire); see Cockburn, *Introduction*, pp. 38–9. The material on conditions in contemporary gaols is voluminous, but for some examples see Cockburn, *Introduction*, pp. 36–41; Lambard, *Constables*, p. 18; *CSPD*, 1625–6, p. 408; *CSPD*, 1627–8, pp. 441, 539; PRO E 215/860, 870–5, 994–5, 1012, 1322, 1511; Henry Brinkelow, *The Complaint of Roderick Mors* (London, 1548); L. Hutton, "The Black Dog of Newgate" and W. Fennor, "The Counter's Commonwealth" in *The Elizabethan Underworld*, pp. 265–91, 423–87.

routine for those who had confessed, been caught red-handed or been accused by "common fame." Freedom was reserved for suspects in less dangerous offenses, for persons trusted in the community and for those accused on "light suspicion" rather than on concrete evidence. The Statute of Westminster provided "a line, whereby the justices of [the] peace are to guide themselves" and the expected procedure was usually clear. But in cases where the decision to free a suspect or to commit him was problematic, Dalton advised that "it behoves the justices of [the] peace to be very circumspect" both against binding suspects over too carelessly and against denying them too frequently.[37]

Dalton's warning indicates a realization that bail was granted too often by local magistrates without proper consideration; as many defendants may have been lost to the courts through defaulted bonds as through negligence in arrests and confinements. The government tried to improve the situation by insisting that justices meet together to make these decisions. The Privy Council repeatedly urged magistrates to take great care to accept only responsible local residents as sureties. Neither plea was effective. In eastern Sussex, at least 60 percent of the justices who ordered bonds or committals for suspects did so on their own authority. Eleven percent of the cases in the Quarter Sessions where the appearance or absence of the defendant is noted lapsed because defendants defaulted on their promises to appear. Moreover, at least occasionally men with suspicious backgrounds of their own were allowed to act as sureties.[38]

Magistrates in eastern Sussex followed the guidelines laid out in handbooks such as Dalton's selectively and with mixed results. None of the six suspects accused of burglary and then bound to appear before the Quarter Sessions defaulted, but 10 percent of those expected to answer charges of grand larceny defaulted. Magistrates were generous to some suspects who had confessed and to others with past histories of accusation; in neither circumstance was that generosity repaid. But a loose interpretation of who

---

[37] Dalton, *Countrey Justice*, pp. 308, 305; the full discussion runs from pp. 304 to 328.

[38] 1 & 2 Philip & Mary, c. 13; 2 & 3 Philip & Mary, c. 10; Dalton, *Countrey Justice*, p. 295; Hawarde, pp. 23–5, 53; Stephen, *History of the Criminal Law*, 1: 237–8. Of 1,045 cases in eastern Sussex in which magistrates can be identified as responsible for committal or bail, 629 cases list only one justice; some additional proportion of those recognizances with two signatures were also probably the product of one man. The files of the Quarter Sessions note 55 cases with defaulted bonds and 54 cases where the defendant is "at large"; only a handful of defaulted bonds survive in the Assizes of Sussex, but 16 percent of the cases there listed defendants as "at large"; in neighboring Surrey and elsewhere on the southeastern circuit, up to 30 suspects per session might default on bonds. Cockburn, *Introduction*, pp. 94–5. For questionable sureties in eastern Sussex: ESRO Q/R/E 43/28, 37; 49/19, 29, 34, 49; 49/18, 31, 72–3, 77. The common practice of using members of a defendant's family as sureties also had its risks, see ESRO Q/R/E 12/6, 46, 82; 36/97; WSRO Q/R/WE 16/6, 22, 26. Some defaulted bonds may represent private settlements rather than simply irresponsibility.

might be granted bond was not the only problem. Popular expectations about reliability also hampered the efficiency of recognizances. Seventy-three percent of the defaults listed in the Quarter Sessions concerned petty thefts, assaults or trespasses, activities where the granting of recognizances was routine. In cases of trespass, the rate of defaults in the Quarter Sessions was more than triple the rate for theft; the rate of defaults for yeomen as defendants was more than double that of any other social group. Whether charged with trespass, assault or theft, yeomen were more likely than other people to default on their promises of appearance. Despite this pattern, yeomen were almost routinely granted bail.[39]

Since most of the suspects who defaulted on their recognizances never appeared in court, it is impossible to speculate about their guilt or innocence. However, the freedom of a recognizance had repercussions for those who honored it as well as for those who abused it. The relationship between being bound over and being exonerated is striking. Seventy-six percent of the cases of felony heard in the Quarter Sessions in which the defendant appeared on recognizance ended with dismissal. In contrast, only 28 percent of the cases in which the defendant had been in gaol concluded without a conviction. Magistrates' perceptions of guilt or innocence, whether accurate or not, were confirmed in the later stages of the legal process.[40]

Despite the complaints of contemporaries such as Sir Francis Bacon about popular apathy, to modern eyes the most striking feature of the system used in early modern England to identify, capture and secure suspects is its broad

---

[39] These figures exclude the Assizes because only 3 defaulted recognizances from that court have survived. Magistrates allowed bond to 18 defendants who had confessed: 4 defaulted. They allowed bond in 63 cases where the defendant had a previous history of accusation (which may or may not have been known to the justice of the peace); 25 of these cases ended in defaults. The crimes concerned in the 55 defaults listed in the Quarter Sessions accounted for 36 percent of the cases of trespass in that court (12 defaults), 11 percent of the assaults (10 defaults), 10 percent of the felonious thefts (15 defaults) and 9 percent of the petty thefts (16 defaults). The other defaults concerned violations of the regulatory statutes. The stated statuses of defendants and the percentage of bonds defaulted within each group were gentlemen, no defaults, yeomen 52 percent defaults (13), laborers, 21 percent (6), husbandmen 20 percent (19), women 14 percent (5), non-agriculturalists 11 percent (11). One default fell into the miscellaneous category. Although no cases in which they were charged with grand larceny ended in default, yeomen defaulted in 60 percent of the cases where they were given bail in petty largenies, 57 percent of the cases where they were given bail in assaults and 83 percent of the cases where they were given bail in trespasses. Three yeomen (of 31 accused) were committed to gaol (one each for grand theft, petty theft and trespass). Since, apart from the gentry, yeomen were bailed more regularly than members of any other social grouping, it is impossible truly to know if other groups, given the opportunity, would have equalled the default rate of the yeomen.

[40] The statistical relationship between form of appearance and verdict is the strongest of the relationships between form of appearance and other variables. In both courts, significance = 0; in the Quarter Sessions, Cramer's V = .47889; in the Assizes, Cramer's V = .53997.

participatory base. The private individual was the most important law-enforcing officer in the community. Public obligation intruded on private life repeatedly. Residents drifted easily between official and private status. At no point in the early stages of accusation did private individuals or public officials completely control the legal process. Private initiative dovetailed with the powers allotted to public officials. Magistrates' decisions concerning depositions, jail, or recognizances depended on the willingness of local inhabitants to serve as witnesses, sureties, and guards for prisoners. The cooperation not only of the law and the aggrieved individual but also of several local residents was necessary for prosecution to go forward.[41] The number of persons involved reinforced the dispersion of authority, although it also frustrated any attempt to systematize the process. The courtroom stood at the end, not at the beginning, of a complex chain of private and public actions. Each actor retained the power to play his part as he saw fit. Each was inspired by his own desires but also constrained by the behavior of every other actor. With the granting of bail or the conveyance of an individual to jail, a suspicion became a formal accusation. A complaint between private individuals became a part of the public record, and whether through indictment, arbitration or default, its resolution was also public. Between this formalization and the date of trial, some bonds to keep the peace were rescinded; some suspects escaped from custody, some victims rethought their interest, but most complaints that reached the point of recognizance or committal remained the responsibility of the court.[42]

[41] Almost half of the known cases (1,135 of 2,412, 47 percent) in eastern Sussex involved witnesses beyond the victim; 44 percent of the Quarter Sessions cases that used examinations recorded at least 3 depositions (118 of 266); 66 percent of the extant bonds for appearance depended on 2 or more sureties (188 of 286, with 68 percent of these relying on parochial rather than on familial intimacy). On gaol conveyances, see note 36 above and ESRO Q/R/E 15/43, 66, 86, 114v.

[42] Only a handful of bonds for the peace were relaxed prior to an appearance; see ESRO Q/R/E 25/46–50; 38/82–3, 87A–B; 49/51–2, 54, 62. The records note only 10 escapes *en route* to jail, and 25 cases in which guards were blamed for an escape *en route* to prison: ESRO Q/R/E 15/8; 21/30; 22/53, 121, 123, 161v; 24/12; PRO ASSI 35/39/7/35, 56; 35/67/8/67–9; 35/76/9/12, 35. In common law, defendants could not be tried *in absentia*; Pollock & Maitland, 2: 581–2, 594–5.

5

From accusation to indictment

The accusation of a suspect in early modern England required cooperation between private individuals and legal officers, but the concurrence of neighbors, constables and magistrates did not guarantee a trial. Before charges had to be answered in open court (arraignment), yet another group of men sitting as a grand jury considered the evidence. The job of the grand jury was to act as a barrier between local gossip and legal process by sifting substantial complaints from casual accusations. Grand juries in theory did not assess guilt or innocence; that job was left to petty jurors. Since grand jurors heard only the evidence for the victim, their conclusions could not be synonymous with conviction or acquittal.[1]

However, the grand jury was enormously important both for individual suspects and for the law in general. The standard metaphor for the role of the grand jury in early modern law was the *primum mobile*, the wheel that allowed all other wheels to begin their turning. The grand jury was considered "the grand spring . . . the key that opens and shuts the proceedings of the court."[2] Grand jurors represented the legal conscience of the shire; their very presence could be a restraining influence on local malice and on magisterial highhandedness. A case dismissed by a grand jury as unreliable (*ignoramus*) was removed from the agenda of the court; the written evidence of accusation was supposed to be destroyed and the suspect was supposed to be freed without further investigation. A suspicion legitimated by a grand jury became a true bill (*billa vera*) and an indictment. The case proceeded either to a summary judgment or to a trial. Grand jurors could neither protect

---

[1] The most extensive study of grand juries in pre-industrial England is Morrill, *Grand Jury*, but see also Cockburn, *Introduction*, ch. 5; R. H. Helmholz, "The Early History of the Grand Jury and the Canon Law," *The University of Chicago Law Review* 50 (1983): 613–27; Stephen K. Roberts, "Initiative and Control: The Devon Quarter Sessions Grand Jury, 1649–1670," *BIHR* 57 (1984): 165–77; J. M. Beattie, *Crime and the Courts in England 1660–1800* (Princeton, 1986), pp. 318–33, 400–6.

[2] Sir James Astry, cited in Morrill, *Grand Jury*, p. 45. For similar views, see Babington, pp. 2–4, 6; *William Lambarde and Local Government, passim.*

suspects from accusations in the future nor guarantee their convictions, but they could and did reject charges they believed to be insufficient, and they could and did mitigate accusations they believed to be miscast.[3]

Only a few charges actually were altered by grand juries, but that should not suggest that contemporary metaphors were mere flourishes. The existence of a panel that had to be convinced before a case could go to trial had its own effect on the place of law in local life. Because such preliminaries meant that not all charges proceeded to judgment, the use of grand juries probably encouraged spurious accusations as tactics in personal quarrels. But, because the decision to indict rested in an authority with a changing membership, the use of grand juries also meant that any complainant interested in seeing a suspect convicted was wise to make as comprehensive a case as possible.

The grand jury was more than the "key" that opened criminal procedure; it had a second, aggressive function that reinforced its position as the legal conscience of the shire. Grand jurors were expected not only to assess complaints brought forward by other people but also to inform the court about activities in the jurors' neighborhoods. Zachary Babington, who served as a lawyer on the Oxford circuit of the Assizes from 1632 until late into the century, compared grand juries to the House of Commons. Both, he said, had the power to present any blemish in any sphere against the crown, public peace, or private dignity. In this capacity, grand juries brought a variety of matters – civil and administrative as well as criminal – before the courts. To men like William Lambard, this accusatory function overshadowed even the confirmatory responsibilities of the grand jury. Lambard told grand jurors in Elizabethan Kent, "think yourselves weeders sent into the cornfield of the commonwealth." In Cheshire, Sir Richard Grosvenor spoke of jurors as "the eyes of your country to spy out and bring such [offenders] to their deserved punishment."[4]

Babington, Lambard and Grosvenor extolled the prowess of grand juries, but their flattery contrasts sharply with their assessments of how well grand jurymen fulfilled these obligations. And they were not alone in their complaints; legal writers in the seventeenth century repeatedly condemned grand jurymen for both their assertiveness and their passivity. On the one hand,

---

[3] Without indictment, there was no protection against re-accusation, Blackstone, 4, p. 301. The problem was not serious in eastern Sussex, but see ESRO Q/R/E 34/36, 98–9, and 38/47; 41/126 and 42/38; 43/4 and 44/9. In 32 cases (2 percent of the indicted) the changes made by grand jurors are apparent. On jury independence, see also Cockburn, *Introduction*, pp. 51–5, 104; Brian Manning, *The English People and the English Revolution* (London, 1976), p. 134; James M. Rosenheim, "Robert Doughty of Hanworth: A Restoration Magistrate," *Norfolk Archaeology* 38, part 3 (1983): 301; Lawson, p. 75; Babington, *passim*; Roberts, *Recovery and Restoration*, pp. 90–3.

[4] Babington, p. 6; *William Lambarde and Local Government*, p. 75; Eaton Hall Grosvenor MSS, "A Charge to the Quarter Sessions 1624."

grand jurors were accused of too often going beyond their proper charge, of offering *de facto* verdicts while assessing accusations of felony. Attempting to discourage such interference, Grosvenor insisted, "it is your parts only to present the truth of the fault and ours to punish or to show mercy where we find cause." On the other hand, grand jurors were accused of negligence where initiative was wanted in the reporting of violations of statutes. In Kent, Lambard claimed:

Every man, I know, will privately at home complain of things amiss and seem heartily to wish amendment, but when it comes publicly to his lot to have both time, place and power to open the grief, then will he rather suffer the sore to fester than make us that be the physicians acquainted with it.[5]

Most contemporary observers overlooked the implicit critique of the legal division of labor in such behavior and instead defined the trouble in terms of the susceptibility of jurors to social pressures. Grosvenor, in the mid 1620s, analyzed the problem in a charge to the grand jury at the Quarter Sessions in Cheshire:

I have observed in my time three main enemies which hinder the perfection of this service: the first is fear to offend great men our superiors; the second is favors and affection we bear towards our friends and neighbors; the third is foolish pity extended where not deserved.[6]

For the government, the solution was to improve the reliability of grand jurors by improving both the quality and the quantity of men willing to serve on grand juries. It was thought that men impervious to pressure from their superiors or peers would be found among the more educated and wealthy strata of society. The goal was more easily recognized than realized; various schemes to broaden participation (rotations, higher required income, enlistment of constables or magistrates) were considered but abandoned. In truth, the goals of quantity and quality were mutually exclusive in a society so solidly hierarchical and so, too, were the demands to increase at once both responsibility and reliability. Complaints about grand jurors in the late seventeenth century echo the problems noted over the previous century.[7]

[5] Eaton Hall Grosvenor MSS, "Quarter Sessions Charge," n.d.; *William Lambarde and Local Government*, p. 74. See also *William Lambarde and Local Government, passim*; Babington, *passim*; Larminie, *The Godly Magistrate*, pp. 16–17; Sir Harbottle Grimston, "Charge to the Essex Grand Jury, Quarter Sessions, 1638," cited in Conrad Russell, *Parliaments and English Politics 1621–1629* (Oxford, 1979), p. 69; "A Relation of a Short Survey of the Western Counties made by a Lieutenant of the Military Company in Norwich in 1635," ed. L. G. Wickham Legg, Camden Society, 3rd series, 52, *Miscellany* 16 (1936): 27; Rosenheim, "Robert Doughty," p. 312, n. 55.

[6] Eaton Hall Grosvenor MSS, "Quarter Sessions Charge," n.d.

[7] On the reluctance of men of quality to serve and attempts to remedy that reluctance, see PRO SP 14/31/55; 14/190/43; E 215/1133; Michael Dalton, *The Office and Authority of Sheriffs*, 2nd ed. (London, 1628), pp. 198–204; Cockburn, *Introduction*, pp. 44–50; Cockburn,

Some grand jurymen were doubtless ignorant, negligent or malicious, but the separation of the task of preparing a case from the task of indicting it encouraged strain between magistrates and grand jurors. Both assessed the reasonableness of suspicions; both kept watch over order in the countryside. But the grand jurors, who were almost always socially inferior to the magistrates, possessed an effective veto over the investigative decisions of their betters. Moreover, this latent tension was exacerbated because each office drew its authority from different sources. The magistracy was legitimate in part because it was exclusive and (despite the fact of yearly appointments) long term. Between 1592 and 1640, only 168 men served as justices of the peace in Sussex and tenures of more than a decade were not uncommon. In contrast, the grand jury was legitimate in part because it was inclusive and short term; its strength came from its comprehensiveness and diversity. More than a hundred different men acted as grand jurors in Sussex in any year between 1592 and 1640; most served on panels that deliberately mixed men of varied experience and geographical origins, and few were called to service repeatedly.[8]

Given such different qualifications for office and such similar responsibilities, magisterial dismay over the decisions of grand juries is unsurprising. Simply in favoring some suspects with pity and others with indulgence, grand jurors exercised a discretion they felt that they shared with other legal officials, but a discretion that discomforted men such as Grosvenor, Lambard and Babington. Believing in a more restricted role for grand juries in the prosecuting process, these men were especially skeptical when grand juries reached conclusions different from their own. Their reaction was to dismiss the dissent as evidence that the grand jurors were overstepping their authority. Such tensions may have been inescapable. Grand jurors were supposed to protect their communities from dangerous individuals and to protect individuals from dangerous claims made in the name of the community. To fulfill these duties, jurors could not avoid interpreting the law. The comments of Grosvenor and others conveyed a mixed message — grand jurors ought to exercise discretionary powers, but do so only in ways that reflected the opinions of justices and judges. Grand jurors, acting as intermediaries between the earlier decisions of individual justices and the collective

---

Assizes, pp. 111–20; Morrill, *Grand Jury*, pp. 12, 15–20; Russell, *Parliaments and English Politics*, pp. 90–1; Hassell Smith, *County and Court*, pp. 118–19; Manning, *English People*, p. 236.

8 In the period under study, 989 men filled 2,430 spaces on grand juries in eastern Sussex. The courts used 82 men on grand juries in 1594, 88 men in 1617 and 93 men in 1637. These estimates do not include the jurors called to the western Quarter Sessions. Moreover, they include only persons who served, not all of those who were asked to serve. On the tenure of grand jurymen, see below, pp. 102, 106; cf. Morrill, *Grand Jury*, pp. 9–11.

judgments of the judiciary, invariably offended if they too regularly exercised the powers that were their reason for being.

The evidence belies the image of grand jurors suggested by many seventeenth-century legal commentators. In early Stuart Sussex, grand jurors were not exceptionally modest or casual about their obligations. John Morrill has found that grand jurymen in Cheshire between 1625 and 1659 were similarly attentive. But the nature, meaning and consequences of service on any jury defy generalization. The job of grand juror fell everywhere mostly to middling freeholders, but who they were and how they responded were matters intimately related to particular circumstances. Some men acted altruistically, but many, probably most, appeared or defaulted for reasons having little to do directly with the task before them. Presence and absence both arose often from personal rather than civic inspirations. Men might serve as grand jurors because they had other business at the court, because they liked the sociability of the occasion, because they wanted to pursue a grievance, or because they feared a fine if they defaulted. They might ignore summonses because appearances not only cost time and money but also could require actions that would offend others. However, such choices were not made in a vacuum; the perceived advantages of public service influenced prospective grand jurors in their responses. Different patterns of participation, both between shires and within them, were reflections of such differences.

Service on a grand jury could bring individual members several benefits. Participation confirmed a man as one of the governors of his locality. Public responsibility was the price of social privilege at all levels, but the equation could also be read the other way; if a man was expected to serve the shire, that expectation suggested that he was one of the better sort. Obligations that the secure disdained could hold an integrative meaning for the newly arrived or the newly placed. Like other symbols of status, however, participation was unreliable in its impact; without a receptive audience, the effect was lost. The potency of participation was highest where other options for displaying status were restricted. Where commissions of the peace and membership on the quorum expanded easily, other forms of service such as membership on grand juries were devalued for men with genteel pretensions. But where the magistracy could be attained only with patience, less exalted positions could not be dismissed so uniformly.

Service on a grand jury offered opportunity as well as prestige. Men who served on grand juries had a structured chance to comment on governance not even available to magistrates. In the parlance of the day, grand juries were likened to local parliaments. Morrill has detailed how grand juries in Cheshire used their position to become a political force within the shire, and a similar sort of activism can be detected in other counties (such as Essex) renowned for a concern with godliness. Petitions from grand juries to Westminster seem to have carried greater weight than independent requests from local justices. The ideal of grand juries as public forums was more than a rhetorical window dressing for routine drudgery. Where men cared deeply about local interpretations of discipline and governance, grand juries were a logical focus for expressing their concerns. At most meetings of the courts, grand jurors dealt with problems that seem far removed from politics. But parliaments devoted most of their sessions, too, to mundane business. However rare the forays made by grand juries into issues formally recognized as constitutional, their right to comment widely influenced the meaning of their participation.[9]

Sussex was a shire with a considerable concentration of active Puritans, a fair amount of economic prosperity and a relatively small and inbred social elite. Moreover, because of the administrative divisions of the shire, the Assizes in Sussex were a uniquely public gathering, unmatched by the local Quarter Sessions and unrivaled as the most important convention of local governors. The meaning of participation in grand juries in Sussex reflects these circumstances: relative to other shires, service on grand juries in Sussex was hierarchical, respectable and undemanding.

Grand jurors had the same responsibilities whether at the Assizes or the Quarter Sessions, and the formal qualifications for participation at each court were identical. In Cheshire, where both the Assizes and the Quarter Sessions could be considered local courts, men willing to be grand jurors served in either forum as needed. In most counties (Sussex among them), the two courts had far less in common, and grand jurors for each tribunal came from discrete social groups. Grand jurors at the Assizes in such shires were routinely men of higher status than grand jurors at the Quarter Sessions. To serve in both courts was unusual; even among the foremen of sessional grand juries in eastern Sussex, no more than 12 percent appeared on grand juries at the Assizes. Of 128 grand jurors from Sussex traced in the Assizes, only

---

[9] On the importance of grand juries in non-judicial matters, see *CSPD* 1627–8, p. 128; 1637–8, p. 557; Morrill, *Grand Jury*, pp. 6, 24–39; J. S. Morrill, *The Revolt of the Provinces: Conservatives and Radicals in the English Civil War 1630–1650*, 2nd ed. (London, 1980), pp. 22, 37, 38, 40, 53–4, 77, 83; Cockburn, *Assizes*, pp. 112–17; Hurstfield, "County Government: Wiltshire," p. 280; Derek Hirst, "Court, Country and Politics before 1629," in K. Sharpe, ed., *Faction and Parliament: Essays on Early Stuart History* (Oxford, 1978), pp. 133–4; Barnes, *Somerset*, p. 226; *Western Circuit Assize Orders*, pp. 76, 253, 254; Hunt, *Puritan Moment*, pp. 174, 204–5, 266, 268; Campbell, *English Yeoman*, p. 344; Anthony Fletcher, *The Outbreak of the English Civil War* (New York, 1981), p. 194; Roberts, *Recovery and Restoration*, pp. 9–11; Silcock, "Worcestershire," p. 81. The prestige attached to serving on a grand jury at the Quarter Sessions is a repeated, if perhaps instrumental, theme in *William Lambarde and Local Government*.

twelve appear in the extant lists of grand jurors for the eastern Quarter Sessions, and ten of these served in the reign of Queen Elizabeth. Such particularity extended beyond grand juries; in Cheshire, no consistent distinction existed between petty jurors and grand jurors, but, in Sussex, a minority of those whose careers can be reconstructed filled both positions. In further contrast to Cheshire, those who accepted both obligations in Sussex served on a grand jury after rather than before they served on a petty jury. Men called as grand jurors in Sussex filled a variety of other local offices but service on juries – grand and trial, Assizes and Quarter Sessions – seems to have followed an unstated but closely adhered to hierarchy.[10]

Morrill has shown that grand jurors in Cheshire were "middling freeholders with income and status well below that of the magisterial class," men at best chosen from "the lowest section of the gentry." More substantial gentlemen seem to have played no formal role in legal process unless they were part of the commission of the peace.[11] Both as cause and effect of more restricted demands of service, the social position of men chosen as grand jurors in Sussex was more diverse than in Cheshire. At the Assizes, many grand jurors outranked middling freeholders, while at the Quarter Sessions grand jurors were normally men of more modest standing than those in contemporary Cheshire.

Among the 128 men who served on ten grand juries studied as a sample from the Assizes of Sussex, many seem to have been a part of the network of "cousinage" that united the gentry of the county.[12] At least thirty-two can be

---

[10] The 128 grand jurors from Sussex served on the only extant panels from the Assizes that list jurors by residence as well as name. These lists, which can be found in PRO ASSI 35, detail the juries used at the Assizes held at Lent, 1588; Lent, 1589; Summer, 1613; Summer, 1616; Lent, 1617; Lent, 1618; Lent, 1623; Lent, 1624; Summer, 1624 and Summer, 1631. Ninety-two of the 128 were residents of eastern Sussex and therefore in theory eligible to be sessional grand jurors. Forty-nine of the 128 (38 percent) may have appeared as petty jurors at the Assizes held between 1558 and 1625, but, since lists of petty jurors contain no information beyond names, this figure represents the maximum rather than the actual percentage of overlap. An earlier summary of biographical information about the men sampled as grand jurors in Sussex can be found in Herrup, diss., pp. 431–57. The ecumenicalism seen in Cheshire is unusual; cf. Morrill, *Grand Jury*, p. 11; Lawson, pp. 146–51; Roberts, *Recovery and Restoration*, pp. 67–81; but also *The Staffordshire Quarter Sessions Rolls*, ed. S. A. H. Burne, William Salt Archaeological Society, 53 (Kendall, 1931), pp. xxx–xxxii; Silcock, "Worcestershire," pp. 66–7; Samaha, *Law and Order*, p. 49. For a different view of this evidence, see Cockburn, *Introduction*, pp. 50–1.

[11] Morrill, *Grand Jury*, pp. 17–18.

[12] The biographical information upon which the following discussion is based relies upon: PRO ASSI 35; PRO E 179/190/283, 179/190/297–9, 179/190/332, 179/190/342, 179/191/361–7, 179/191/368–76, 179/191/377a, 179/191/390; E 178/5675; PROB 11; ESRO W/A7–28; index of ecclesiastical deponents (composed by Brian Phillips); Q/R/E 1–50; WSRO STC I–III; Q/R/WE 16, 31; *Alumni Oxonienses (1500–1714)*, ed. and comp. J. Foster, 4 vols. (Oxford, 1891–2); *Alumni Cantabrigienses*, ed. and comp. J. Venn and J. A. Venn (Cambridge, 1922), part 1, 4 vols.; *A Register of Admissions to Gray's Inn 1521–1889*, ed.

found in the Visitation of Arms completed in 1634, and sixteen more were identified in wills or testimony before the ecclesiastical courts as gentlemen. Ties of blood or marriage bound more than half of the 128 to one another or to magistrates of the same generation; ties of friendship or service united still others. Twenty-seven of the sampled jurors had been or had sent their sons to a university, the inns or court or both; thirty others were literate enough to sign their names. Almost all of the grand jurors listed in the local subsidies were assessed above the minimum rate, and some held estates valued elsewhere as highly as £1,000.

The grand jurors in Sussex who served at the Assizes seem more of a piece with the men of the magistracy than do their counterparts in Cheshire. Many foremen of the grand juries in Sussex were esquires of rank close to the justices. Three grand jurors became magistrates (although only one achieved that position before 1642) and thirteen had sons who became justices and/or members of Parliament. Seventeen whose families had gone unnoticed in 1634 gained official recognition in the herald's visitation in 1662. In fact, in Sussex the social distance between grand jurymen at the Assizes and local justices of the peace was not so great as the chasm between grand jurors at the Assizes and those at the eastern Quarter Sessions. Grand jurors at both the eastern and the western Quarter Sessions were chosen from among the hundredal constables. Rather than minor gentry, most were from the more modest tiers of the yeomanry. They substituted the experience of parochial office for the grander training of the universities, and their social lives focused most often on the neighborhood rather than on the county.

The ideal of a hierarchical division among participatory obligations seems so natural an outgrowth of contemporary social theory that it may have existed in many shires. As a palatinate, Cheshire was in many ways *sui generis*. But in maintaining a hierarchy that encompassed esquires as well as minor yeomen, Sussex rather than Cheshire was the anomaly. The more common situation was probably one similar to that described for Devon in 1625 by Robert Oland:

At our assizes [in times] passed our grand jury have been esquires and gentlemen of quality and the best farmers and yeomen to serve at sessions and none but freeholders

J. Foster (London, 1889); *Students Admitted to the Inner Temple 1547–1660*, ed. W. H. Cooke (London, 1878); *Register of Admissions to the Honourable Society of the Middle Temple*, ed. H. A. C. Sturgess, 3 vols. (London, 1949); *The Records of the Honourable Society of Lincoln's Inn: Admissions*, ed. W. P. Baildon (London, 1896), vol. 1; *The Visitations of the County of Sussex . . . 1530 and 1633/4*, ed. W. Bruce Bannerman, Harleian Society 53 (London, 1905); *The Visitation of Sussex, Anno Domini 1662*, ed. and ann. A. W. Hughes Clarke, Harleian Society 89 (London, 1937); *Calendar of Sussex Marriage Licences Recorded in the Consistory Court of the Bishop of Chichester for the Archdeaconry of Lewes August 1586 to March 1642/3*, ed. E. H. W. Dunkin, SRS 1 (Lewes, 1902); Fletcher, *Sussex*, pp. 348–54. See also Appendix 2 below.

in both; but now the case is altered. If there be three or four gents at the assizes the rest are yeomen. Gentlemen count themselves too high for that service and farmers [being] the best yeomen of £100 a year, think it too base to attend at sessions, for they say a clerk of the peace will record their appearances for five shillings yearly.[13]

In Sussex, too, sessional grand jurors were rarely "best yeomen of £100 a year," but the grand jurors at the Assizes in Sussex seem, in the light of Oland's comments, quite distinctive.

Conceivably, this peculiarity reflects only the corruptness of local clerks, but more plausibly the full explanation lies in a particular balance of policy and circumstances. Oland's comments confirm the importance that contemporaries attached to the social interpretation of public responsibilities. What distinguished that interpretation in Sussex? The administrative structure of the shire, its size and relative conservatism meant that a public presence at the Assizes may have been less troublesome and potentially more useful than in other places. Because of the importance of the Assizes as a communal forum in Sussex, service that elsewhere was considered humiliating and unnecessary could retain value. Because the commission of the peace did not expand as dramatically or as regularly as in other counties, alternatives to prove one's social standing publicly were somewhat limited.[14]

Moreover, the presence of men interested in the godly governance of Sussex was very influential, perhaps the more so for being tightly concentrated in the eastern division of the county. The Quarter Sessions in eastern Sussex in the 1630s were allegedly controlled by a clique of Puritan magistrates "steered rather by humor and faction than justice," according to one of their frustrated opponents, and "grown so strong that such as are moderately disposed were not able to withstand it."[15] Surely not coincidentally, a man closely associated with these justices, Thomas Jefferay of Chiddingly, esquire, dominated the chairmanship of the grand juries at the Assizes from 1622 into the 1640s. Jefferay chaired twenty-two of the thirty-six juries convened between

[13] Cited in Roberts, *Recovery and Restoration*, p. 89. Oland was the father of a hundredal constable and sessional grand juror. Evidence of the status of men serving as grand jurors in other counties can be found in *The Harleian Miscellany*, ed. W. Oldys (London, 1808–11), 3: 396 (Huntingdonshire); Manning, *English People*, p. 236; Lawson, pp. 146–50; Silcock, "Worcestershire," pp. 66–7; Samaha, *Law and Order*, pp. 49–52.
[14] The working commission of the peace in Sussex increased by 127 percent between 1562 and 1621, when it reached its largest size before the 1640s. See Gleason, *Justices of the Peace*, p. 49. His analysis includes three shires (Kent, Somerset, Worcestershire) with more modest rises (120 percent, 76 percent and 105 percent respectively) and three shires with more dramatic increases (Norfolk, 206 percent, Northamptonshire, 218 percent, North Riding of Yorkshire, 182 percent) but if one uses Gleason's terminal dates rather than those showing the greatest extremes, all of these counties save Somerset increased their commissions more dramatically than did Sussex; Fletcher, *Sussex*, p. 348; PRO ASSI 35/78/8; 35/78/9.
[15] PRO SP 16/442/137; Fletcher, *Sussex*, pp. 239–43; *CSPD*, 1640, p. 520; Thomas-Stanford, *Sussex*, p. 28; T. W. Horsfield, *The History and Antiquities of Lewes and its Vicinity*, 2 vols. (Lewes, 1824–7), 1: 202, n. 1.

1622 and 1640 and he was a member of four more. He left no explanation for his exceptional dedication, but as foreman of the jury he was theoretically in a position to accomplish at the Assizes some of what his magisterial counterparts hoped to accomplish at the Quarter Sessions. The presence of someone such as Jefferay, interested enough to take on the burden of governance, but flexible enough to take it on outside of the commission of the peace, is exceptional, but the climate that made his actions viable was less fortuitous. Jefferay was only one of several esquires who sat on grand juries at the Assizes in Sussex in the early seventeenth century; in their company, participation could hardly be derogatory.[16]

The qualities that kept duty at the Assizes in Sussex respectable were reinforced by their own influence. As long as gentlemen served on grand juries, that service could help to verify gentility. Once tainted with men of lesser status, an office could easily gain a different social meaning. Such an erosion of status may help to explain the distance of substantial gentlemen from minor legal offices in Cheshire as well as the ecumenical nature of official obligations there. It reveals a deep irony in the notion of a "gentility of social function." The connection between status and recruitment also sheds light on a scheme proposed in Devon to add luster to grand juries at the Assizes; men of special eminence were to receive personal invitations to participate rather than routine summonses from shrieval underlings.[17]

Additionally, and dependent on equally circular reasoning, men of high status were more willing to serve where their obligations were limited, although, in fact, such restricted tenure was feasible only where enough men of high status were willing to serve. Only as long as enough men were available to allow a division of labor among the various juries needed in a county could service on one grand jury be free of the taint of Pandora's box. In Sussex, where such a division existed, the average tenure of grand jurors at the Assizes was less than three terms (2.4); in Cheshire, the average length of service was more than twice that (5.7 terms) and a relatively small number of families shared the duty of staffing not only grand juries at the Assizes and the Quarter Sessions but also petty juries and other minor legal offices.[18]

[16] Herrup, diss., pp. 445–6; Fletcher, *Sussex*, p. 222. Jefferay was a provost marshal in the shire in the 1620s, a member of the County Committee in the 1640s and 1650s and a justice of the peace from 1644 to 1660. Other grand jurors listed as esquires in the records of both the Assizes and the Heralds were Richard Alfrey, Richard Bartlett, John French, Richard Michelbourne, John Stapley and John Whitfield. Jefferay was not the only grand juror who considered himself part of the godly community; see, for example, the comments on John Everenden, John French, Richard Michelbourne, and William Newton in Fletcher, *Sussex*.

[17] Morrill, *Grand Jury*, pp. 16–19; Roberts, *Recovery and Restoration*, pp. 89–90; see also PRO SP 14/190/43.

[18] Morrill, *Grand Jury*, pp. 9–10, 57. Among the grand jurors used as a sample from Sussex, the average length of service was 4 terms rather than 2.4, but the contrast with Cheshire is still

Prosopography cannot reveal how grand jurymen performed their duties; without the faith of the early modern governing classes in a direct correspondence between status and responsibility, one must rely on other evidence for such information. Magistrates in Sussex attended the Assizes more regularly than did their colleagues elsewhere; lesser gentlemen in lesser offices seem to have been similarly conscientious. Recorded fines for defaults by grand jurors at the Assizes were relatively uncommon, but even if they matched the level of about 30 percent which Cockburn has posited for the Home Circuit between 1558 and 1625, attendance among grand jurors at the Assizes would have been more reliable than it was among members of the commission of the peace.[19]

The benefits of service at the Assizes in Sussex, however, were not duplicated at the Quarter Sessions. The Quarter Sessions, while important as a regional occasion, were neither as public nor as all encompassing as the Assizes. The presence in eastern Sussex of so many godly magistrates also may have dampened the sense of urgency among the godly about participation. But the most important influence on the social status of grand jurors at the Quarter Sessions in eastern Sussex was the identification of the position with the responsibilities of the hundredal constables. This merger tied service on a grand jury in the quarterly court to an office routinely shunned by substantial yeomen. If, in Cheshire, more established gentry chose not to participate save as justices of the peace, in eastern Sussex the more established yeomen seem to have roused themselves to be grand jurors only if called to the Assizes. In Kent, where sessional grand juries were also recruited from the constabulary, Lambard expressed the wish in 1599 that both positions be reserved to "such only as can both write and read and is withall assessed to the subsidy at 6 or 8 li lands or at the double thereof in goods . . . " That standard was never achieved in eastern Sussex, nor, most probably, in Kent.[20]

---

striking. Each county had a core of men who served well beyond the expected tenure; in Cheshire 18 percent of the grand jurors sat on 11 or more grand juries; in Sussex 13 percent of the sampled grand jurors sat on 8 or more panels; in Hertfordshire, the comparable figure was 12 percent. The demands of service at the Assizes throughout the Home Circuit seem to have been roughly as in Sussex; see Cockburn, *Introduction*, p. 54; Lawson, p. 142.

[19] Cockburn, *Introduction*, pp. 44–6, n. 18; Samaha, *Law and Order*, p. 51; default fines for grand jurors from eastern Sussex can be found in PRO E 137 and E 368; the 6 courts for which fines are extant from the 1590s list 50 defaulting grand jurors; the 22 Jacobean courts list 7 defaults and the 5 Caroline courts list 2 defaults. In Cheshire grand jurors were even more attentive to their duties: Morrill, *Grand Jury*, pp. 11, 19. On the behavior of justices at the Assizes in Sussex, see above, pp. 61–2.

[20] *William Lambarde and Local Government*, p. 138. Lincolnshire, Kent and the city of Coventry used juries of constables as they were used in Sussex. In Middlesex juries of constables were used as hundredal juries separated from the sessional grand juries. Unlike the grand juries in Sussex, Lincolnshire, Kent and Coventry, juries of constables seem to have dealt only with business outside of felonies. See Morrill, *Grand Jury*, p. 43; Webb and Webb,

The modest standing of the constables should not blind us to their influence; hundredal constables in eastern Sussex normally belonged to the elites of their villages. From the standpoint of those who ruled the nation or the shire, the qualifications of such men may have been insignificant, but recent studies of villages such as Terling in Essex have left little doubt about the impact such men had on local life. Within the world of the parish or the hundred, the influence of these men easily matched that which their more exalted brethren claimed over wider areas. Most of the constables studied in eastern Sussex had spent their adult lives in the hundred that they represented; almost all had filled administrative offices such as the positions of churchwarden or headboro. Lambard would have described these men as uneducated and unsuccessful, but in a sample of fifty-nine grand jurors who served at the Quarter Sessions from three hundreds in eastern Sussex more than 40 percent paid above the minimal assessment in the subsidies, and at least 30 percent could sign their names.[21]

More striking than these shared characteristics, however, are the differences that distinguished the grand jurors of each hundred from one another. Since grand jurymen were also hundredal constables, it is not surprising that the economic and administrative structure of each hundred, rather than any generalized standard, determined the men most likely to appear as grand jurors.

Looking at the grand jurors selected from three of the hundreds (Hawksborough, Buttinghill, Whalesbone) cited most regularly as scenes of illegal activities, the diversity within eastern Sussex is clear. In Hawksborough, grand jurors were almost always the elders of the local landholding community. In Buttinghill, the grand jurors were younger and richer than their colleagues from Hawksborough, but part of a less exclusive governing group. In Whalesbone, which was dominated by the town of Brighton, the grand jurors were the officials of that seaport, men more concerned with fishing and the peculiar problems of an urban center than with the institutions of the

---

The Parish and the County, pp. 460, n. 2, 464–5; *Quarter Sessions Indictment Book, Easter, 1631 to Epiphany, 1674*, eds. S. C. Ratcliff and H. C. Johnson, Warwick County Records 6 (Warwick, 1941), pp. xxi–xxiv; *Staffordshire Quarter Sessions*, vol. 54, pp. xxx–xxxv; *Minutes of Proceedings in the Quarter Sessions Held for the Parts of Kesteven in the County of Lincoln 1674–95*, ed. S. A. Peyton, Lincoln Record Society 25 (Lincoln, 1931), pp. lxx–lxxiii.

21 Wrightson and Levine, *Poverty and Piety, passim*; Campbell, *English Yeoman, passim*. The sample of sessional grand jurors here includes all men chosen for service at the eastern Quarter Sessions from the hundreds of Hawksborough, Buttinghill or Whalesbone in the years 1594 to 1640. For the status of sessional jurors in counties where constables were not drafted for this purpose, see Lawson, p. 143; Roberts, *Recovery and Restoration*, pp. 72–3, 116–17; Silcock, "Worcestershire," p. 67.

shire. Table 5.1 details these comparisons, which seem closely related to the economic situation in each hundred.[22]

Hawksborough, situated almost exactly in the center of eastern Sussex, was a hundred rich in land for mining and for grazing. Each of its three parishes housed a growing population interested in the diverse economic opportunities of the region. Since the hundred included one of the largest commons in the shire, thefts of sheep dominated the crimes reported from Hawksborough. The constableship shifted fairly regularly among the parishes of Hawksborough, but access to the job within each parish was restricted. Although the economic standing of the twenty-five grand jurors from the hundred was relatively modest, all seven of the men for whom some information on age is available were forty-five or older when they became hundredal constables. At least five had earlier been headboros and others had served as churchwardens. Eight of the twenty-five were particularly familiar with the legal procedures concerning larcenies because they had themselves been victims.

Moreover, the sessional grand jurors from Hawksborough seem to have identified themselves as a coherent group. Six of them made their wills in the presence of other local grand jurors or named fellow grand jurymen from Hawksborough as overseers of their estates. And, just as the grand jurors at the Assizes in Sussex shunned other forms of legal service, grand jurymen from Hawksborough imposed a hierarchy of their own upon legal obligations. Although as many as six grand jurors from the hundred may have been petty jurors at the Assizes, none appeared as petty jurymen in the Quarter Sessions. That service was usually performed by men of lower local standing. The common interest among the men who dominated the constabulary in Hawksborough is reminiscent of that discerned among the parochial elite in Terling by Keith Wrightson and David Levine. And several sessional grand jurors have left evidence of a shared religiosity. The wills of William Pun and William Barham of Hawksborough and of John Haynes of Whalesbone include bequests, respectively, for repairs for the church, extra preaching and the maintenance of a lecturer. Some of the repercussions of this cohesiveness were also similar. The constables of Hawksborough showed little interest in pursuing vagrants or illegal cottagers, but they were a vocal presence in local attempts to control the sale of beer and ale.[23]

---

[22] Except as noted, the discussion below relies on the sources cited in footnote 12 and *VCH*, VII, IX; WSRO Ep II/10/1–3; ESRO ADA MSS 56; 143; SAS Acc. Box 1; ABER 1–3; BL Additional MSS 33,174; 33,058; for materials relating to Brighton or Whalesbone, the biographical index of John Farrant relating to Brighton and transcripts made by John Farrant and Christopher Whittick of court rolls in the possession of the ESRO (SAS uncatalogued, Dyke Hutton 1121–3) have been indispensable; for Hawksborough, see also Herrup, diss., pp. 457–63.

[23] Wrightson and Levine, pp. 73–143; ESRO Q/R/E 102/8.

Table 5.1. *Sessional grand jurymen*

	Hawksborough	Buttinghill	Whalesbone
Number of grand jurors	25	26	8
% of constables sworn to grand juries	81	87	53
Social status	3 gentlemen 11 yeomen 1 butcher 1 husbandman 9 unknown	1 gentleman 14 yeomen 1 husbandman 10 unknown	— gentlemen 1 yeoman 5 fishermen 1 mercer 1 unknown
No. in Visitations (1634 or 1662)	1	2	—
No. at universities and/or inns of court	1	1	—
% serving 3 or more sessions as grand jurors	24	31	37.5
% assessed above the minimal rate in subsidies	33 (of 18)	53 (of 19)	43 (of 7)
% able to sign their names	69 (of 16)	71 (of 7)	66 (of 3)
% resident locally less than 10 years in year of service	33 (of 6)	0 (of 4)	0 (of 2)
Known residences of grand jurors	9 of Heathfield 5 of Burwash 4 of Warbleton 7 unknown	10 of Cuckfield 5 of Hurst 2 of Slaugham 2 of Keymer 1 of Balcombe 6 unknown	all of Brighton
Range of ages at first jury service	45–59	36–48	35–66
Commonest other public offices prior to grand jury	churchwarden headboro	churchwarden trial juror	churchwarden subsidy assessor
Crimes reported to Assizes or Quarter Sessions	60% thefts 10% disorders 22% statutory 6% homicides 1% vs. constables 1% misc.	51% thefts 30% disorders 12% statutory 3% homicides 3% vs. constables 1% misc.	23% thefts 32.5% disorders 32.5% statutory 6% homicides 6% vs. constables
	No. = 79	No. = 145	No. = 52

The hundred of Buttinghill, which stretched from the border with Surrey south to the edge of the downlands, was almost three times the size of Hawksborough and considerably more diverse. Buttinghill contained the oldest (and by 1600 the least profitable) forges in Sussex, some of the most intractable areas of local forest, and valuable land for grazing. Within the hundred, competition for good land could be intense; greater extremes of both poverty and wealth existed than in Hawksborough. The crimes reported to the courts from Buttinghill reflected this disparity; compared with Hawksborough, there were more thefts of food, clothes or money as well as more complaints of trespass, hunting and assault. The backgrounds of the grand jurymen contrast with those of the men who served in Hawksborough. Only one of the three grand jurors for whom information on age is available was forty-five or older when he became a constable. More than half of the grand jurors from Buttinghill paid above the minimal rate in the subsidies. Of the three hundreds studied, Buttinghill seems to have produced the largest percentage of men who were able to sign their names.

The geographical position and the administrative history of Buttinghill encouraged a different attitude towards legal obligations than in Hawksborough. Buttinghill was adjacent to the hundred of East Grinstead, which was the normal venue for the Assizes; five of the sessional grand jurors may have also been grand jurymen in the Assizes and as many as seven may have been petty jurors there. Convenience was probably as important as credentials in explaining this unusual situation, but the overlap also reinforces the notion that the constableship in Buttinghill and Hawksborough belonged to different sorts of men. Ironically, although men of higher status dominated the constabulary in Buttinghill, the fact that the hundred was also a liberty, i.e. a discrete legal franchise, made the separation between service on a grand jury and service on a trial jury, so clear in Hawksborough, untenable. Each of the two liberties in eastern Sussex provided a list of eighteen potential trial jurors for every Quarter Sessions; the number of men necessary to meet such an obligation made it impossible to use juries to express any fine gradations of local status. Sixteen of the twenty-six grand jurymen from Buttinghill appear on extant panels of petty jurors from the liberty and at least half of these men were sworn as petty jurors. The distinctions drawn in Hawksborough between service on different sorts of juries found expression in Buttinghill in distinctions drawn between different levels of the constabulary; in contrast to Hawksborough, no grand juryman from Buttinghill seems to have had experience as a headboro.

The young, established men who were sessional grand jurors from Buttinghill justified their position by status rather than by experience. And, although grand jurors in Buttinghill were more likely than those in Hawksborough to live in the same parish, there is little to suggest that the jurors from Buttinghill saw themselves as a discrete social group. None of the grand jurors from Buttinghill entrusted their fellows with major responsibilities over their estates and only two called upon their colleagues as witnesses to important occasions. The evidence is stronger in fact for bonds in Buttinghill between grand jurors and petty jurors; three grand jurors named petty jurors as either the overseers or the executors of their estates. For the constables of Butting-hill, neither common residence nor common office provided the basis for other social bonds.

The grand jurors called to the Quarter Sessions from the southern hundred of Whalesbone were yet another sort of local elite. The small parishes in Whalesbone outside of Brighton, although fertile, were sparsely populated. Brighton was relatively prosperous, but its prosperity was not an unmixed blessing. Disagreements between those who worked on land and fishermen were chronic, the town was allegedly "overcharged with the multitude of poor people" and the fishermen at least believed themselves to be "diversely charged and burdened with service of her majesty in 'sizes, sessions and other courts and other services . . . "[24] When the inhabitants of Whalesbone appeared before the courts, they complained most often of assaults, corruption or negligence by legal officers or of unfair economic competition. Local tensions are clear in such an agenda, although only a small number of complaints of thefts or vagrancy rounded out the list of grievances.

The constabulary in Whalesbone was not an elective office as it was in Buttinghill or Hawksborough. Instead, the position rotated among the members of the governing council of Brighton ("the twelve"). Although, after 1618, constables were paid a salary for their trouble, the job remained an offshoot of other, larger responsibilities. This merger of official duties meant that the constables of Whalesbone tended to be men established in the area but preoccupied with local problems. Five of the eight constables who served as grand jurymen from Whalesbone were fishermen; at least three of the eight were assessed above the minimum for subsidies and the two who appeared as witnesses before the ecclesiastical courts were both considered literate. Grand jurors from Whalesbone were neither as young as their counterparts from Buttinghill nor as mature as those from Hawksborough; the ages of grand jurors and constables from the hundred ranged from thirty-five to sixty-six.

The grand jurymen from Whalesbone were the same sort of men chosen for office elsewhere but, both personally and officially, they had less involvement with the criminal courts than did their counterparts. Only two of the grand jurors were members of petty juries assembled for the Assizes or the Quarter Sessions and none of them seems to have served as a local headboro. Men from Whalesbone appeared only rarely in the ecclesiastical courts as witnesses and none used the Assizes or the Quarter Sessions to avenge personal injustices. The constables of Whalesbone were less likely than other constables to attend the Quarter Sessions and, when they did appear, they were less likely to be sworn to grand juries. The schedules of men who spent some

---

[24] "Costumal of Brighthelmston," cited in J. A. Erredge, *History of Brighthelmston* (Brighton, 1862), pp. 36, 37.

From accusation to indictment   109

part of each year at sea explain part of this apparent lack of interest, but the peculiar concerns of urban life added to the isolation. All of the grand jury-men from Whalesbone lived in Brighton, but they did not form a discrete group within the community. The relationships outlined by their wills and marriages suggest a broader set of linkages encompassing all of those from the hundred who participated in the Assizes or the Quarter Sessions.

The label governing classes cloaks the diversity of the elites in eastern Sussex; in age, wealth and experience, the grand jurors of Hawksborough, Buttinghill and Whalesbone were quite different from one another. In all three hundreds, however, service as a grand juror was an obligation reserved for the local elite. In all three places, most grand jurors were established resi-dents well-qualified to speak for the propertied men of their hundred. These details suggest the challenge any grand jury confronted in working together and they indicate the dilemma each grand jury faced as well. Grand juries that reflected only local interests were ill qualified to judge offenses unrelated to their localities, but grand juries that reflected only broader interests were ill qualified to present offenses based on personal knowledge. Each grand jury had to strike a balance between parochialism and disinterest.

One apparently effective solution to the conflicting demands of interest and impartiality seems to have been the use of hundredal juries to provide grand juries with information. Hundredal juries supplemented the grand jurymen's obligation to make presentments, and they assured that, regardless of the geographical composition of the grand jury, some formal outlet would exist for voicing local complaints. It is unclear why some counties used hundredal juries and others did not, but their impact on business is unquestionable. In shires such as Essex, Kent, or Hertfordshire, where grand jurors and hun-dredal jurors shared the burden of presentment, complaints of violations of statutes were routinely more comprehensive than in shires such as Sussex or Cheshire, where the geography of presentments paralleled the geographical origins of the grand jurors. Morrill concluded that in Cheshire grand jurors from particularly troublesome sections of the shire were sworn deliberately to assure the courts information about such areas. This may have been so, but the inverse is equally likely; certain parishes might appear as troublesome from presentments because of their regular representation on grand juries.[25]

---

[25] Morrill, *Grand Jury*, pp. 13, 31–3. Sussex and Cheshire appear to have been in a minority of shires that did not use hundredal juries in the early seventeenth century; among the counties known to have had hundredal juries at that period are Essex, Kent, Hertfordshire, Devon-shire, Wiltshire, Derbyshire, Warwickshire, Dorset, Norfolk, Northamptonshire, Somerset, Yorkshire, Surrey and Lancashire. See Lawson, pp. 172–6; Roberts, *Recovery and Restoration*, pp. 68, 76–7, 105–6; Campbell, *English Yeoman*, p. 341; Hassell Smith, *County and Court*, pp. 87, 91; Webb and Webb, *The Parish and the County*, pp. 456–62; Wrightson,

The responsibility of presenting offenses from personal knowledge (whether left to grand jurors alone or to grand jurors and hundredal jurors) seems to have been attended to selectively in every shire, but the range of concerns exhibited in eastern Sussex is particularly narrow. The jurors showed none of the assertiveness or creativity that Morrill found, for example, among later grand juries in Cheshire. Table 5.2 provides a rough breakdown of the topics of presentments in eastern Sussex. Grand jurors confined their comments to specific violations of one or another of the regulatory statutes; they said little that could be construed as political and they showed no interest in supervising the conduct of other legal officers. Moreover, the grand jurors used their powers of presentment not primarily to discipline the poor, as seems to have been the case in shires such as Hertfordshire and Essex, but to regulate the behavior of the middling sort. More than 60 percent of the extant presentments list complaints against engrossing, recusancy or neglect of roads and bridges. Unlicensed alehouses, or illegally crowded dwellings accounted for only one in every three complaints. Such casualness seems inconsistent with the care taken in deciding whether to indict suspects, but the priorities suggested by both patterns are complementary. The attitude toward the meaner sort that prompted vigilance in other shires was perhaps less strident in eastern Sussex; in indictments and presentments as well as in the larger pool of accusations, the offenses for which men of higher status were likely to appear (assaults, trespasses, neglect of highways), all actions tinged with economic tension, aroused the ire of grand jurors far more regularly than did thefts. The various lesser offenses characteristic of the poor inspired greater sympathy than did other categories of illegal activity. Undoubtedly grand juries supported many accusations that originated in malice, pettiness or social prejudice, but the presentments show little evidence of any sustained effort at local reformation.[26]

Detailing how grand jurors interpreted their responsibility to indict or to dismiss accusations is an exercise as frustrating as it is important. The decision to dismiss charges against a suspect was always multifaceted. No single quality ensured the rejection of a case. No combination of characteristics could guarantee the same outcome before two grand juries. Each case was

"Two Concepts of Order," pp. 26–7; *Quarter Sessions Indictment* (Warwick), pp. xxi–xxiv; cf. also *Minutes . . . Lincoln*, pp. lxx–lxxiii and *Staffordshire Quarter Sessions*, pp. xxx–xxxv.

26 See Morrill, *Grand Jury*, pp. 27–36; Lawson, pp. 174–87; Wrightson, *English Society*, pp. 165–70; Wrightson, "Two Concepts of Order"; but cf. Cockburn, *Introduction*, pp. 53–4 and, for a slightly later period, Roberts, *Recovery and Restoration*, pp. 67–72, 93–4. Even in Sussex, grand jurors made political statements occasionally: *CSPD*, 1640, pp. 520–2, relates the jurors' fury over a sermon preached at the Assizes.

Table 5.2.* *Presentments in eastern Sussex*

Complaint	No.	%
Neglect or abuse of roads or bridges	103	36
Unlicensed alehouses	69	24
Recusancy (by household)	66	23
Unlicensed building of cottages or keeping inmates	24	8
Engrossing	12	4
Illegally leaving service	4	1.5
Hunting	3	1
Official negligence	3	1
Miscellaneous	4	1.5
Total	288	100

*The 56 courts with presentments extant (33 Quarter Sessions, 23 Assizes) include 288 complaints, 186 from the Quarter Sessions and 102 from the Assizes, an average respectively of 6 complaints and 4 complaints each. The work of 12 Quarter Sessions can be followed from the Indictment Book of the 1620s and early 1630s (ESRO QI/EW1), but all business noted follows the same pattern. The nature of presentments makes their quantification somewhat problematic; these figures are best considered approximate, not exact. On the difficulty of quantifying presentments: Morrill, *Grand Jury*, p. 54.

unique, each aggrieved victim approached his situation differently, each panel of grand jurors provided a particular combination of education, values, sympathy and disapproval. The evidence accompanying the extant bills highlights some of the facts that influenced indictments, presentments and dismissals, but too much is hidden by time to recreate exactly the mix of chance and logic that produced any one decision.

Some part of the internal dynamics of each grand jury permanently eludes us. Moreover, what is known about the environment in which grand juries worked makes the unknowable all the more frustrating. Discussions among grand jurors were unrecorded and carried on outside the courtroom. Because a grand jury that worked too slowly risked returning indictments after many potential petty jurors had already left for home, the most effective grand juries were those who acted quickly. To help assure the flow of business, courts received decisions from the grand juries in clusters; trials on indicted cases proceeded while grand jurymen continued to work through their agendas. A foreman, chosen for his social status, experience, or legal expertise, presided over each grand jury and probably presided over the consideration of evidence. The foreman spoke for the jurors in the courtroom and at least occasionally used his position to win approval for his interpretation of a case. For some grand jurors, such persuasion was harassment, but for others it was probably light cast on a path of brambles. Since grand jurors returned indictments on the basis of reasonable suspicion, not guilt or innocence, they heard only the evidence for the crown. Grand jurors examined alleged victims and their witnesses in person, relying only occasionally on written examinations. Testimony was given under oath, but evidence was neither public nor final, and the laws against perjury were not always an effective spur to honesty. A malicious accusation could do considerable harm with little easy recourse. Juries had to be on guard against men like Richard Marshall, a yeoman from Rodmell, who allegedly boasted that "He cared not for the said oath nor perjury for that the same could be no where punished and that any man might swear what he would at any Sessions of the Peace how untrue soever it was ... "[27] Grand jurors also had to contend with other problems: absent or too obviously present magistrates, frightened or furious victims, intimidating or intimidated witnesses. These problems were somewhat eased because only the concurrence of twelve men, not every member of the jury, was necessary for an indictment. Since larger juries could speed the decision-making process, few courts impaneled grand juries of just twelve men. The exact number of grand jurors varied from court to court and from county to county, but most panels included between thirteen and twenty-one men. At the eastern Quarter Sessions in Sussex, the average number of grand jurors sworn was fifteen; at the Assizes, it was seventeen.[28] When a grand jury retired to deliberate, it conducted business in an atmosphere not necessarily conducive to careful consideration.

An outline of the priorities of grand jurors can be inferred from their decisions, but even that outline is incomplete because clerks were supposed to "rent into pieces immediately" any suspicion that had been dismissed as *ignoramus*.[29] Despite that injunction, more than three hundred rejected accusations from eastern Sussex do exist, but two facts undermine the typicality of these materials. Only sixty-six bills returned *ignoramus* in the Assizes have survived, almost all concerning cases with multiple suspects in which some individuals were dismissed and others were indicted. How the culpability of one person differed from another in these charges cannot be assessed because the files of the Assizes contain no depositions. Conse-

---

27 PRO STAC 8/128/04. On procedure, see BL Lansdowne MS 49/59–60; T. W., *The Office of the Clerk of the Assize* (London, 1676), pp. 5–7, 53–6; Cockburn, *Assizes*, pp.110–11; Lambard, *Eirenarcha*, p. 213; *Life of Adam Martindale*, pp. 59–60; and, for a later example of the organization of evidence for a grand jury, Macfarlane, *The Justice and the Mare's Ale*, pp. 98–9.

28 The range of sizes for juries in Sussex was from 11 men (on three occasions) to 22 men in the Quarter Sessions and from 15 to 20 men in the Assizes. This was slightly smaller than the average in other shires; cf. Cockburn, *Introduction*, p. 46; Lawson, p. 139; Babington, p. 4; Morrill, *Grand Jury*, p. 11; Roberts, *Recovery and Restoration*, p. 68.

29 Smith, p. 80.

quently, information from the Assizes has been used sparingly in the following discussion and has been eliminated entirely from the accompanying tables. The more plentiful records of the grand juries in the Quarter Sessions are the best sources for studying the process of indictment, but, since virtually all of the extant materials from the Quarter Sessions relate to the reign of Charles I and the vast majority come from the years 1636 to 1640, only a static analysis is possible.[30]

This evidence, albeit limited, reveals some fascinating patterns. Despite the pressures under which they labored and in contrast to the image of simple men passing along accusations sent them by their social betters, grand jurors in the Quarter Sessions of eastern Sussex seem to have worked from a set of consistent, if informal, evidentiary guidelines that encompassed both the form and substance of accusations. If judged by their decisions, grand jurymen were neither capricious, timid, nor overly concerned with the opinions of the social or legal establishment. Between 1625 and 1640, the grand jurors in the Quarter Sessions of eastern Sussex rejected a full quarter of the cases that they considered, a proportion showing quite clearly that indictment after accusation was not "but a matter of course, a ceremony, matter of form" as it became by the eighteenth century. Nor were the grand jurymen in eastern Sussex unique; grand jurors in Worcestershire in the same period were almost as active in rejecting complaints. Estimates of the *ignoramus* bills returned to the Assizes in various places are only slightly lower.[31]

That grand jurors did make decisions, however, reveals little about the basis on which they made them. The consistency of their choices as well as the number of *ignoramus* bills suggests the attention grand jurors paid to their obligations. Grand jurors in eastern Sussex infused the law with common-

---

[30] The 66 cases from the Assizes include 24 naming persons charged only as accessories and 39 naming persons involved as co-principals with others. Of the 275 *ignoramus* bills extant from the Quarter Sessions, 1 dates from the 1590s, 8 from the reign of James I, 61 from the years 1625–35 and 205 from the years 1636–40. In the analysis that follows only the materials from the reign of Charles I have been used since only for these years can we have any sense that the records are complete.

[31] *A Guide to Juries: Setting forth their Antiquity, Power and Duty, from the Common Law and Statutes* (London, 1699), p. 41. Sessional grand jurors in Worcestershire rejected 15 percent of the business before them in the years 1591–1643, *Worcester County Records*, 12, p. liii; see also Lawson, p. 164; Ingram, "Law and Disorder," *Crime in England*, p. 133 (28 percent). Morrill, *Grand Jury*, p. 21, estimates an "absolute minimum" rejection rate for grand juries in Cheshire at 8 percent; Cockburn, *Assizes*, p. 127, estimates a rate of 12 percent for the Home Circuit Assizes. Roberts found that in the 1650s and 1660s, grand jurors at the Quarter Sessions in Devon rejected as many as two-thirds of the cases presented to them (*Recovery and Restoration*, p. 71, n. 23). Cf. Beattie, "Crime and the Courts in Surrey 1736–1753," *Crime in England*, p. 163. In the last year for which information on the business of grand juries in Great Britain is available (1930), neither the Assizes nor the Quarter Sessions rejected more than 1 percent of the cases presented to them; *Parliamentary Debates*, 261 HC Deb.5s (London, 1932), pp. 1802–3.

Table 5.3. *Quarter Sessions: indictments according to category of crime*
1625–1640

*Category of crime	% of accusations returned *billa vera*	Total no. cases
Felony without clergy	25	24
Clergyable larceny	65	124
Petty larceny	58	199
Disorderly offenses	82	480
Offenses against the communal peace	87	234
Other offenses	89	9
Total	76	1,070

*For an explanation of these categories see Table 2.1, p. 27.
  Chi square = 0, Cramer's V = .3173.

sensical notions of both culpability and prudence. They eliminated a small number of cases for technical reasons, but deficiencies in evidence were behind most rejections. The essential demand was for a cohesive charge that interlocked crime, alleged criminal and, if relevant, stolen possessions. Jurors disliked suspicions based upon opportunity or circumstance as well as charges made from malice. They were not generally receptive to accusations made too quickly or too slowly or to those lacking supporting witnesses. Jurors were willing to bend strict definitions of liability when special circumstances seemed to render mercy the better part of justice. The translation of the idea of reasonable suspicion into the working life of the legal structure was not an easy task. The attempt of grand jurors (consciously or not) to impose a coherent set of standards upon indictments is a touchstone for their effect on the administration of criminal justice in early modern England.

Indictment, of course, meant different things in different sorts of accusations. A charge such as assault usually translated into a fine for the defendant, but a charge such as grand larceny could put a defendant at risk of his life in jail awaiting trial as well as at the trial itself. The frequency with which different sorts of suspicions became indictments suggests how seriously grand jurors considered these distinctions. Table 5.3 shows clearly that grand jurors in eastern Sussex responded most readily to accusations that carried financial rather than corporal penalties; only 25 percent of the most serious accusations, those for felonies without clergy, were returned *billa vera*. Indictment was more likely than dismissal for every suspect, but the grand jurors showed sympathy most regularly to those facing the most severe of charges.

The pattern of indictment arose from the origins of the accusations as well as from the priorities of the grand jurors. In contrast to accusations of thefts, charges for statutory offenses surfaced usually when one person confronted another during an illegal act. Unlike discoveries of theft, the detection of crime and suspect in statutory offenses was one event, and consequently more of these sorts of charges were uncontestably legitimate. The accusations that produced indictments most regularly, offenses against the communal peace, were also those most frequently supported by the personal knowledge of a grand juror or another constable. Since such transgressions were technically victimless, hundredal constables assumed the responsibilities left to the alleged victim in a theft. The high rate of indictment for these cases may reflect the attention grand jurors gave (whether from respect or expediency) to complaints presented by fellow officials. Moreover, although they usually belonged to the social groups most likely to be victims of theft, the grand jurors were generally willing to err on the side of mercy in serious charges. Such compassion might have been balanced by unremitting harshness in more serious cases at the Assizes (although no evidence suggests that), but the grand jurors of the Quarter Sessions seem to have been routinely more sympathetic to suspects accused of acts associated with poverty than they were to suspects more like themselves. This "foolish pity," as Sir Richard Grosvenor dubbed it, led to fine distinctions separating even crimes within a single general category. Charges of official negligence, of rescues from custody, or of failures to repair local thoroughfares produced indictments more regularly than did accusations of harboring inmates, building unlicensed cottages, or operating illegal alehouses. In eastern Sussex grand jurors were receptive to charges of illegally practiced trades only when such practices directly involved food or drink. The realities of deference and power in the early modern countryside cannot be discounted, but the behavior of grand jurors suggests that they recognized what it meant to be indicted for even a minor larceny and that this awareness inspired a particular care in defining reasonable suspicion.[32]

However, grand juries neither operated within a social vacuum nor, in a society that equated social standing with character, would that have been considered desirable or rational. Grand juries looked for probabilities not certainties, and in applying that standard, the statuses of alleged victims and of suspects were themselves part of the evidence. Rates of indictment fluctuated most clearly by alleged crimes, but the stated statuses of the accused and

---

[32] The rate of indictment in these smaller categories was: official negligence (85 percent, 27 cases), assault to rescue (93 percent, 43 cases), neglect of highways or bridges (90 percent, 10 cases), illegal inmates or cottages (83 percent, 35 cases), unlicensed alehouses (77 percent, 35 cases), illegal trades involving grain (100 percent, 29 cases), other illegally practiced trades (55 percent, 22 cases).

Table 5.4.* *Indictments according to category of crime and suspect's stated status: Quarter Sessions 1625–1640*

Percentage of accusations returned *billa vera*

	Gentlemen†	Yeomen	Husbandmen	Laborers	Non-agricultural	Legal officers	Women	Overall rate of indictment	No. of accusations
Felony without clergy	—	—	29	60	11	—	—	25	24
Clergyable larceny	—	40	63	72	68	—	59	65	124
Petty larceny	—	75	45	80	67	—	42	58	199
Disorderly offenses	80	88	76	90	82	40	85	81	453
Offenses against the communal peace	100	96	76	93	85	80	25	87	224
Overall rate of indictment	67	90	67	81	76	67	69	75	
No. of accusations	43	150	291	124	270	15	131		1,024††

*This table and its counterparts in later chapters should be treated skeptically for two reasons. First, since only indictments with a status listed for defendants were legitimate, the accuracy of that information is suspect; see Cockburn, "Assize Records." Second, the use of cross-tabulations reduces the number of cases in any single category. Percentages have been used for clarity, but the numbers themselves are too small to be given weight as true statistics. For Table 5.4, following the order of the table, the number of accusations is: gentlemen (1, 1, 6, 30, 5), yeomen (1, 5, 8, 51, 85), husbandmen (7, 41, 56, 137, 50), laborers (5, 29, 44, 31, 15), non-agricultural (9, 31, 54, 121, 55), legal officers (0, 0, 0, 5, 10), women (1, 17, 31, 78, 4). The relationships seem to me to be worth plotting despite these difficulties, particularly since the stated status of a defendant was what was presented to the jurors. See Appendix 2 below for an explanation of the categories used here.
†Status categories are explained in Appendix 2 below.
††Total differs from Table 5.3 because of cases with unknown status for suspects (37) and because the category of "other offenses" was too small to be included as percentages (9).
　Chi square = significant only for petty larceny: .0004, Cramer's V = .4133

Table 5.5.* *Indictments according to category of crime and complainant's stated status: Quarter Sessions 1625–1640*

Percentage of accusations returned *billa vera*

	Gentlemen	Yeomen	Husbandmen	Laborers	Non-agricultural	Legal officers	Women	Overall rate of indictment	No. of accusations
Felony without clergy	—	67	50	—	20	—	—	36	14
Clergyable larceny	92	79	50	67	26	50	75	63	89
Petty larceny	74	69	33	60	39	—	71	59	135
Disorderly offenses	84	57	82	100	72	90	79	81	244
Offenses against the communal peace	75	100	100	—	50	100	—	86	36
Overall rate of indictment	81	78	63	77	49	89	75		
No. of accusations	125	89	104	13	82	36	69		518†

*Because the status of a victim was not necessary to an indictment, this information, while available less regularly, is more reliable than information on the status of defendants. The problem of reducing each category to small numbers is, however, exacerbated. For Table 5.5, following the order of the table, the number of accusations is: gentlemen (0, 12, 46, 63, 4), yeomen (13, 29, 32, 7, 18), husbandmen (4, 16, 27, 56, 1), laborers (0, 3, 5, 5, 0), non-agricultural (5, 19, 18, 32, 8), legal officers (0, 2, 0, 29, 5), women (2, 8, 7, 52, 0).

†Total differs from other tables because of cases where complainant's status is unknown.

Chi square = significant for clergyable larceny: .0007, Cramer's V = .5843; assault: .0001, Cramer's V = .4502; trespass: .0012, Cramer's V = .6225.

the complainant were influential. Table 5.4 illustrates how the stated statuses of suspects might affect their chances of indictment; Table 5.5 traces the influence of the stated statuses of complainants. Certain patterns are clear, although the distinctions are not uniformly strong enough to be statistically significant. The yeomen who dominated the grand juries in eastern Sussex made few decisions that subverted their own interest, but neither did they ignore the disruptiveness of the ruling classes nor the possibility of legitimate grievances from below. In cases of theft (nonclergyable felony, clergyable larceny and petty larceny in Tables 5.4 and 5.5), suspects identified as laborers were the most vulnerable to indictment, but a handful of yeomen (eight, but 57 per cent of the yeomen accused) also found themselves awaiting trial. Grand jurors indicted yeomen and gentlemen regularly for disorderly offenses and offenses against the communal peace. They were similarly impatient of disruptive women, although in thefts they favored female accusers and protected female suspects. Men identified as husbandmen earned less than average rates of indictment in almost all categories of accusation, but, surprisingly, they seem to have had little credibility as complainants. This inconsistency is odd given the frequent appearances of men identified as husbandmen both as suspects and as accusers. Perhaps most interestingly, the vulnerability of men identified as working outside of the agricultural community stands out whether the men were accused or accusers. The susceptibility of such men to indictment arose in part because many men wandering in the county in search of work undoubtedly called themselves clothworkers, ironworkers, etc., but the bad luck of tradesmen not only as suspects but also as victims suggests a more fundamental conservatism. The lack of sympathy grand juries showed to these men complements the lack of interest shown by the constables of urban Whalesbone in their obligations to the court. Both as users of the court and as its representatives, men from outside the agricultural community in eastern Sussex seem to have been marginal.

Grand jurors clearly considered social status to be relevant to their decision-making, but it is impossible to measure precisely the influence of such considerations. In a legal structure where many, perhaps most, suspicions never reached a court, a high rate of indictment attests neither to exceptional cruelty nor exceptional sensitivity. In a system in which the dominant felony was theft, the predominance of the rich among the victims and the poor among the suspects is as logical as it is harsh. The specific crime carried more weight with grand jurors than did social status, but, since the accusations themselves favored certain social groups, this provides no evidence of objectivity. Grand jurors were not expected to separate themselves from their environment; they were representatives not judges. Their willingness to indict some established members of the community and to protect some of the less respected, suggests simply that, in tandem with their own self-interest, grand jurors could show compassion.

The details apart from category of crime and social status that influenced grand jurors confirm the importance of such ideals. Within the constraints intrinsic to their notion of social organization, grand jurors made sustained efforts to decide each case on its merits. Grand jurors looked at how well concrete evidence supported the charges; they demanded a coherent link between a suspect and illegal activity. They considered the motives for accusations, realizing that not every suspicion was made innocently. On occasion they even set aside a standard of reasonable suspicion for a standard adjusted to the capabilities of a suspect. The decision to indict a suspect or to dismiss him was far more complex than an equation between culpability and social status.

Grand jurors cared more about the substance of an accusation than about its technical accuracy. Only one charge refused and then reinstated changed in legal formula but not in substance. No statistically significant difference exists between rates of indictment for accusations accurate in every detail and rates of indictment for charges obviously misstating the status or residence of the accused. In fact, faulty charges became indictments more frequently than did perfect ones. Grand jurors did show concern for the proper use of categories of accusation, but the fastidiousness was selective. In thirteen accusations that carried corporal penalties, grand jurors dismissed the charges until the accusations resurfaced in later courts renamed to carry only financial penalties.[33] In the three known cases in which errors favored the suspect rather than the alleged victim, the grand jurors indicted charges as they stood. The sample is too small to suggest a deliberate policy, but in every known case reevaluation worked in the suspect's favor, suggesting that, while grand juries often ignored technical inadequacies, they were also willing to exploit flaws in the name of leniency.[34]

The connection between an acceptable accusation and the time taken to investigate a case reveals the tension between a system of detection that necessitated patience and a system of evaluation that demanded a clear link between a suspect and an alleged crime. Quick discovery often produced a confession, and suspects who confessed, for obvious reasons, were normally indicted. Other suspicions developed rapidly were particularly prone to rely upon communal prejudices or circumstantial evidence; grand juries heard about only 4 percent of the sampled accusations within five days of the alleged incident and only 73 percent of these cases became indictments. Cases pieced together too slowly had other problems; they were often difficult to corroborate; grand juries accepted only 72 percent of the charges considered after more than three months (the usual lapse of time between Quarter Sessions). The rate of indictment was highest for accusations based upon

---

[33] Fifty-eight percent of the cases in which the information in the indictment matches that of a recognizance ended with indictments; 71 percent of accusations with faulty information were indicted. See *Reports of Sir John Spelman*, ed. Baker, 94, p. 301, but also Quintrell, "Essex," p. 72. ESRO Q/R/E 47/1, 24 was the single accusation where only a formula was altered; cf. Q/R/E 20/2 and 20/7; 34/36, 98–9 and 38/47 (3 defendants); 41/126 and 42/38 (5 defendants); 44/15 and 44/24 (3 defendants); 44/12 and 44/23, cases dismissed, represented and indicted under new criminal categories.

[34] Q/R/E 41/37; 41/25, 74 were cases where recognizances indicate an error in the formal accusation that favored the suspect; see also PRO ASSI 35/38/8/17, 36; 35/38/8/13, 60.

sedate but not delayed investigations; grand juries indicted 83 percent of the cases presented between six days and six weeks after the alleged crime.[35]

The dispute between Walter Mace, a shoemaker living near the border between Kent and Sussex, and Thomas Hall, a shoemaker from Mayfield (who was probably once Mace's apprentice), shows the need for prompt responses to an alleged crime. After living with Mace for a time, Hall (according to Mace) left suddenly without explanation. Mace claimed that he then discovered that a silver spoon was missing from his house, but he did not take any action against Hall despite a suspicion that his departed assistant was the culprit. Two years after the men parted, Mace heard that Hall, in Mayfield, had pawned a silver spoon engraved with the initials E.H. He proceeded immediately into Sussex to question the custodian of the spoon. When interrogated later, Hall explained that the utensil had been a gift years earlier from his dying sister and that he used it as collateral for loans of ready money. With so much time between crime and accusation (during which Hall would have had ample opportunity to engrave his sister's initials on the spoon), the case came to one man's word against another's. The grand jury gave Hall the benefit of the doubt and dismissed the matter without indictment. English common law had no formal statute of limitations and not all postponed prosecutions failed, but long delays decreased a victim's credibility.[36]

Another measure of the soundness of a case was the willingness of local people to participate actively in the accusation. The alleged victim, witnesses and the committing magistrate all influenced cases brought before grand juries. The victim played an essential role in the successful detection of a suspect, but, once a complaint reached the courtroom, it became an offense against the crown as well as the grievance of an individual. The evidence does not allow any firm conclusions about the effect of the default or attendance of the victim, but the very small sample available suggests that the absence of the aggrieved party was not necessarily fatal to a case. Victims may have been reduced to the role of key witnesses once accusations arrived at court; their personal absence could be offset by other witnesses or by the presence of an interested magistrate. More than half of the cases heard by grand juries included witnesses for the crown besides the alleged victim, and grand juries

[35] The breakdown of indictment dates and grand jury hearings was: within 5 days: 32 cases of 44 indicted (73 percent); 5 days–6 weeks: 367 cases of 441 indicted (83 percent); 6 weeks–3 months: 160 cases of 247 (65 percent); over 3 months: 222 cases of 307 indicted (72 percent). These figures must be used cautiously given the apparently casual attitude of clerks in assigning dates to crimes in court records. However, statistically a significant relationship exists between alleged crime dates and grand jury hearings (significance = .0, Cramer's V = .23866).
[36] ESRO Q/R/E 28/14, 69, 74; Stephen, *History of the Criminal Law*, 1: 1–2. See also ESRO Q/R/E 27/8; 34/39, 88; 36/15; 38/27, 101–3; 39/7; 41/132; 44/13; 45/13; 45/7; 45/11, 69; 49/24.

were more willing to indict accusations supported by unconcerned parties than those that rested only upon a victim's word.[37]

The large number of indictments carried in the absence of the committing magistrate (19 percent) confirms the unimportance of the justice of the peace as a prosecutor, but the ability of individual magistrates to round out evidence in investigations could affect the persuasiveness of suspicions presented to grand jurors. Among cases supervised by five of the most scrupulous magistrates on the commissions of the peace in Sussex under Charles I, the percentage of indictments returned varied widely. John Baker, for example, who attended seventeen of the eighteen Quarter Sessions between 1636 and 1640 for which records are available, saw only 56 percent of the thirty-three accusations he had investigated become indictments; Herbert Hay, whose presence was equally reliable, saw seventeen out of twenty-four accusations (71 percent) passed on for trial. The cohesiveness of a case, not simply the presence of a magistrate willing to press the matter, was what counted.[38]

The ambiguities that plagued early modern criminal investigations often resulted in vague suspicions that grand juries did not accept as substantial enough to support indictments. In accusations of larceny, the strength of a case depended on questions similar to those involved at earlier stages of detection. Were stolen goods recovered? If so, could they be positively identified? Was there proof that someone knowingly had taken property rather than simply happened upon it? If no direct link between an alleged thief and missing possessions could be established, was there other reasonable cause to suspect the accused individual? Police today rely regularly upon similar deductions. The evidence culled from examinations suggests that early

---

[37] Only one case in which a victim's default is known is included in this sample and that case was indicted. Seven indicted cases relied only on the testimony of constables and 7 more listed victims as unknown; the numbers of similar cases rejected by grand juries were 1 and 5 respectively, but cf. ESRO Q/R/E 38/24, 64, 107 and also 25/4, 68–9; 49/20 where the victims died between the accusation and the trial date (both cases were rejected by grand juries). Seventy-one percent of cases with no supporting witnesses (48 percent of the sample) were indicted; 79 percent of cases with such additional backing (52 percent of the sample) were indicted. Between jury choices and number of witnesses, significance = .0026, Cramer's V = .11483.

[38] The 5 men accounted for 15 percent of the court's business and were all scrupulous in attending Quarter Sessions meetings. They were: Anthony Fowle, who was excluded from the commission for 4 of the 18 sessions while he served as sheriff, but appeared at 9 courts as a magistrate, 83 percent of the 37 cases he oversaw indicted; Herbert Hay, 17 courts, 71 percent of 24 cases indicted; John Baker, 17 courts, 56 percent of 33 cases indicted; John Wilson, 18 courts, 49 percent of 39 cases indicted; and Anthony Stapley, 14 courts, 42 percent of 26 cases indicted. Magistrates could, of course, intervene in favor of dismissal rather than indictment. Among cases where magistrates were named (426), however, there was a greater chance of indictment if the justice did appear in court (70 percent for cases with magistrates present, 62 percent for cases with magistrate named but absent), but no significant relationship exists between the appearance in the courtroom of the committing magistrate and indictment.

modern grand jurors, working with much cruder evidentiary tools, seem to have remained aware of the uncertainty of many suspicions, and to have insisted upon an accusation linking crime, suspect and circumstance.

One of the strongest pieces of evidence in a charge of larceny was the recovery of stolen possessions from the suspect. Most cases sent on for trial relied heavily on this proof. The absence of booty did not negate a suspicion, but, without the missing property or some remnant thereof, it was difficult to show conclusively either that a theft had been committed or that a suspect was truly the thief. Grand juries were cautious about endorsing true bills that rested only on circumstance. William Edwards, a petty chapman who worked near Lewes, found himself "vehemently" suspected of theft because the complainant said that he had seen Edwards and "diverse others" pass his store several times the day of the break-in. The grand jurors dismissed the accusation. The charges against Elizabeth King, a peddler near Ticehurst, rested on the fact that, having been given directions between two houses, King preferred an alternative route through a wooded area. The grand jurors returned the bill as *ignoramus*.

People whose behavior was considered odd were vulnerable to accusation when a theft occurred even if they had not been seen at the site of the alleged crime. Richard Underwood blamed John Girdler for stealing clothes and money because Girdler, a local thresher, had asked the Underwoods where they would be working the next day. Underwood argued that such curiosity was abnormal and that, since Girdler knew that no one would be home on the day in question, he was undoubtedly the felon. The connection was not enough to support an indictment. The accusation of John Longley of Wadhurst, charged with stealing small iron tools from Robert Manser, rested on two points of alleged evidence: Longley had not been home when Manser went to look for him, and Longley had been seen carrying a heavy bag of goods that rattled. The grand jury rejected Manser's suspicions.[39]

Without aids such as fingerprints or polygraphs, the identification of stolen property relied basically upon the testimony of witnesses; if goods had been permanently modified, the determination of original ownership was extremely difficult. Investigators worked with a broad definition of suspiciousness; it was up to the grand jurors to divide probabilities from facts. Generally, the more valuable a piece of property, the more likely a grand jury was to indict someone accused of its theft, but nevertheless grand jurors clearly recognized the problems of identifying stolen goods and often

[39] ESRO Q/R/E 25/2, 64–5, 73 (Edwards); 22/34, 104, 113–15 (King); ESRO Q/R/E 23/33, 97 (Girdler); 27/5, 60 (Longley). Only the case of Elizabeth King involved a theft valued at less than 1 shilling, i.e. a petty larceny. On the importance of the recovery of goods, see pp. 78–9 above. See also ESRO Q/R/E 22/32, 124–5; 25/4, 71; 34/33, 92; 34/39, 88; 33/15, 86, 88, 90; 35/12, 89; 35/91; 36/40; 37/15, 66; 45/72; 46/30; 49/20.

made their decisions accordingly. For example, Ann Hasting, a widow from Folkington, was accused at the Quarter Sessions for Michaelmas, 1626, of stealing a cock from Roger Breecher. Breecher had searched the area for his missing rooster; he believed that Hasting was the culprit because he had found the bones of an animal in the ashes of her fireplace and a discarded liver outside her door. Hasting said that the remains came from a pair of rabbits, not a cock and that they had been a gift (and a meal) about a week earlier. The grand jury excused the accusation. In the case of John Longley of West Hoathly, the jurors were at least equally generous. Henry Herbert claimed that Longley had stolen a sheep. The searchers found several pieces of mutton in Longley's home, but he said that they came from a sheep bought legitimately to feed his workers after harvest. When the headboro asked for the sheepskin, however, Longley said that he had pulled all of the wool off; when the officer wanted to see the pelt, Longley claimed his dog had eaten it; when the constable inquired after the sheep's wool, Longley could find none. The testimony of two laborers who had been treated to a feast of mutton at Longley's home added to the evidence, but the grand jurors did not allow the indictment; Longley clearly had a sheep, but nothing proved that his sheep was the one lost by Henry Herbert.[40]

Table 5.6 provides context for these anecdotes by showing how rates of indictment for larceny varied according to the type of property in question. The most commonly contested goods (food, small livestock) were not those most commonly indicted. Several facts, including the stated statuses of both suspect and victim, the value of the contested property and the probable motive for alleged thefts, help to explain this pattern, but food and small livestock were among the goods hardest to recover intact and most difficult to identify positively. The low rate of indictment for other categories of goods that were either hard to personalize and/or easy to transform into new shapes or sizes (small iron tools, clothing, wool, malt, etc.) confirms the importance of the issue of identification. So, too, does the reluctance of grand jurors to forward accusations involving money, the most uniform and easily convertible commodity in early modern England.

The possibility that goods claimed as stolen had been innocently misappropriated created another challenge for grand jurors. Livestock in eastern Sussex grazed in many places on public commons and often shared communal pens. Labor was paid in kind probably as often as in currency. Such circumstances provided numerous opportunities for bad feelings, and disputes over proper ownership often became stalemates. Grand juries

---

[40] ESRO Q/R/E 24/9, 76 (Hasting); 39/10, 99–101 (Longley). See also ESRO Q/R/E 22/33, 120; 22/30, 135; 24/5, 45, 63, 77; 34/40, 88; 34/55, 89, 93, 35/21; 34/38, 91; 39/8, 49, 98; 45/11, 69; 45/72, 46/30; WSRO Q/R/WE 16/8, 41; 16/7, 38.

Table 5.6. *Quarter Sessions: indictments according to categories of stolen property 1625–1640*

Category of stolen property	% of accusations returned *billa vera*	Total cases
Food, poultry	60	95
Sheep, pigs	62	78
Wool, malt, wood, etc.	58	33
Iron	57	26
Household items	72	25
Cloth	70	23
Clothing, shoes	50	20
Money, jewels, plate	47	19
Cattle	75	4
Total	60	323*

*Excludes thefts for which benefit of clergy was not available, i.e. breaking and entering, theft of horses, cutpursing (together 17 cases, 35% indicted).

frequently dismissed such controversial accusations. In April, 1639, Sara Muddle accused Jane Glasier, of Rotherfield, of the theft of a tablecloth from Sara's mother, Mary Muddle. The daughter said that the linen had disappeared from her mother's cupboard. On search the constable found the covering at Glasier's. Glasier, "being asked where she had it [the cloth], she replied if it were hers [Muddle's] she should have it." The suspect added, however, that the cloth was her payment for nursing services rendered to the Muddles. Mary Muddle was not examined nor did she appear in court (the illness in question may have been her last). Her daughter Sara was either ignorant of the payment arranged for Glasier, or indignant at the results of Glasier's services. The grand jury dismissed the matter.[41]

A well-constructed case, of course, was not necessarily a legitimate one. Criminal charges could arise from fear, anger, or a desire to discredit an opponent in legal suits elsewhere. Accusations in disputes over land spawned ancillary accusations; sometimes both charges were supportable, but malice often prompted second or third complaints. Since witnesses or magistrates might support such tactics, grand juries were left to try to separate honest suspicions from those that were sideshows to other disagreements. Their

---

[41] ESRO Q/R/E 45/12, 71; see also Q/R/E 15/20, 85; 16/4, 28, 46; 19/82–3v; 21/54, 74, 111–12; 22/30, 35, 85, 106; 22/56, 71–2, 107–8, 130–1; 24/23, 71–3; 25/26, 78; 26/24, 50–1; 26/39–40, 49; 27/5, 26, 59–60; 29/30, 63–4; 35/4; 35/42, 93; 36/46, 81, 99; 36/50, 104–5; 37/97; 38/27, 101–3; 38/57, 105–6; 47/10–15, 51.

success or failure is not quantifiable, but the evidence shows that some effort was made to uncover the true stories behind complex accusations.

Because the accessibility of the court increased the ease with which people could use the legal process to prosecute vague prejudices or to vent unjustified grudges, perhaps the simplest measure of the efforts of grand juries to distinguish truth from malice is geographical. Areas within easy reach of the Quarter Sessions at Lewes had the highest percentage of dismissed charges. Because the preferment of complaints was more difficult for individuals who lived far away from Lewes, charges from these distant hundreds were probably more substantial, and they were more frequently endorsed.[42] But the distance that an alleged victim traveled to prosecute his case might test determination rather than sincerity. Some cases were part of a wider web of bad feelings and no simple measure of convenience could separate harasser from harassed. Determining the validity of such charges was often difficult. In obvious cases, a suspect answered an accusation with an exact countercharge, asserting the same illegal act, involving the same persons, on the same day, as the original complaint, but related cases could also be dated weeks or months apart, could allege crimes of unequal magnitude and could accuse different individuals. Grand jurors sometimes threw out all of the tainted accusations, but more often they tried to sort legitimate complaints from those that stemmed merely from later anger. The deliberateness with which grand jurors approached such problems can be inferred from the fact that most double suspicions were heard by a single grand jury, making the jurors privy to both sides of a contested story. Few of these cases have left ancillary evidence, but, where witnesses beyond the victim were available to testify, the side with supporting parties invariably received the true bill. Although dates given in indictments are not a reliable judge of the actual beginning of a dispute, grand juries seem also to have given greater credence to the earliest dated accusations.[43]

Not every local argument, however, produced charges and countercharges before a single court. At the Quarter Sessions held at Michaelmas, 1627, David Fairman accused his neighbor, John Rolfe, of a destructive trespass. Despite the presence of a supporting witness, the grand jurors dismissed the case. Fairman's accusation might well have been discounted because of his

---

[42] Hundreds with rates of indictment lower than 60 percent were Streat, Swanborough, Younsmere, Danehill Horsted, Bishopstone, Flexborough, Loxfield Dorset, Hartfield, and Netherfield. Those with rates of indictment higher than 90 percent were Longbridge, Bexhill, Burleigh Arches, Portslade, Willingdon, Henhurst, Ninfield, Guestling, Staple and Goldspur. Significance = .0075, Cramer's V = .12920. See Figure 2.1, p. 27 above.

[43] ESRO Q/R/E 21/11 and 21/12; 21/9 and 21/10, 28–9; 24/6 and 24/13; 36/30–1 and 36/32; 41/40 and 41/127; 41/25 and 41/131; 43/4 and 43/12; 45/4 and 45/14–15; 49/26 and 49/32; 50/8, 22 and 50/24; cf. Q/R/E 29/10; 29/19; 41/46; 41/132; 45/6; 45/7; 49/19; 22; 49/34. On the validity of dates in indictments, see Cockburn, "Assize Records."

longstanding animosity toward John Rolfe. Ten years earlier, in one of the few charges of witchcraft extant from eastern Sussex, Fairman had claimed that Rolfe and two others had tried to bankrupt him through sorcery. Those charges resulted in indictments and acquittals; by 1627, the other accused sorcerers were dead, but Fairman and Rolfe were obviously still uneasy neighbors.[44]

A different type of malice underlay the accusations between two families in Ticehurst, the Hosmers and the Puxtys. Mary Puxty, a widow, charged that Edward and Grace Hosmer broke into her house in the dark of night and stole enough butter and cheese to merit a charge of grand larceny. Puxty told the examining justice that a hole had been made in the wall of her milkhouse. She explained that she suspected the Hosmers because they had earlier killed her dog and had treated her with "great scorn and derision" in later boasting of the act. Grace Hosmer admitted that she had taken an axe to the widow's animal but, in regards to the theft, she claimed "the said widow of malice towards this examinate has framed these reports to accuse her and her husband wrongfully." Testimony by a former servant of Puxty's that the widow had staged the theft by breaking her own wall in order to revenge herself on the Hosmers verified Grace Hosmer's suspicions. The grand jury dismissed the case without indictment.[45]

The intentions of Mary Puxty or David Fairman might have been fairly transparent; some arguments were far more complicated, spanning not only years, but also a variety of legal forums. A handful of complaints, entered in the Jacobean Court of Star Chamber, reveal instances in which criminal charges were used to harass individuals in eastern Sussex. Grand juries managed to weed out some false accusations, but they doubtless did indict phony charges that were supported by corrupt witnesses. The larceny alleged by Sir Benjamin Pellat of Bolney against Samuel Wilkinson, the local curate, emphasizes the need for vigilance by grand juries and the difficulties of dividing true disputes from diversionary tactics. Pellat accused Wilkinson of stealing a plate and linen from his manor house in Bolney. He condemned Wilkinson, who had only recently come to the area, as a "naughty pilfering fellow." Wilkinson said there had been no theft, but that Pellat had brought a constable to the vicarage and taken away Wilkinson's own property, challenging it as stolen and threatening to indict the cleric unless he moved to another parish. The problem, Wilkinson explained, was not his honesty, but rather his zealous attention to the infrequent attendance at church of the

---

[44] ESRO Q/R/E 18/26–7, 28, 31, 59–60; 28/12; BT/XE 1/302/2; W/A25; WSRO Ep II/9/14/1, 19; 9/23/44; see also Macfarlane, *Witchcraft*, pp. 147–200; Thomas, *Religion and the Decline of Magic*, pp. 535–70; above Chapter 2, pp. 32–3.
[45] ESRO Q/R/E 25/4, 68–9, 71–2.

Pellats. The knight denied this, but Wilkinson explained that a prominent local churchman and a justice of the peace had both assured him that Pellat would not press any charges if Wilkinson would leave the area before the next Quarter Sessions. When the cleric arrived at the court, moreover, two of Pellat's men allegedly threatened him. "Being a very simple and inexperienced man in such courses," Wilkinson testified later, he decided that Pellat had turned the magistrates against him. Overcome by such fears, he left Lewes without fulfilling his promise to appear. Pellat pressed this advantage to have Wilkinson indicted for not one, but two, separate, larcenies. The grand jury endorsed both bills as true, either because of Wilkinson's default, or, as the cleric claimed, because Pellat produced false witnesses.

Wilkinson next hid for three weeks with some sympathetic persons, one of whom, John Dumbrell, was himself a frequent grand juror at the Assizes. Perhaps at Dumbrell's urging, Wilkinson eventually surrendered himself before two magistrates, Sir Walter Covert and Sir Thomas Eversfield. In the week before the Assizes, Pellat allegedly continued to harass Wilkinson, even (according to Wilkinson) bringing the common stocks of the parish into the parlor of the vicarage, locking the cleric inside of them and leaping and dancing about all night around him. At the Assizes, three indictments were presented, the two against Wilkinson sent from the Quarter Sessions and now a third by Wilkinson against Sir Benjamin Pellat for conspiracy. A special trial jury acquitted the cleric of larceny, and the Bench rejected the conspiracy charge as technically insufficient. At the next Assizes, Pellat again was accused and this time indicted for conspiracy. Pellat had the charge removed into the Court of King's Bench where he was acquitted. Still undeterred, Pellat began a suit against Wilkinson in the Court of the Star Chamber, but it also was dismissed as unwarranted. Wilkinson then countersued in the same court. The results of this proceeding are unknown. This contest of wills spanned at least four years, three magistrates and four courtrooms. It reveals the complexity that could hide behind a simple charge of larceny as well as the legal machinations of which grand jurors could unwittingly be a part.[46]

Grand juries affirmed the plausibility of suspicions, but sometimes grand jurors dismissed charges regardless of their validity. Suspects who were willing to help in the prosecution of others, for example, often earned sympathy. The use of witnesses who traded preferential treatment for information was an accepted part of the English common law; testimony so arranged was not on the face of it considered tainted. The records of the Assizes and Quarter Sessions never refer openly to such arrangements, but on occasion an accusation rejected by a grand jury coincided with the appearance of the

[46] PRO STAC 8/242/5; 8/294/23; ASSI 35/50/9/1, 9–10. For other attempts to deceive local grand juries see PRO STAC 8/111/04; 8/224/1; 8/208/14; 8/128/04.

suspect as a witness against his own companions. At the Quarter Sessions in 1618, Robert Lowle and John Cressey were indicted in five cases of stealing sheep. William Cogger apparently bought the animals, and then resold them at a profit. Cogger was originally accused with Lowle and Cressey, but the grand jury freed him with a bill of *ignoramus* and he appeared as a witness against the others. Since Lowle and Cressey denied any impropriety, Cogger's evidence was probably crucial for a successful prosecution. Thomas Shoulder received lenient treatment in a similar situation. Shoulder, identified in the records as a victualler from Piddinghoe, earned a reprimand in 1627 for running an unlicensed alehouse. He was given the statutory penalty (three days in jail, a fine of twenty shillings and demand for a promise of no future misbehavior). However, a second charge against him, for running a disorderly alehouse, was dismissed. It is probably not accidental that this rejection coincided with Shoulder's testimony against two other men for brewing illegally.[47]

The default of defendants dissuaded grand juries from indictments in at least seventeen instances, although in general a suspect's disappearance was taken as confirmation of the charge against him. Grand juries on occasion felt that the practical problems of law enforcement outweighed the demands of strictest justice. In the fall of 1637, Charles Turner accused Jane Farnes of picking his pocket at a local fair. Turner noticed the woman, he said, because she stood near him for a long time while he bought a hat. When he found his keys and money gone, he asked the nearest constable to arrest Farnes. The officer questioned the woman and, much to Turner's dismay, released her. Turner persisted in his accusations although Farnes offered to pay him if he would stop harassing her. Finally Turner, Farnes and the constable took the matter to John Wilson, a justice of the peace. Farnes told Wilson that she was recently widowed, that she lived in London, that she had been to Sussex only once before, and that she did not normally frequent fairs or fairgrounds. She claimed to have come to Horsted Keynes to collect a debt owed her late husband; she insisted that the money she carried was her own. Since Wilson was skeptical of her story he ordered her held until the next Quarter Sessions. But a week later, a second magistrate, Thomas Middleton allowed her to go free once she had provided a bond for her appearance. When the court convened the next month, Farnes was absent. It is certainly possible that Jane Farnes was, as Charles Turner and perhaps John Wilson suspected, a petty thief, but she may have been, as the actions of the constable and Thomas Middleton suggest, an innocent victim of circumstance. Given conflicting opinions and

---

[47] ESRO Q/R/E 19/30–4 (Lowle and Cressey); 27/2, 20–1 (Shoulder) and, for other examples of probable exchanges of information for dismissal, ESRO Q/R/E 36/11; 42/27; 48/5, 26; 49/18, 77, 81; PRO ASSI 35/57/7/26–33. On the legal position of such witnesses, Dalton, *Countrey Justice*, p. 297.

the enormous task of finding Farnes in London, the grand jury, reluctant to pursue the matter beyond the boundaries of the shire, dismissed the charge with an *ignoramus.*[48]

In addition to times when practical considerations worked against indictment, situations existed when indictment, while justified, would in fact be an injustice. The common law dictated no official allowance for immaturity beyond the age of seven, but Sir William Blackstone noted that, in England, culpability was "not so much measured by years and days, as by the strength of the delinquent's understanding and judgment." Grand juries were reluctant to indict adolescents or children. Six bills marked *ignoramus* survive in which the accused not only confessed, but also appeared in court; at least four of these suspects were under sixteen years of age at the time of their offenses. Agnes Barton, whose theft of a coin during a Christmas dinner was discussed in Chapter 4, was twelve and one-half when she had that fateful meal. John Ball, who with his sister Ann gleefully threatened to attack and jail William King was "twelve or thereabouts" when he was examined for his thievery. Physical maturity aside, one example will illustrate why adolescents were more vulnerable to temptation than older persons. In July, 1626, Jane Tully was accused and dismissed for stealing £4 from Anne Dimock, a widow from East Grinstead. Dimock, it seems, was about to marry Jane's father. Another local woman, Joan Harriden, had warned Jane that once Tully and Dimock married, Dimock would "get from him [Tully] all his goods and convert it to her own children's use." Jane and her siblings would be disinherited. Harriden offered to save Jane from this fate by keeping her possessions secretly until the girl came of age. She advised Jane to get some of Dimock's goods immediately. Jane obeyed, but soon discovered her gullibility. Harriden took what Jane had stolen and "threatened her that if ever she did make it known to any what was become of the money she would kill her." According to the parish register, in 1626 Jane Tully was not quite sixteen years old. In five of the cases known to involve adolescents, the teenager was the partner in crime of an older person who had actively encouraged the younger suspect. In every instance, both child and adult were excused by the grand juries.[49]

---

[48] ESRO Q/R/E 39/15, 55, 96, 104, 107, 110. See also ESRO Q/R/E 22/31, 61–2; 24/3, 33; 24/5, 45, 63, 77; 28/16, 72; 35/9, 36–40; 35/13–14, 36; 37/17, 68; 44/10; 44/14; WSRO Q/R/WE 16/6, 22, 26; and ESRO Q/R/E 20/3, 30, 55, 71; 21/57, 102–5, 113 where a defaulted defendant was recharged and indicted when new evidence became available. Of 90 cases with alleged defendants recorded as at large, 81 percent were indicted.

[49] Blackstone, *Commentaries,* 4: p. 23; ESRO Q/R/E 20/4, 54, 69–70 (Barton); 34/37, 94–5 (Ball); WSRO Q/R/WE 16/6, 22, 26, 42 (Tully); see also ESRO Q/R/E 12/45, 60–1, 73, 102–3; 24/7–8, 70, 75; 36/93–5. For the ages of the accused see ESRO parish registers and bishops' transcripts and the registers in the publications of the Sussex Record Society (vols. 7, 13–15, 21). See also Ingram, "Wiltshire," pp. 347, 355–6. It is uncertain why the elder

The decisions of grand juries at the Quarter Sessions in eastern Sussex reflect the particular priorities of the governing classes in a particular shire, but these decisions also have wider ramifications. Both the indictments and presentments reveal how men of property flexibly defined their needs for peace. As expressed in eastern Sussex, that need was more selective than the stereotypes of either contemporary social organization or contemporary religiosity might lead us to expect. The grand jurors surrendered at times to pettiness, laziness and prejudice, but they could also show concern for a more abstract ideal of fairness.

The job of the grand juror, as indicter and presenter, differed decisively from the task of the petty juror. Petty jurors confirmed a decision that in theory was self-evident – defendants deserved criminal punishment or they did not, and any honest man who knew the defendant's background and heard his defense could fairly judge him. The distinction between reasonable suspicion and flimsy allegation theoretically was more delicate than the gap between guilt and innocence. Grand jurors, consequently, needed not to be men of a set neighborhood, but rather men who were distinguished for their discernment, "the most discreet, able and sufficient persons, both for their estate and understanding."[50] As Lambard said, they did truly need to be "weeders" of the commonwealth, sifting wheat from chaff in both accusations and presentments. A suspect brought to the grand jury left either free or defendant, a complainant went out humiliated or symbolically supported by the outrage of the king. Grand juries alone, however, could not seal the fate of defendants.

---

partner in these situations escaped indictment but, if the instigator had acted overtly only as an accessory, he or she may have been saved by the rule that accessories could not be convicted unless the principal was.

[50] PRO SP 14/190/43.

6

From indictment to conviction

The rituals of criminal trials in early modern England emphasized the responsibilities of petty jurors. At least three separate times in a trial, juror and defendant confronted one another. When suspects were ready to stand trial, the potential jurors and the arraigned defendants approached the Bar of the courtroom. The two groups stood face to face while the clerk presented the jury to the defendants: "These good men," he said, "that were last called, and have appeared are those that shall pass between our Sovereign Lord the King and you upon your lives and deaths . . . " Unlike grand jurors, who were sworn collectively, petty jurors made their promises individually, each with his hand upon the Bible. The accepted procedural manual for clerks of the courts in the late seventeenth century recommended not only that a juror touch the Scriptures as he swore, but also that he look directly into the faces of the defendants. Any defendant could dismiss up to twenty potential jurors without specific cause by challenging the candidates when they moved forward to take the oath of office. To emphasize further the solemnity of the occasion, after taking their oaths, the petty jurors stood to either side of the Bar with the persons to be tried in between them. One by one, each prisoner was brought forward and instructed to raise his hand. "Look upon the Prisoner you that be sworn and harken to his cause," the clerk instructed the jurymen. The clerk declared that each prisoner had pleaded innocent to the crime alleged against him and had chosen to be tried by "God and the Country, which Country are you." After a jury reached its verdicts, petty jurors and defendants once more came face to face. Before the foreman announced the decisions, the clerk again advised the jurors, "Look upon the Prisoner." In these encounters, both sides were forced to confront the somberness of their relative positions. Early modern criminal trials were loosely structured and rapidly conducted. The care taken to ensure ritualized personal contact between jurors and defendants indicates the importance attached to the formal role of petty juries in the sixteenth and seventeenth centuries.[1]

---

[1] T. W., *Clerk of the Assize*, pp. 11–13, 16, 66–73, is the standard contemporary account of a

The authority of the petty jurors differed from the authority of both their medieval and their modern counterparts. The medieval juryman was chosen because he knew the circumstances surrounding a particular charge. He pronounced judgment on the basis of previously attained information. In contrast, the modern juryman is excluded from service if he is acquainted with an issue or its contestants; he bases his decision on information received in the courtroom. In the early modern era, jurors were neither so familiar with the circumstances of cases as medieval jurors nor so distant as modern ones. Except on juries convened to investigate sudden deaths or to try local misdemeanors, "men of the neighborhood" were simply men from the county, not men from the vicinity of an alleged crime. Even in shires such as Sussex where geographical considerations affected the composition of juries, a match between the scene of an alleged crime and the homes of the jurors was fortuitous. However, jurors who did live near the victim or the defendant or who were familiar with the case in question were not automatically eliminated from a jury. The ideal of the jury as a *tabula rasa* was not yet in place, but the older base of power, information not presented in the courtroom, had been largely lost.

At least three practical considerations rendered the older ideal unworkable. By the late sixteenth century, even in courts with modest agendas, the number of defendants tried was substantial. The Assizes in Sussex often oversaw the trials of fifteen or twenty defendants, and the Quarter Sessions normally handled the cases of four or five individuals. To impanel petty juries from the locality of each crime would have been a clerical nightmare. The ease with which men and women in early modern England changed their residences suggests a second reason for the obsolescence of the medieval system; a jury of the neighborhood worked only if local residence ensured reliable knowledge of an alleged crime, criminal, victim, or witnesses. Where recent immigrants, temporary residents, or total strangers were a routine part of the local population, common residence was less likely to translate to common experience. As society itself became more fluid, the advantages of trial by neighbors diminished. The importance of local juries may also have been inhibited by a growing social distance between petty jurors and defendants. Everyone agreed that substantial yeomen from a prisoner's neighborhood made the best jurors, but writers such as Sir Thomas Smith acknowledged that such jurymen rarely knew defendants personally. These jurors, Smith

trial. The best modern accounts of trials are Cockburn, *Assizes*, ch. 6; Cockburn, *Introduction*, pp. 100–13, and, for a slightly later period, Beattie, *Crime and the Courts*, ch. 7. Challenges seem to have been uncommon in simple criminal matters, but not unheard of; see ESRO Q/R/E 2/1, 5; 4/3; 17/26; 21/50, 58; 37/34, 99; 39/41, 50; 40/29, 35; 44/32, 70; 49/44, 93.

explained, were "men acquainted with daily labor and travail, and not with such idle persons as be ready to do such mischiefs."[2]

But legal as well as sociological changes separated the jurors of early modern England from their predecessors. Medieval jurors controlled trials (and to some degree the evolution of the law as well) through their monopoly on facts. The Marian legislation requiring written examinations in all felonies nullified that monopoly and denied jurors the privacy to interpret facts and law free from judicial scrutiny. Moreover, once liberated from reliance upon jurymen for their own information, judges and justices could test the decisions of petty jurors against judicial interpretations of cases. Disagreements between juries and judges or magistrates over verdicts became more obvious and differences more easily degenerated into contests for control of the courtroom. The period of transition, when the petty jurors' monopoly on information had ended, but their right to find any verdict free of judicial interference had not yet been secured, was an uncertain one in terms of the relationship between judicial officials and petty jurors.[3] The men willing to serve on petty juries changed along with the nature of that service. The use of discretion did not disappear in the early seventeenth century, but mitigations granted by judicial officials came to be seen as proper exercises in mercy, while increasingly mitigations from the broader bases of grand juries or petty juries were dismissed as signs of perversity or ignorance.

Commentators in early modern England discussed petty juries with the same mixture of hopefulness and dismay that infused their writings about grand juries; they bemoaned the allegedly tepid public spirit of sufficient freeholders, and they idealized the place of petty juries in the English law. The consensus was that the best jurors were substantial yeomen, men "more apt and fit to discern in doubtful causes of great examination and trial, than are men wholly given to moiling [laboring] in the ground, in whom that rural exercise engenders rudeness of wit and mind." Simpler men, James I declared in his proclamation on the status of jurors, were "almost at a gaze in any cause of difficulty." The concern over ability stemmed not only from prejudices about the relative merits of the rich and the less rich, but also from worries that poorer men were more vulnerable to corruption. Zachary

---

[2] Smith, p. 91. The best recent summaries of social conditions in the period are Wrightson, *English Society*, and D. M. Palliser, *The Age of Elizabeth: England under the Later Tudors 1547–1603* (London, 1983).

[3] The most comprehensive discussion of the implications of such changes is Green, *Verdict According to Conscience*, especially ch. 4, but see also Langbein, *Prosecuting Crime*, pp. 104–28; Cockburn, *Introduction*, chs. 8, 10; Babington, "The Author to the Reader," (no pagination), p. 205; Sir John Hawles, *The Englishman's Right: A Dialogue Between a Barrister at Law and a Juryman* (London, 1732), pp. 13–14, 52; Quintrell, "Essex," p. 83; Eaton Hall Grosvenor MSS, Quarter Sessions Charge.

Babington complained that jurors at the Assizes in the middle years of the seventeenth century "seldom serve, but to serve a turn . . . to obey a superior, pleasure a friend, or to help away a quick dispatch of practice." He insisted further that "some serving had more need to be relieved by the eight pence [dinner money] than discretion to sift out the truth of the fact." James I urged potential jurors to recognize that they held a power "no less important to the sum of justice than the true and judicious exposition of the Laws themselves." But even the king recognized that many of his subjects persisted in what he dismissed as "that vain and untrue conceit, that they are in any ways disgraced or disesteemed, if they be called upon or used in this part of justice . . . " A chronic shortage of jurors made a mockery in many places of the exhortations of the government.[4]

Individuals avoided petty juries for many reasons. Impanelment disrupted daily life; it required time and money to appear at court. Inconvenience, of course, affected grand juries as well as petty juries, but, in general, grand juries were less onerous and more prestigious to serve on than their counterparts. Grand jurors began their work early in the proceedings of a court. They could be dismissed when all pending accusations had been presented. Petty jurors were not even sworn until the grand jurors had returned some indictments. No petty juror could predict at what point in a session he might be impaneled; on more than one occasion, men called to court as jurors simply left when the waiting lasted longer than their patience. And, although grand juries operated under pressure to produce indictments quickly, they were independent compared to petty jurors. The stipulation that petty jurors have "neither bread, drink, meat nor fire" was irrelevant in routine cases, which were decided in minutes rather than in hours, but in cases requiring extensive deliberations, jurors could be held virtually as prisoners until they returned a verdict.[5]

Not even the verdict necessarily ended the discomfort of being a juror. Because the decisions of petty juries were generally irreversible, individual jurors shouldered a greater personal responsibility than did grand jurors. Judges at the Assizes or justices at the Quarter Sessions actually sentenced

---

[4] BL Harleian MS 38/153. This distinction was drawn from Sir John Fortescue's fifteenth-century comparison of English and European legal systems, but his justification for restricting impanelment to the relatively wealthy still resonated in the early modern era; cf. Sir John Fortescue, *Learned Commendation of the Political Laws of England* (London, 1567), fos. 65–69v; "A Proclamation for Jurors 1607," in *Royal Proclamations of King James I 1603–1625*, eds. James F. Larkin and Paul L. Hughes (Oxford, 1973), pp. 168, 169; Babington, pp. 12–13; see also Hawles, *The Englishman's Right*, pp. 10, 45–7; Richard Bernard, *A Guide to Grand Jury Men, Divided into Two Books* (London, 1627), p. 25; Cockburn, *Introduction*, ch. 6, n. 83.

[5] "Notebook of a Surrey Justice," p. 180; Smith, pp. 92–3; Hawarde, pp. 230–2; but, for a different view of normal process, see Cockburn, *Introduction*, pp. 110–12.

convicts, but the judiciary acted within constraints set by petty juries. Some men preferred to avoid such responsibilities entirely; the burden may also explain what one grand jury in Essex considered the "perverse delight" of trial jurors in acquitting felons whom the grand jurors considered to be obviously guilty. Every petty juror, sensitive or not, would have preferred to avoid the anger that decisions occasionally ignited in judges, victims, defendants or spectators. Thomas Fuller wrote that a yeoman on a jury cares "not whom he displeases so he pleases his own conscience," but for most men independence was hard to maintain in the face of verbal or even physical assaults. Most criminal decisions proceeded without incident, but judges were known to malign petty jurors publicly, to insist that they revise decisions and to censure them before the Court of Star Chamber. In non-criminal matters, unhappy litigants on occasion formally charged juries with corruption or physically attacked jurymen. William Harrison, citing a story of jurors carted from town to town on the order of a judge who hoped to influence their verdict, claimed that fear of such harassment was what kept substantial yeomen away from juries.[6]

Bullying was not the normal response to the decision of a petty jury, but the possibility of such unpleasantness reinforced the belief that those who could ought to avoid impanelment. This lack of enthusiasm increased the burden of service. The Assizes and Quarter Sessions in eastern Sussex called about twenty panels of jurors (over 400 men) for criminal business annually; that only a small proportion of those summoned would be sworn just added insult to injury. By the early seventeenth century, the problem had become as circular as the problem of finding proper participants for grand juries; unless men of substance served, trials would be left in the hands of the less respected, but as long as men of modest standing dominated petty juries, more substantial men would not join them. In many shires, two sorts of men increasingly dominated juries; novices impaneled *ad hoc* in the courtroom and men "so accustomed and inured to pass and serve upon juries . . . [as to] make the service, as it were an occupation and practice."[7]

6 The relationship between jurors and the judiciary is more fully discussed below, pp. 158–64. Contemporary anecdotes about the tensions of the relationship include PRO ASSI 35/70/8, cited in Quintrell, "Essex," p. 83; Thomas Fuller, "The Holy State," cited in Campbell, *The English Yeoman*, p. 341; Harrison, *Description of England*, p. 91; Smith, pp. 100–1; *CSPD*, 1629–31, p. 74; Hawarde, pp. 62, 230–2; Hawles, *The Englishman's Right*, pp. 1–3; John Walter, "Grain Riots and Popular Attitudes to the Law: Maldon and the Crisis of 1629," in Brewer and Styles, eds., *Ungovernable People*, p. 78; Cockburn, *Introduction*, pp. 70–1; Lawson, pp. 191–2.

7 *Royal Proclamations*, ed. Larkin and Hughes, p. 169; Cockburn, *Assizes*, pp. 118–20; Cockburn, *Introduction*, pp. 57–63. In the Quarter Sessions for eastern Sussex, where information both on juries summoned and juries used is available for 7 years, the number of men called to court ranged from 270 to 342, with about 20 percent of those summoned actually participating in trials. In the Assizes no information on summoning is extant, but between 35

In contrast to duty on grand juries, duty on petty juries was hard to make prestigious. Conscience and experience were the petty juryman's stock in trade. His contribution to the law rested on the illusion that he was the common respectable man, pure in insight in part because he was not burdened with the subtleties of formal learning. Nicholas Breton's fictitious yeoman of the seventeenth century explained:

We can learn to plow and harrow, sow and reap, and prune, thrash and fanne, winnow and grind, brew and bake, and all without book; and these are our chief business in the Country, except we be jury-men to hang a thief, or speak truth in a man's right, which conscience and experience will teach us with a little learning.

James I likened the authority of petty jurors to his own, remarking that "For even that judgement which was given by a King in person, and is so much commended in the Scriptures, is not any learned exposition of the law, but a wise sifting and examination of the fact."[8] To yeomen anxious to prove their uncommonness, such analogies held no attraction.

The usual qualification for service on a petty jury was possession of a freehold worth forty shillings annually. But, by 1608, the government estimated that no more than half of the eligible men appeared on lists of freeholders. Men who came to the courts as victims, witnesses, constables, spectators, or jurors for common pleas increasingly risked being drafted as petty jurors in criminal cases. By the 1620s, such *ad hoc* jurors tried most of the criminal cases on the western circuit of the Assizes. The problem allegedly discouraged men in Essex from appearing at the Assizes to prosecute defendants and it also had repercussions beyond the legal process. In Somerset, a candidate for the House of Commons complained that voters would avoid the election if the sheriff used the opportunity to collect the names of freeholders. On at least one occasion, copyholders rejected the king's offer to convert their lands to freeholds explicitly because the change would bring added responsibilities such as service on petty juries.[9]

The symbiotic relationship of prestige and participation is clear in the

and 95 men a year were sworn in the 16 years from which both meetings of the court survive; see Herrup, diss., ch. 5, n. 20.

8　Nicholas Breton, "The Courtier and the Countryman," cited in Campbell, *The English Yeoman*, p. 263; *Royal Proclamations*, ed. Larkin and Hughes, p. 168.

9　*Royal Proclamations*, ed. Larkin and Hughes, pp. 167–71; Cockburn, *Assizes*, pp. 118–19; Derek Hirst, *The Representative of the People? Voters and Voting in England under the Early Stuarts* (Cambridge, 1975), p. 243, n. 29; PRO SP 14/59/44, cited in Campbell, *The English Yeoman*, p. 138; see also *CSPD*, 1637–8, p. 425; *Western Circuit Assize Orders*, pp. 283–4; Smith, pp. 75–7; Harrison, *Description of England*, p. 91; PRO SP 14/31/55; E 215/1133; KAO Sackville MS U269/M258; Babington, pp. 12–13; Russell, *Parliaments*, pp. 90–1; Samaha, *Law and Order*, pp. 50–1; Alan Hassell Smith, "The Elizabethan Gentry of Norfolk: Officeholding and Faction" (Ph.D. dissertation, University of London, 1959), p. 95; J. F. Pound, *Poverty and Vagrancy in Tudor England* (London, 1971), p. 66; Green, *Verdict*, p. 22.

experience of jurors from eastern Sussex. In contrast to the Assizes elsewhere on the Home Circuit or in the west and to the Quarter Sessions in counties such as Warwickshire and Lincolnshire, men summoned as potential jurors from eastern Sussex seem to have appeared regularly enough to eliminate any steady need to impanel individuals in the courtroom. In both courts in Sussex, the distribution of service was geographical. Each of the six rapes provided roster. Officials hoped to spread the burden of impanelment throughout the liberties of Buttinghill, Loxfield and Manwood each sent lists of eighteen persons. Juries at the Assizes routinely included men from different rosters; jurors at the eastern Quarter Sessions normally came entirely from one region. Officials hoped to spread the burden of impanelment throughout the division. Most juries had a life spanning two or three meetings of the court. Once the jurors handled any business, the court dissolved the panel and the cycle began again. Four of the six jurisdictions in eastern Sussex provided eighteen rosters each to the Quarter Sessions between 1594 and 1640. Each hundred within a rape or liberty normally contributed only one or two men to a petty jury, further emphasizing the ideal of shared service. Among the parishes in each hundred and among the villages in each parish enlistment also followed some semblance of rotation. Not surprisingly, men who lived near the venue of either the Assizes or the Quarter Sessions had more than their fair share of impanelments, but the imbalance was not as marked as in other shires. Forty-nine percent of the juries used in trials at the eastern Quarter Sessions came from outside of the rape of Lewes; the average rate of attendance among all petty jurors summoned in the division was 58 percent.[10]

Although no full rosters of potential jurors called to the Assizes in Sussex have survived, there too the problem of attendance seems to have been less serious than in other shires. The pattern of tenure among petty jurors at the Assizes in Sussex shows neither of the extremes evident elsewhere on the Home Circuit between 1559 and 1603; in three of the other four shires the Assizes relied more heavily than in Sussex on jurors used in just one court and

[10] On juries in Sussex: Herrup, diss., pp. 202–6, 466–78; ESRO Q/R/E 10/94v; KAO Sackville MS U269/M258;Cockburn, *Calendar, Sussex: Elizabeth I*, 1209. Information on eastern Sussex relies upon 108 panels prepared for the eastern Quarter Sessions in seven years for which complete annual records are available (1594, 1615, 1626, 1627, 1637–9). If the occasional use of men called for petty juries at the Quarter Sessions as *ad hoc* grand jurors is included in the geographical analysis, the proportion of panels sworn from outside of the rape of Lewes rises to 62 percent. On juries outside of Sussex: Cockburn, *Introduction*, pp. 79–80; *Quarter Sessions Indictment* (Warwick), p. xxiii; *Lincoln*, p. lxxiii; *Staffordshire Quarter Sessions Rolls*, vol. 54, pp. xxxii–xxxiii; *Worcester County Records*, 12, pp. xxiii–xxiv; Roberts, *Recovery and Restoration*, pp. 77–9; Morrill, *Grand Jury, passim*; Samaha, *Law and Order*, pp. 50–1; Beattie, *Crime and the Courts*, pp. 378–95. Cheshire, Staffordshire and Worcestershire like Sussex relied on geographical considerations as an important part of impaneling.

on jurors who served more than ten times. In fact, in 1623 the grand jury at the Assizes in Sussex complained that, since the under-sheriff failed in his summons to differentiate men to be sworn from the rest of those impaneled, too many men appeared in court, so that "the country is much wronged and abused, in that they come far off and are never called to appear or do any service."[11]

If the pattern of tenure in Sussex differed from the situation in other counties, part of the explanation lies in who was willing to serve as a petty juror for the shire. The concerns that determined the prosopography of grand jurymen in eastern Sussex (geography, hierarchy, friendship) influenced the staffing of petty juries as well. Petty juries were drawn from the bottom ranks of the parochial elite. Without precise definitions for terms of status such as substantial or modest, any attempt to measure jurymen against the charges of their detractors is somewhat artificial, but the men sworn as jurors in eastern Sussex seem to have been middling freeholders rather than men of meaner standing. The backgrounds of eighty-six men who were sessional jurors from the major parishes within the hundreds of Hawksborough, Buttinghill and Whalesbone show that while the jurors were not the substantial freeholders of governmental fantasy, neither were they marginal farmers nor quasi-professionals impaneled for need of money.[12]

Table 6.1 outlines what we know about these men; in almost every indicator available, sessional petty jurors rank lower than the hundredal constables who were sessional grand jurors (detailed in Table 5.1), but the discreteness, while clear, is hardly overwhelming. The same social divisions evident among grand jurors from different hundreds can be found among the petty jurors from different villages, but the similarities among the petty jurors are more striking than the differences. Tradesmen were more prominent among the petty jurors than among grand jurors (especially in Brighton), but at least 66 percent of the petty jurors whose status can be traced considered themselves yeomen. Fewer petty jurors than grand jurors have left their signatures but, among those for whom any evidence on literacy exists, 68 percent could sign their names. According to the assessments for the subsidies, petty jurors were less affluent than their neighbors who were hundredal constables and grand jurors but, since 35 percent were assessed

---

11 PRO ASSI 35/65/7/32; Cockburn, *Introduction*, pp. 57–63.
12 The biographical information below relies upon the sources listed in Chapter 5, nn. 12 and 22 above, pp. 99–100, 105, and ESRO PAR 372/1/1/1; *The Parish Registers of Cuckfield, Sussex 1598–1699*, ed. W. C. Renshaw, SRS 13 (Lewes, 1911); *The Parish Register of Brighton in thje County of Sussex, 1558–1701*, ed. Henry D. Roberts (Brighton, 1932); W. V. Cooper, *A History of the Parish of Cuckfield* (Hayward's heath, 1912); J. A. Erredge, *History of Brightelmston* (Brighton, 1862); for an earlier examination of the jurymen from Heathfield, see Herrup, diss., pp. 463–6; cf. Lawson, pp. 144, 161–3. See also Appendix 2 below.

Table 6.1. *Sessional petty jurymen*

	Heathfield (Hawksborough)	Cuckfield (Buttinghill)	Brighton (Whalesbone)
Number of trial jurors	9	62	15
% of those impaneled who were sworn	75	66	68
Social status	4 yeomen 5 unknown	1 gentleman 29 yeomen 1 yeoman/husbandman 1 yeoman/weaver 7 tradesmen 1 husbandman 22 unknown	2 yeomen 1 yeoman/fisherman 6 tradesmen 6 unknown
% serving more than once as a juror	11	14	0
% assessed above the minimal rate in subsidies	40 (of 5)	35 (of 29)	33 (of 6)
% able to sign their names	33 (of 3)	71 (of 14)	100 (of 2)
% resident locally less than 10 years in year of service	0 (of 1)	22 (of 9)	0 (of 2)
Range of ages at service	43–44	26–49	44–50
Most common other public offices	manorial juror churchwarden headboro petty juror/Assizes	manorial juror churchwarden petty juror/Assizes	manorial juror churchwarden petty juror/Assizes subsidy assessor

above the minimum rate at least once, the difference is of degree not kind. This distinction can be seen clearly in the records for the subsidy of 1626, the most extensive of the period. Heathfield, Cuckfield and Brighton note 136 assessments in this subsidy, half at the minimal assessment and half above that level. The names of fifty-seven grand or trial jurors in the sample appear on the list for the subsidy; among the grand jurors (36), 39 percent paid more than the minimum; among the trial jurors (21), 29 percent paid above the minimum. Almost half of the petty jurors left wills or inventories concerning their estates. Many of these include references to leases held and loans forgiven and to lands within several parishes. Bequests of cash commonly accompanied bequests of property and several jurors mentioned servants among their beneficiaries. Forty-eight percent of the petty jurors leaving wills set aside at least five shillings for the local poor.

Petty jurors in eastern Sussex differed from the sessional grand jurors in the experiences they brought to their obligations as well as in their social standing. Petty jurors seem to have been on average slightly younger than grand jurors. Slightly more than a third of the petty jurors from the Quarter Sessions seem to have done similar service at the Assizes, but almost half of the sessional grand jurors had done so. This distinction is one of the few clues available about the identity of jurymen at the Assizes in Sussex; it suggests that the discreteness of the groups who served as grand jurors in the two courts repeated itself among the men chosen as petty jurors. The hierarchical division appears in other offices as well; few petty jurors became hundredal constables and more petty jurors than grand jurors served as local headboros. Tellingly, tenure as a headboro normally preceded impanelment as a petty juror, while tenure as a constable normally followed that service. Very few petty jurors held positions with hundredal authority (such as assessor of the subsidies) but many came to the Sessions having served as local church-wardens or as manorial or leet jurors.[13] Moreover, the petty jurors were knowledgeable not only about their parishes but also about one another; their lives reveal the same sort of interconnections that marked the lives of the gentry. More than 40 percent of the petty jurors were bound to their colleagues by blood, marriage, or close friendship; 14 percent could boast of similar ties to sessional grand jurymen. And, among petty jurors as among grand jurors in eastern Sussex, scattered evidence suggests the prominence of the godly among those who took their legal obligations most seriously. The will of Thomas Brockett, a petty juror from Cuckfield, expressly mentions his election. His fellow juror, Robert Weekes, showed faith by baptizing his sons Increase and Restored. John Gower and Alexander Rodes, both petty jurors from Heathfield named their children, respectively, Rejoice and Fearnot. At the Assizes held in the summer of 1640, in a sermon preached to the court, the son of the late Bishop of Bangor attacked Sussex jurors for their opposition to tithes and their animosity towards the clergy.[14]

---

13 Half of the trial jurors from Heathfield and Brighton had been both leet jurors and church-wardens for their localities. Local service was less evident among the men from Cuckfield (in part because fewer records from the leets survive) but these two positions were the most common preparation for duty on a petty jury at the Quarter Sessions. At least 10 jurymen (2 from Brighton, 4 from Heathfield, 4 from Cuckfield) were headboros before they were jurors; 5 men (1 from Brighton, 4 from Cuckfield) followed service on a jury with a term as a hundredal constable. Sixteen jurors may have also been jurors for the Assizes (3 from Brighton, 4 from Heathfield, 9 from Cuckfield). Only 3 (all from Brighton) acted as assessors in any collection of the subsidy. Trial jurors were less prominent as victims of crime than were grand jurors; 10 men (2 from Heathfield, 8 from Cuckfield) prosecuted cases in the Assizes or the Quarter Sessions.

14 *CSPD* 1640, p. 520. Nine jurors named other jurymen as executors or overseers of their wills, 7 married or saw their daughters marry someone in the immediate family of another petty juror, 4 used other petty jurors as witnesses to their wills or to their marriages, 10 were mem-

The typical petty juror from eastern Sussex, then, was a minor yeoman or a tradesman. He was hardly unacquainted with the law nor was he necessarily cowed by the task before him. His standing, however much it dismayed the officials in Westminster, gave him an acute interest in local stability. The elaborate division of labor (both hierarchical and geographical) among the variety of juries sworn in eastern Sussex doomed to failure the hope that substantial yeomen would dominate most legal obligations, but it also seems to have freed impanelment of the taint of impressment. Despite the gradations of status, in eastern Sussex petty juries, like grand juries, were part of the agenda of obligation for middling landholders. As long as that was so, petty jurors would expect their position to be substantive, not ceremonial. Controlling the decisions of these men would be a complex and a piecemeal process.

Petty jurors judged defendants in an atmosphere at times both chaotic and intimidating. The early modern trial, like the early modern religious service, resembled a multi-ringed extravaganza more than a distinct, solemn ritual. The legal process was never segregated from the other businesses of life. While trials went on at the central Bar, spectators, legal officials, waiting defendants and potential jurors milled in and out of the courtroom, gossiping, commenting and conducting personal business. Since judges pronounced sentences only after all pending trials had been completed, any individual hearing might be interrupted by confessed or already convicted defendants who, standing to one side, sometimes chained together, might use the opportunity to plead for mercy from the judges. In front of the Bench, clerks scribbled frantically to keep pace with the stream of paperwork. To many spectators and most defendants, trial was but a part of the blur and bustle of activity in the courtroom. Until the reforms of the nineteenth century, most hearings proceeded at a pace so breathtaking that they might be likened to "a wild elephant [rushing] through a sugar plantation."[15]

Despite such conditions, and even though the defendant was allowed no counsel or sworn witnesses, every suspect had a chance to convince his audience of his sincerity. The crucial opportunity for the jurors to evaluate the accused came through what Sir Thomas Smith described as the "altercation" between a defendant and his accusers. The defendant had free rein to tell his

bers of the same families. Links with men who were only grand jurors rather than both grand and petty jurors were more tenuous: 2 petty jurors oversaw the estates of grand jurors and 2 more named grand jurymen to do the same task for them; 2 acted as witnesses for grand jurors and 2 called on grand jurors as witnesses; 2 petty jurors were related by marriage to grand jurors and 2 more were related by blood.

[15] Cited in Cockburn, *Assizes*, p. 122. The trial description below relies on Smith, pp. 91–2; T. W., *Clerk of the Assize*, pp. 13–17, 66–72; cf. Cockburn, *Introduction*, pp. 100–13; Beattie, *Crime and the Courts*, ch. 7.

story. He had the added freedom to interject comments during the testimony of victims or witnesses (although his accusers and his judges were equally free to intervene). The speed and style of the entire process encouraged jurors to rely on an impression of penitence or suspiciousness culled from the performance of a defendant. The sweeping nature of the charge to the jury, which focused on the general issue of guilt or innocence rather than on extenuating circumstances, reinforced the tendency towards personal evaluations. The personal interaction emphasized in the ritual of initiation for each juror was realized in the freewheeling Socratic exercise that was the process for trying criminals in Tudor–Stuart England.

The power of an individual petty juror to convert an impression into a verdict, of course, depended on the concurrence of the other jurymen, but the power of a jury as a whole to convert its impressions into punishments was also limited. The division of labor within the courtroom and the peculiarities of the statutes governing the uses of benefit of clergy worked to ensure shared responsibility between the different groups making decisions, in most trials. To understand what happened in an early modern courtroom one must understand the restrictions on petty juries as well as the scope of their power. Even then, it must be remembered that the idiosyncratic pressures of acquaintance and dependence, of prejudice and superstition, are largely unrecoverable.

A petty jury had the right to convict anyone whom it considered to be guilty and to acquit anyone whom it considered to be innocent, but on its own, a jury could guarantee neither the execution nor the immediate delivery of a defendant. A judge or a justice was free to sponsor any convict for a pardon; conversely, he could make the delivery of an acquitted party conditional on one of a variety of minor disciplinary actions. The decision of a jury similarly limited the actions of the Bench. If a jury returned an acquittal or a partial verdict, in theory the defendant could not be exposed to any formal punishment more serious than a whipping, a month in the local house of correction, or an escorted trip back home. And no judge or justice had the power simply to free a defendant if a jury convicted him. Judges and juries had various means to frustrate the desires of one another; ideally, defendants went to the gallows or returned to their normal lives only when both the Bench and the petty jury agreed on the proper resolution of a case. The way that responsibility in decision-making was dispersed within the courtroom worked to legitimate the choices made there as well as to guarantee outbursts of frustration from the professional caretakers of the legal process. Given a system that teamed men who prided themselves on legal expertise with men who were often skeptical of such subtleties, it is surprising how few decisions have left overt signs of tension.

The exact division of power between the petty jury and the Bench depended upon the crime being contested. As the categories of convicts excluded from pleading benefit of clergy grew throughout the sixteenth century, the situations in which a jury might chastise a defendant without condemning him grew fewer. By reducing a charge of homicide to one of manslaughter, a jury could convict someone of violence without marking him for execution, but in many types of major thefts, the statutes made such mercy difficult. Burglary, highway robbery and cutpursing were all crimes excluded from benefit of clergy; to convict a defendant of one of these and still hope to spare his life, a jury had to reduce the allegation to some form of larceny without violence. Since the amount of goods stolen was irrelevant to the definition of thefts without clergy, often a jury faced the choice of convicting a defendant for a capital offense or for a petty larceny. In the case of the theft of horses, even this option was unavailable; regardless of the value of the animal or the circumstances of the crime, an accusation of stealing a horse could produce only a capital conviction or an acquittal.

Most striking of all, until 1624, benefit of clergy was unavailable to women, so that defendants who were female had no hope of routine mitigation. Even after 1624, no woman accused of the theft of goods valued at more than ten shillings could ask benefit of clergy, so that for many alleged crimes, and particularly for allegations of violence, juries still had no easy way to punish a woman without placing her life at risk.[16] In analyzing the choices that juries made, it is important to recognize that each choice occurred within the specific options allowed by the formal legal structure. Juries, judges and justices could only decide the cases that grand jurors presented to them, and often the specific accusation presented restricted them. The adjustments that jurors made to compensate for these restrictions show how the law and the balance of responsibility within the courtroom acted as unstated boundaries within which jurors evaluated each alleged crime and each defendant.

To discover how jurors made their decisions about life, death and punishment, one must first acknowledge some modern boundaries. Jurors assessed not only fact but also character, yet the historian cannot see what they saw or hear what they heard. In the written record, the defendant is often mute; confessions offer the most direct link to the defendant's story but, in most instances, confessions precluded the need for trials. The lack of direct evi-

---

[16] Women received the right to plead benefit of clergy in small felonies by 21 James I, c. 6, because "many women do suffer death for small causes." Full rights to clerical privilege were denied to women until 3 William & Mary, c. 9 (1691). Benefit of belly was not the equivalent of benefit of clergy; it postponed rather than voided a sentence of death (although judges did not always enforce the sentence) and it involved a test more complex, more humiliating and probably less open to manipulation than the test administered for benefit of clergy; see above, pp. 48–50.

Table 6.2. *Verdicts in cases tried in the Assizes and the Quarter Sessions of eastern Sussex**

Category of crime	% of cases convicted among those tried	No. of cases tried
Murder	63	27
Infanticide	53	15
Felonious killing	61	18
Theft without clergy	63	166
Grand larceny	59	300
Petty larceny	66	105
Miscellaneous felony	26	23
Other†	24	45
Total	58	699

*The only major distinction between the rates of conviction in the two courts was in the treatment of grand larceny; at the Assizes, 66 percent of the cases tried ended in convictions; at the Quarter Sessions, only 43 percent of the cases ended in convictions.
†This includes 23 cases where the defendants were identified as only accomplices and 22 trials for disorderly offenses or offenses against the communal peace (traverses).
  Chi square = 0 in both courts, Cramer's V = .4559 for the Assizes, .3455 for the Quarter Sessions.

dence is complicated by problems in interpreting the indirect evidence: no sure method divides sincere verdicts from those that worked as mitigations, nor can one always distinguish collusion between a petty jury and the Bench on the proper moment for extending mercy from a disagreement between the deciding parties about the proper degree of punishment. Consequently, any assessment of decisions by petty juries is generally rather than specifically accurate. Groups of decisions suggest how jurors evaluated cases, but the decisions themselves are not predictable; the essence of a trial, however speedily conducted, was an unpredictable confrontation between hostile and often frightened individuals; any reconstruction artificially smooths out that volatility.

  Despite these limitations, some inferences about the decisions of petty juries in the early seventeenth century can be made. In general, verdicts reflect a mixture of prejudice, legal rules and common sense. The particular crime alleged, the quality of the evidence supporting the accusation and the behavior of the defendant were crucial components in decisions. The stated statuses of alleged victims and defendants influenced verdicts, but social status was not as important to the process as has at times been suspected. Jurors in eastern Sussex were unsympathetic to most defendants, but the fre-

Table 6.3. *Verdicts in the Assizes and the Quarter Sessions according to categories of stolen property**

Category of stolen property	% of cases convicted among those tried	No. of cases tried
Sheep, pigs	66	118
Food, poultry	53	78
Clothing, shoes	61	44
Household items	65	43
Cattle	68	38
Cloth	57	28
Money, jewels, plate	62	26
Iron	32	19
Wool, malt, wood, etc.	82	11
Total	61	405

*This table includes cases of clergyable theft only; it excludes items stolen in alleged cases of breaking, burglary, cutpursing, or the theft of horses.

quency with which juries convicted suspects varied depending upon the type of crime involved. Although among commonly tried accusations, the range of rates of conviction was fairly narrow, the alleged crime of a defendant had the most powerful effect upon a verdict. Jurors reacted to crimes as disturbances in the community, but their responses seem to have taken into account the likely punishment in each case as well. As Table 6.2 shows, they acted most readily not against the accusations of grand larceny, which comprised roughly half of the cases tried in the Assizes and the Quarter Sessions, nor against accusations of more heinous crimes such as homicides, but rather against charges of petty larceny. In these cases, a conviction ensured that a defendant would be punished and yet protected against execution. Jurors were generally more lenient in crimes carrying punishments over which they had less control, even if the threat to local peace was more severe.

This sensitivity to the law extended beyond general categories of crime into the way that jurors handled specific sorts of larceny. Rates of conviction increased slightly with the stated value of the contested property, but where a verdict would endanger the defendant's life, as in the theft of horses, the rate of conviction was relatively low. Defendants sold all sorts of items for profit and they could convert almost any item into cash that might be spent on food but, as Table 6.3 shows, a rough correspondence existed between rates of conviction and the likelihood of need. Goods most directly useful to the poor (food, iron tools) had much lower rates of conviction than did goods more easily turned into profit (cattle, sheep, household items). These priorities were constant throughout the period studied here; moreover, they were not unique to eastern Sussex.[17]

No decision, of course, was a response simply to the alleged crime; in all categories of accusation, at least one in every three cases ended with acquittal. Where testimony provided specific physical evidence, such as footprints, a jury usually agreed with the findings such information implied. Most accusations, however, relied on details needing interpretation. Defendants might offer explanations that were as plausible as those offered by their adversaries. Some of the ways that juries resolved such contradictions can be seen by comparing four separate charges of theft made over a period of six months against a single man, Francis Pankhurst of Heathfield. At the Quarter Sessions held in October, 1637, Pankhurst was accused by John Ellis for, first, the theft of several bushels of wheat and, secondly, the taking of a goose from Ellis' father, Thomas. Three months later Pankhurst was back at the Quarter Sessions, this time at the demand of Anne Williams, who claimed that he had stolen an iron pot and, on another occasion, feathers worth four shillings. A grand jury rejected the charge against Pankhurst for the larceny of the goose; the trial for the theft of the pot ended in an acquittal. The other two cases brought convictions; one was eased by the petty jurors who revalued the stolen property to ten pence instead of three shillings, and the other was softened by the justices of the peace who accepted Pankhurst's plea for benefit of clergy.

These diverse decisions reflect contemporary standards of condemnatory evidence. The most serious charge against Pankhurst, and the one for which he was most severely punished, was the theft of the feathers from widow Williams. Anne Williams told Justice Thomas Pelham that she had suspected Pankhurst as soon as she discovered the theft, but had taken no immediate action against him. When Pankhurst heard of her suspicions, he went to her house to deny them. According to Williams, however, he arrived with "the down of the feathers upon his head and about his clothes whereby she charged him the more." When he left, she followed him to the home of a local alehousekeeper where she found a sack, the feathers, and the mistress of the house who said she had bought the goods from Pankhurst. Although no confession by Pankhurst has survived, Williams contended that he did admit the

---

[17] Fifty-nine percent of the cases tried concerning the theft of horses (56) ended in convictions. The general rate of convictions for grand larcenies of goods valued under £5 was 59 percent; over £5 it rose to 61 percent. See also Samana, *Law and Order*, pp. 119–33; Sharpe, *Essex*, pp. 96, 98, 109, 134; Lawson, pp. 166–72; Beattie, *Crime and the Courts*, pp. 167–92, 199–236 for similar, but not identical, responses elsewhere. The relationship between both types of goods and verdict and cost of goods and verdict was statistically significant throughout most of the period under study.

sale. The jury convicted Pankhurst, and, without the intervention of the Bench, he would have been hanged.[18]

The evidence against Pankhurst in the other accusation accepted by the jury was less definitive, but still reasonably conclusive. John Ellis' suspicions were aroused when he discovered wheat at a local miller's that resembled his own. The miller told Ellis that the grain had been brought by Francis Pankhurst's daughter. Pankhurst, when confronted, denied any theft. He explained that the wheat looked familiar because it had been gathered from loose pieces found on the lands of Ellis and several other local farmers. The jury convicted Pankhurst, but cut the value of the wheat to one-third of the appraisal stated in the indictment; this reduced a felonious larceny to a petty larceny and the jurors were able to punish Pankhurst without condemning him.

The other two charges rested on even more circumstantial evidence. John Ellis discovered half a goose in Pankhurst's home during the search for his lost grain, and in a similar situation Anne Williams found the iron pot that she claimed as hers, saying it had been stolen three years earlier. In neither case was there written testimony beyond the word of the alleged victim that the discovered goods were the stolen properties, and in both cases Pankhurst denied the thefts. The relationship between the four verdicts and the evidence is obvious. Only if they were certain of the circumstances did jurors risk condemning a defendant to the gallows. On less conclusive evidence, they preferred to alter charges and to impose less than final punishments.[19]

Jurors seem to have responded to defenses with similar caution. In sixty-five cases of alleged theft heard by petty juries at the Quarter Sessions, evidence survives of the probable explanation given by the defendant. These depositions record explanations made outside of the courtroom, but since no transcripts of actual trials exist they are the only suggestion of arguments heard in court. The explanations offered fall generally into three groups: claims that the goods in question had been legitimately obtained, claims that the goods had been found and accepted as a windfall, and denials of any knowledge of the contested goods.

The first defense was the one most commonly offered; in thirty cases, defendants said that the contested goods had been bought or given to them. Jurors regularly accepted such explanations; they dismissed twenty-three of the thirty such cases (77 percent) and reduced the charges in three more to petty larceny. The distinction between the answers accepted and those rejected was fairly constant; all but one of the acquitted defendants could name the person from whom he claimed to have received the contested property. Of the seven convicted defendants, three said that their sources were strangers, three more named individuals also under indictment and one,

---

[18] ESRO Q/R/E 40/33, 64. [19] ESRO Q/R/E 39/49, 98; 39/8, 98; 40/32, 64.

who changed his story during interrogation, said that he bought his goods from his accuser. With the exception of the last case, the defense of having bought goods from an identifiable party held up equally well whether the defendant named the accuser or an unsuspected individual as the last custodian of the items. And, without corroborative testimony, juries were rarely sympathetic when employers accused former employees of pilfering.

Less common and less successful were suspects who claimed to have innocently found stolen property; jurors responded favorably in only five of the thirteen cases (39 percent) where suspects offered this defense, and in three of these instances the indifference of the victim undoubtedly helped the defendant's case. Jurors were even less tolerant of defendants who denied knowledge of the goods in question. Eight defendants claimed to know nothing of stolen property; the only two defendants jurors delivered in these circumstances were both men of standing in their villages. Four of the six convicted defendants may have undermined their own credibility by accusing their co-defendants while insisting upon their own innocence.

The handful of less regular explanations offered by defendants was equally unsuccessful. When Thomas Wiggins, a forgeman from Frant, said that he had owned for twenty years the tools challenged by William Fowle, a local esquire, the jury released him, but other defendants were not so lucky. For example, Mary Tuppin, a spinster from Lewes, said that she had mistakenly picked up some new cloth with her own goods when she visited the shop of Thomas Gun; she found herself convicted and whipped for petty theft. William Peckham, a millwright from West Hoathly, told how, after he had refused to watch over their goods, two soldiers had left some peas, a winnowing sheet and the remains of a sheep in a boarded-over hole near his house. Peckham, like Tuppin, was convicted of petty theft.[20]

An idea of reasonable proof clearly stood behind the decisions of petty juries, but no jury had to deliver a verdict strictly in accord with the evidence. James I's Proclamation for Jurors, issued in 1607, made clear their autonomy:

[to jurors] also the Law of this our Realm does ascribe such trust and confidence, as it does not so absolutely tie them to the evidences and proofs produced, but that it leaves both supply of testimony, and the discerning and credit of testimony to the juries consciences and understanding.[21]

In many cases all of the available evidence was circumstantial; the decision turned on the trustworthiness of the subject and the victim. Since grand juries weeded out accusations that rested merely on suspicion, what remained was often the word of one person against another. Consequently, the impression

[20]   ESRO Q/R/E 35/42, 93 (Wiggins); 16/18, 71 (Tuppin); 44/28–9, 59 (Peckham).
[21]   *Royal Proclamations*, ed. Larkin and Hughes, p. 168.

that the defendant made upon the jurymen was crucial. The evidence from eastern Sussex suggests that early modern jurors relied on judgments of character formed in the courtroom just as earlier petty jurors had relied on reputations built over a lifetime of observation. No jury, however, tried cases in a social vacuum; character was a composite of social position and demeanor. What a jury saw in the behavior of a defendant reflected its expectations of what was appropriate to a specific person. No system of courts occupied so heavily with thefts could avoid the logic of poorer people accused of stealing from richer people. The expense of prosecuting cases favored the better sort for the role of prosecuting victim as the power of social prejudice favored the meaner sort for the role of defendant. Even before a jury gathered, there was a sifting of cases based partially on status. Both individuals of exceptionally high statuses and individuals of exceptionally modest statuses were unlikely to trust their fates to petty juries. Cases in which the imbalance of power was exceptionally wide, regardless of who appeared as the victim and who as the defendant, were those most likely to be settled privately. The greater the social position of the alleged victim, the greater the likelihood that a defendant would surrender the right to trial by making a confession. This pattern may be a measure of fear, or of *noblesse oblige*, or simply of a practical calculation as to whose opinions would most likely count in the courtroom. Status always mattered, even if alone it determined little.[22]

Neither the gender nor the stated social position of a defendant or a victim had a statistically significant relationship to the behavior of petty juries, but petty jurors were hardly blind to status. Table 6.4 compares rates of conviction for defendants of different statuses. Excluding the tiny group of defendants listed as gentlemen, the rate of conviction for men corresponds with contemporary notions of respectability, while the rate of conviction for women was lower than that for most men. The special treatment accorded women as defendants reflects both the social and the legal worlds of which the petty jurors were a part. Jurors favored wives over widows and widows over spinsters. They returned convictions in 16 percent of cases in which defendants were identified as wives, in 40 percent of cases in which defendants were identified as widows and in 54 percent of cases in which

---

[22] Confessions can be matched with the stated statuses of victims in 53 cases; 66 percent of these (35) involved gentlemen or yeomen, 13 percent (7) involved husbandmen, 13 percent (7) involved non-agricultural workers and 4 percent (2) involved laborers. Only one defendant accused of a crime against a woman confessed in lieu of trial; one victim's status fell into the "other" category. According to the indictments, 38 of the cases with confessions were petty larcenies, 13 were grand larcenies, 1 was a burglary and 1 was a case of bigamy. This distribution suggests that willingness to confess often earned the suspect a judicious assessment of the stolen goods. For similar evidence elsewhere, see Lawson, pp. 133–4; Cockburn, *Introduction*, pp. 65–70.

Table 6.4.* *Convictions according to category of crime and defendant's stated status*

	Gentlemen	Yeomen	Husbandmen	Laborers	Non-agricultural	Women	Overall rate of conviction	No. of cases tried
Percentage of cases tried ending in convictions								
Murder	100	—	83	67	60	38	62	26
Infanticide	—	—	—	—	—	53	53	15
Felonious killing	—	67	—	86	75	—	61	18
Thefts without clergy	—	—	50	66	79	36	63	166
Grand larceny	100	—	60	67	54	40	59	298
Petty larceny	—	25	50	75	64	68	66	105
Overall rate of conviction	100	27	56	68	62	47	61	
No. of cases tried	2	11	88	315	117	95		628

*These figures differ slightly from those in Table 6.2 because of the exclusion of the "miscellaneous felony" and "other" categories and the exclusion of three defendants whose stated statuses fell into a miscellaneous category.

As noted above, p. 116, the sample here is very small and cross-tabulations of crime and stated status must be treated cautiously. For Table 6.4, following the order of the table, the number of cases tried is: gentlemen (1, 0, 0, 0, 1, 0); yeomen (0, 0, 3, 1, 3, 4); husbandmen (6, 0, 3, 18, 47, 14); laborers (6, 0, 7, 109, 153, 40); non-agricultural (5, 0, 4, 24, 59, 25); women (8, 15, 1, 14, 35, 22). See Appendix 2 below on these categories.

defendants were called spinsters.[23] But, beyond these preferences, the verdicts reflected the limited ways in which convicted women might escape execution and perhaps some sense that women involved in felonies were not entirely responsible for their actions. In allegations such as petty larceny, where gender did not define punishment, petty juries convicted men and women with about equal frequency; however, in felonies juries hesitated over convicting females more than over convicting males. They hesitated most regu-

---

[23] Women identified differently also favored different sorts of crimes, although in all three categories trials for grand larceny predominated. While women called spinsters appeared accused in every category of crime, wives appeared in any numbers only for grand larceny, petty larceny, burglary and murder. Widows appeared rarely except in cases of grand larceny; see Lawson, p. 168.

larly of all in accusations such as murder and burglary where deliberation rather than passion was considered crucial to a defendant's motivation.

Very few men identifying themselves as gentlemen or yeomen ever became defendants in the Assizes or the Quarter Sessions. The privileges of status were clearest in accusations of petty theft, where the rate of conviction was generally quite high; on occasion, juries acquitted yeomen despite behavior that would have doomed more modestly placed individuals. John Wicker, the yeoman from Worth whose servant suspected him of stealing sheep, was a case in point. The searchers found no identifiably stolen goods when they visited Wicker's house, but they discovered a slaughtering room in a small upper chamber. In an old covered well beside the house, they found numerous horns from sheep and old rotten sheepskins. "The well smelled so ill," the constable later testified, "that they were not able to endure it." Wicker's behavior was equally suspicious. He evaded the constable's questions and, once he realized that he might be arrested, he jumped on his father's horse and rode away. The trial had to be postponed for three months because of his escape. The case against Wicker was only circumstantial, but often juries equated disdain for the legal process with guilt. However, the petty jury acquitted yeoman Wicker.[24]

Jurors were less understanding when privileged men were accused of violence. Defendants styled gentlemen and yeomen made up a disproportionate number of the accusations and the convictions for murder and felonious killing in eastern Sussex; they accounted for 2 percent of all cases tried in eastern Sussex, but 9 percent of the cases tried for murder or felonious killing and 11 percent of the convictions in these two categories. While the sample is too small to be conclusive, the evidence suggests that petty jurors were willing to punish their social betters in such circumstances. Since gentlemen and yeomen convicted of felonious killing almost routinely received benefit of clergy, the willingness of jurors to convict suggests a desire to impose public humiliation upon important residents who had violated the local peace.[25]

When faced with defendants from outside of the agricultural community, petty juries reversed these priorities. The rate of conviction for men indicted as tradesmen, craftsmen, or industrial laborers was relatively low in homicides. No single non-agricultural occupational group accounted for as many trials of homicide as did laborers or husbandmen, so this leniency is not

---

[24] ESRO Q/R/E 35/31; 36/102–3; that same year Wicker was one of six persons charged with an assault and affray. All of the defendants confessed and were fined; PRO ASSI 35/79/2/43. For the treatment of others who behaved as Wicker did, see above, pp. 74, 128.

[25] Jurors convicted 3 of the 4 gentlemen or yeomen tried for murder or felonious killing; all of the convicted received benefit of clergy. Gentlemen or yeomen appeared as defendants in 21 percent of the indicted assaults. Branding in open court was distasteful enough to cause some gentlemen to seek pardons from it; see, for example, PRO C 66/2468.

surprising. In simple larcenies, juries were also relatively lenient, but men identified as being outside the agricultural community were quite likely to be convicted for any accusation of theft, even though such men did not account for a disproportionate number of these accusations.[26]

The reaction to defendants identified as being from outside of the agricultural community reflects the circumstances that brought such individuals to the courts. On the one hand, many accused tradesmen may have been receivers, not principals in thefts. The English law protected a receiver until the conviction of the principal; if the principal escaped trial, then the receiver was immune from prosecution. J. S. Cockburn has argued that many defendants indicted as principals actually were receivers whose manipulated indictments alone brought them before the law. Ninety-three percent of the defendants indicted as butchers and charged in thefts at the Elizabethan Assizes in Sussex, for example, were accused of stealing livestock and all of the curriers charged were accused of stealing hides. Since juries rarely demanded the full punishment of receivers, relatively low rates of conviction would have been natural for these defendants. By the 1590s in Sussex, the relationship that Cockburn suggests was less clear, but the correspondence between certain occupations and certain types of thefts was still too close to be accidental. Only 25 percent of the crimes allegedly committed by tradesmen, craftsmen, or industrial laborers seem tied to the needs of occupation, but among those identified as butchers, millers and others involved in provisioning, the percentage of suspicious accusations rises to 60 percent.[27]

On the other hand, petty juries rarely convicted any defendant of felony if he was accused simply of stealing food, and many ironworkers and defendants from the building trades were as likely to appear accused of stealing food as of stealing occupational materials. Twenty-four percent of the thefts and burglaries credited to tradesmen, craftsmen and industrial laborers concerned food (40 percent if one includes the theft of sheep, which when

[26] Men identified as working outside of the agricultural community accounted for 19 percent of the cases tried. They were most prominent in trials for petty larceny (24 percent of the cases) and they accounted for 22 percent of both the trials for unclergyable theft apart from burglary, and felonious killing, 20 percent of those for grand larceny, 19 percent of those for murder and 9 percent of those for burglary. Burglaries and grand larcenies attributed to men from outside of agriculture were blamed most frequently upon men identified with ironworking and petty larcenies were associated most often with men identified with one of the building trades. Other sorts of accusations fell relatively evenly upon men of various occupations; see Lawson, p. 169.

[27] Cockburn, "Trial by the Book," pp. 66–7. Over the entire period for both Assizes and Quarter Sessions, some link between occupation and items stolen can be made in 60 percent of the charges against men associated with food and drink (20 cases), but in only 33 percent of the cases against men associated with working in cloth (9 cases), 16 percent of the cases against men associated with ironworking (38 cases), and 13 percent each of the cases against men associated with either construction or retailing (24 and 15 cases respectively).

stolen alone were commonly slaughtered and eaten), and among men identified with working in construction the proportion was even higher (54 percent, 67 percent with edible animals). Some of these men were undoubtedly transients following seasonal movements of labor. As the rates of conviction for the more serious forms of theft suggest, however, sympathy had strict limits. In accusations of heinous crimes, a link between stolen property and a defendant's stated occupation worked against him rather than for him because the legal use of goods was less probable; a smith accused of stealing horses, for example, was more likely to be seen as a thief who called himself a smith than as an honest tradesman who had just been careless about his customers. The particular harshness of juries trying men from outside of the agricultural community for serious crimes may reflect the fear of migrants so common in early modern England, but it seems also to complement the division noted earlier between men primarily identified with agriculture and men with more varied loyalties.[28]

Table 6.5 compares rates of conviction for victims of differing status and reinforces the impression given by Table 6.4; status mattered, but other facts were equally important influences on verdicts. In cases of homicide, for example, juries reacted uniformly across lines of status; they reserved their tolerance for a handful of cases against women. In prosecutions for theft, husbandmen and males outside of the agricultural community were most effective at prosecuting cases. Despite their higher status, yeomen and gentlemen elicited less sympathy from petty juries. This was true even in accusations such as burglary and petty theft, where a high rate of conviction was normal and yeomen and gentlemen were prominent as victims. The pattern complements the high rate of indictment for yeomen and gentlemen. Crimes against men of substantial property violated social norms as well as the local peace, and grand jurors may have allowed a disproportionate number of loosely investigated cases with such victims to go to trial. Since substantial yeomen and petty gentlemen controlled most grand juries, self-interest encouraged a broad definition of reasonable suspicion in cases against men like themselves. The result was that petty juries, manned by men of more modest standing, were left to sift the weak accusations from the well-proven ones.

Although yeomen and gentlemen were prominent as victims in most seriously treated categories of crime, their ineffectiveness as prosecutors

---

[28] Men who were identified as other than farmers were particularly prominent in the theft of horses; they were the defendants in 23 percent of the tried cases. The harsh punishment accorded to such thieves by statute meant that jurors acquitted a relatively high proportion of the defendants, but 77 percent of the charges of stealing horses lodged against men outside of the agricultural community (10 of 13 cases but only 3 of 6 defendants) ended in convictions.

Table 6.5.* *Convictions according to category of crime and victim's stated status*

	Percentage of cases tried ending in convictions							
	Gentlemen	Yeomen	Husbandmen	Laborers	Non-agricultural	Women	Overall rate of conviction	No. of cases tried
Murder	—	—	—	100	100	60	80	10
Felonious killing	—	—	100	100	—	—	100	3
Theft without clergy	53	47	56	—	77	67	59	70
Grand larceny	48	33	88	100	59	44	55	113
Petty larceny	44	65	60	50	86	50	65	54
Overall rate of conviction	49	45	76	67	75	57	60	
No. of cases tried	51	65	45	9	52	28		250

*This table excludes infanticide because its victims had no status in the usual sense of the word. They did, of course have different genders. Among the 16 victims of infanticide (1 infanticide involved twin girls), 10 were female, 5 were male and the gender of one is unknown. Five of the 9 defendants accused of killing girls and 2 of the 5 defendants accused of killing boys were convicted.

See n. above, p. 116. For Table 6.5, following the order of the table, the number of cases tried is: gentlemen (0, 0, 15, 27, 9); yeomen (0, 0, 15, 33, 17); husbandmen (0, 2, 9, 24, 10); laborers (1, 1, 2, 3, 2); non-agricultural (4, 0, 17, 17, 14); women (5, 0, 12, 9, 2).

might arise less from their statuses than from their specific complaints, which were often those least likely to arouse sympathy among petty jurors. Sixty-eight percent of the alleged thefts in which gentlemen or yeomen appeared as victims involved food, iron, or small livestock.[29] Yeomen and gentlemen were more likely than others to complain of such thefts. Money, cattle and miscellaneous goods valuable for resale appeared in trials most often with victims identified as husbandmen, tradesmen, craftsmen, or industrial laborers; yeomen and gentlemen were the prosecuting victims in less than

[29] Among cases tried, yeomen and gentlemen accounted for the following percentage of the charges in the following sorts of larcenies: iron, 63 percent; food, 32 percent; sheep, 24 percent; cattle, 21 percent; horses, 20 percent; money, jewels, or plate, 10 percent; household items, 9 percent; cloth, 7 percent; clothing and miscellaneous, 5 percent.

20 percent of such trials. Since such thefts were always taken very seriously by petty juries, the most frequent prosecutors of such thefts would logically have the highest rates of conviction. However, neither the prominence of women as victims of serious types of thefts nor the tenuous economic position of the widows who made up the bulk of the female victims seems to have earned women much respect from petty juries. Women accounted for 11 percent of the victims studied here, but for higher proportions in most serious allegations of crime: 50 percent in murders (no widows), 17 percent in burglaries (all widows), and 14 percent in other nonclergyable thefts.[30] Their relative ineffectiveness as prosecutors might be, in part, a response to their relative success in gaining indictments. But women were essentially outside of the process of legal decision-making and thus particularly dependent upon public sympathy for help in avenging wrongs. Both the frequency with which widows appeared as victims and the relative good fortune of their alleged adversaries attest to the ambiguous position that single women held in early modern England.

Evidence, crime and status are the aspects of cases most amenable to historical analysis, but to a petty jury the attitude of defendants was equally important. Since no transcripts of trials in the Assizes or the Quarter Sessions exist, the impact of the accused's behavior can only be inferred, but the extant evidence implies that, at least in eastern Sussex, most juries waited to be shown a defendant's innocence. Although juries probably did not expect that all of the felons whom they convicted would be hanged, in most cases they did leave convicts vulnerable to execution. Juries responded to a wide range of specific extenuating circumstances, but they showed few signs of general sympathy. They convicted almost everyone whose behavior betrayed duplicity rather than submission or simple defiance. The case of Anne Brasier, the widow who tried unsuccessfully to hide her possession of missing mutton by throwing it out of the window of her bedroom has already been cited. Brasier's alibi, that she had found the stolen animal while she was nutting and had hidden it from the law in fear, was, in fact, quite reasonable, but her earlier actions made the story seem disingenuous. Brasier's fate was typical of such cases; she was convicted, but a judicious undervaluation of the lamb limited her penalty to a whipping.[31]

Submission to the law enhanced a defendant's credibility, but it did not earn a defendant the right to mercy. A confession made trial unnecessary, but where the confession seemed suspicious and the defendant trustworthy, judges or justices might allow a trial. In eastern Sussex, juries decided at least

---

[30] Twenty-one of the 28 female victims who have left information on their marital status were widows (75 percent).

[31] ESRO Q/R/E 36/50, 104–5.

forty-nine cases (21 in the Assizes, 28 in the Quarter Sessions) in spite of confessions. All of the defendants were alleged thieves, almost all were local residents and several had either offered to return stolen property or had made
dramatic pleas for mercy. That trials were possible despite confessions shows
how subjective considerations might offset more objective evidence, but the
fact that petty jurors returned convictions in 80 percent of these cases
suggests the difficulty of that task. If defendants confessed, juries often protected them from execution by reducing their culpability, but only rarely did
jurors accord such defendants the comfort of an acquittal.[32]

Two pieces of indirect evidence reinforce the impression that, when left to
their own devices, petty jurors were more skeptical than sympathetic about
the character of defendants. Juries normally listened to several cases before
returning any verdicts; only crimes of particular complexity were dealt with
seriatim. The sole written aid to memory was the indictment, and the more
cases that jurors heard in one sitting, the less able they were to recall individual defendants. Most panels at the Assizes handled the cases of at least six
suspects collectively; at the Quarter Sessions, with its smaller agendas, the
standard number of defendants dealt with jointly was still three or four. The
way that jurors responded to the problems of recollection is revealing; in both
courts, more business meant higher rates of convictions and lower rates of
partial verdicts and devaluations of goods. The shift is best seen in the willingness of juries to mitigate felonies. When they heard one to three cases
together, petty jurors altered more than one-third of their convictions in
felonies but, as the number of cases increased, the likelihood of such interventions declined. Juries with the longest agendas (eleven or more cases in a
sitting) softened their verdicts in less than one-tenth of the felonies brought
before them.

The files of the Quarter Sessions, which record the residences of jurors, provide further evidence of the same attitude. If larger agendas had bred severity
merely because experience jaded jurymen, then a similar harshness should be
clear among the juries that served the court most frequently. In fact, the
opposite is true. The rape of Lewes and the borough of Lewes together provided slightly more than half of the juries for the quarterly meetings studied
here; their residents served on juries more frequently than men from other
areas, and they returned slightly more than half of the verdicts recorded in the
extant records. Nevertheless, and despite the relatively high number of

---

[32] In charges of nonclergyable offenses (17 cases), juries returned acquittals in only 2
instances, but partial verdicts in 11 more. In more routine felonies (24), they acquitted in 6
cases and reduced verdicts in 9 more. In petty larcenies (8 cases), 2 cases ended in acquittals.
Six of the 13 defendants convicted of felonies seem to have been executed; 6 were granted
benefit of clergy and 1 was remanded to prison. See also the similar case cited in Hunt,
Puritan Moment, p. 308.

alleged crimes reported from Lewes and its environs, these jurors convicted substantially fewer defendants than did jurors from other sections of eastern Sussex. It was jurymen from the liberty of Loxfield, which produced far fewer panels, who returned convictions most regularly, almost twice as frequently as did men from Lewes. Experienced jurors were the ones most likely to recognize subtle differences between defendants. The fact that experienced jurors returned more acquittals rather than more convictions suggests that severity, not mercy, was the jurymen's first response.[33]

Whatever their suspicions of the men and women brought before them, petty jurors were not uniformly unforgiving. As well as delivering some defendants whose prior confessions suggested guilt, juries, by returning partial verdicts, mitigated the punishment of some defendants who pleaded innocent. In thirty-two cases of felony (6 percent of the felonies tried), juries rather than judges or justices determined a defendant's basic punishment. Judges and justices controlled the most popular means of mitigation (benefit of clergy), but petty juries, through their power to define guilt, could determine who was eligible for benefit of clergy. The granting of benefit of clergy by a judge or a justice in a further fourteen felonies depended upon a partial verdict returned earlier by a petty jury.[34] These figures, moreover, are minima; they include only cases tried as felonies and only cases where the action of the petty jury was recorded. The true scale of such changes can never be recovered.

The alterations that can be studied show the attention juries paid not only to crimes and statuses but also to the particulars of each defendant's situation. Since 38 percent (12 cases out of 32) of the felonious charges in which

[33] Juries from Lewes rape and Lewes borough tried 54 percent of the cases at the Quarter Sessions; the rate of conviction for the juries from the rape was 48 percent and for the juries from the borough 38 percent. In contrast, juries from the liberty of Loxfield heard 8 percent of the cases tried and had a rate of conviction of 92 percent. The distinction holds for individuals as well as at the aggregate level; Lewes borough, whose jurors produced the lowest rate of conviction, boasted the highest proportion of experienced jurors (57 percent). Experienced jurors were less common on panels from Lewes rape (12 percent), but rarest of all on juries from Loxfield (2 percent).

[34] These cases divide about evenly between the two types of courts, but those tried at the Assizes include 9 alleged cases of burglary and 1 alleged case of breaking, as well as the more common charges of grand larceny. Since the Assizes tried so many more felonies than did the Quarter Sessions, juries clearly played a less regular role in mitigation there, but all 14 of the cases combining partial verdicts and the granting of benefit of clergy occurred at the Assizes. In his new book, John Beattie points out that, assuming the availability of benefit of clergy, a conviction for petty larceny brought greater physical harm to a defendant than did a conviction for grand larceny. This is an important insight, but two further points deserve consideration. Unless benefit of clergy was granted automatically, and by right, conviction for clergyable larceny entailed psychological as well as physical discomfort. Second, whipping, while usually more severe than branding, was not necessarily so, and, more importantly, whipping left no disfigurement obvious to one's acquaintances. See Beattie, *Crime and the Courts*, pp. 419–30.

jurors returned partial verdicts were also cases in which defendants had provided confessions, the value of cooperation is obvious. But petty jurymen were also sympathetic to actions born of need or immaturity, and, somewhat surprisingly, to those inspired by the tensions of relationships between masters and their dependents. Despite the relatively small percentage of thefts of food among serious crimes, juries mitigated 31 percent of those tried as felonies. They acquitted Arthur Blaker, a sixteen-year-old who had confessed to having cut a local husbandman's purse and to having spent all of the contents. They were almost as kind to Robert Leigh when they reduced his indictment for breaking and grand larceny to a conviction for petty theft. The victim, who had hired Leigh as a temporary laborer, referred to him as "a boy." No defendant who confessed to cheating a master or employer was left to the mercy of judges or justices; juries acquitted only two of these suspects, but they protected four others from the risk of execution. The situations for which petty jurors had less tolerance are equally clear.[35] Neither the three men who confessed to stealing horses nor anyone else whose motive in theft seemed clearly to be profit earned mercy. The concern is obvious in the contrast between the way that petty juries treated defendants accused of larceny and those accused of burglary; in larcenies concerning food, juries monopolized mitigations, but in burglaries of food, half of the mitigations resulted only from the intervention of the Bench.

As a group, juries were unlikely to release suspects without some sense of extenuating circumstances and the most pertinent circumstances were those that reflected upon the defendant's motives and character. The crime alleged and the social position of the two contending parties influenced jurors, but the most critical evidence often came from the defendant. Juries united their medieval role as evaluators of character with the more modern task of evaluating presented evidence. The character of the defendant and the sincerity of his remorse, the harm an alleged crime caused locally and the finality of potential punishments all affected the decision. Many petty jurors had little empathy for those who came before them, but the opportunity that a defendant had to impress the jury offered at least some chance of a sympathetic hearing.

In the sixteenth and seventeenth centuries, as the independence of petty jurors came increasingly under siege, the balance of power in the courtroom shifted towards the judiciary. Thomas Green has demonstrated how the increased regulation of punishment in the sixteenth century undermined the position of the jury. John Langbein has contended that the end of the autonomy of the

---

[35] ESRO Q/R/E 18/34, 56–7, 62–3 (Blaker); 25/35, 67 (Leigh); 16/12, 65; 16/19, 70; 17/6, 8–9, 34–8; 21/56, 114; 48/27, 61–2, 90.

jury coincided with the rise of a judicial prosecutor who presented cases to uninformed jurors. J. S. Cockburn has shown that by the 1580s in the Assizes held nearest to London, the press of business encouraged judges to try to find ways of entirely bypassing juries. Juries existed to speak as men unschooled in the niceties of the law, but, increasingly, petty jurors found themselves pressed to echo the opinions of legal professionals. Intentionally or not, judges cut into the sacrosanct authority of amateurs in the legal process. Their actions were a pragmatic response to the shortage of jurors and perhaps an inevitable result of increased judicial access to investigative information, but, since it lessened the importance of petty juries, judicial behavior probably heightened rather than eased the problem of finding suitable jurors. Fine words about the importance of duty could not attract substantial yeomen to a position with little prestige and waning independence.[36]

But the attempt to control early modern juries was neither uniform nor uniformly successful. In many places, judges and magistrates had no interest in deciding cases themselves. Few of the cases tried in the Assizes or the Quarter Sessions had any legal importance and the jurors were far more likely than the judges to suffer if guilty parties went free. Green, moreover, has demonstrated elegantly the resilience of the idea of the authority of petty juries and the persistence of their claim to independence. He argues both that jurors were less autonomous than they believed themselves to be, and that the judiciary was less influential than it imagined. The evidence from eastern Sussex reinforces his view; in routine trials, no single source of authority dominated the processes of the courtroom.

Jurors at the Assizes in Sussex apparently avoided some of the pressures applied by judges elsewhere on the Home Circuit. By offering to trade confessions for mercy, and by increasing the business assigned to each panel, the Bench in these other shires encouraged defendants to avoid trials and encouraged petty jurors to rely upon judicial advice. In contrast to the situation in Essex, Kent, Surrey and Hertfordshire, the number of prisoners assigned to individual juries in Sussex declined in the early seventeenth century. And confessions at the Elizabethan or the Jacobean Assizes in Sussex never significantly undermined trials.[37] Tensions between the Bench and petty juries existed in Sussex as in other places; however, since the courts had dockets that were relatively brief and jurors who were relatively respectable, in Sussex conflicts were more likely to end in accommodations than in judicial victories.

The relative independence of petty jurors in eastern Sussex is clear in the

---

[36] Green, *Verdict*, especially ch. 4; Langbein, *Prosecuting Crime*, especially pp. 104–28; John H. Langbein, "The Criminal Trial Before the Lawyers," *University of Chicago Law Review* 45 (1978): 284–300; Cockburn, *Introduction*, chs. 6, 8 and conclusion.

[37] Cockburn, *Introduction*, pp. 63–70; see also Silcock, "Worcestershire," p. 193.

way that the jurors made decisions. If justices of the peace acted even informally as prosecutors, and if their influence was as overwhelming as claimed, verdicts should have varied according to the presence or absence of the prosecuting magistrate. In the serious cases tried at the Assizes, however, the presence of individual justices had no traceable impact on verdicts. At the Quarter Sessions, jurors were more likely to return convictions when interested justices were present, but the change from a rate of conviction of 43 percent to one of 49 percent was hardly overwhelming.[38] Since it is unreasonable to assume that magistrates were consistently ineffective as prosecutors, their negligible influence suggests that petty juries generally made their own decisions, regardless of the involvement of local justices.

Jurors were only slightly more dependent upon information provided by examinations or eyewitnesses than they were upon magisterial interventions. Examinations, except in extraordinary circumstances, were intended as guarantees of future personal testimony rather than as substitutes for appearances in court. While jurors were reluctant to allow executions without some evidence from third parties, they were unwilling for witnesses to be the determining balance in the basic matter of guilt or innocence. Recourse to local opinions was inevitable since individual jurors rarely had personal knowledge of defendants, but only slightly more than half of the trials in eastern Sussex involved active witnesses, and their effect was exactly opposite from what might have been expected. Juries reached a verdict of guilty in 65 percent of their decisions, but in issues where at least one witness (besides the victim) spoke, the rate of conviction dropped to 52 percent. The reasons for this pattern are unclear. The drop is reminiscent of the medieval suspicion against anyone without a clear self-interest who volunteered information but it may also suggest that local testimony often revealed malice rather than evidence as the basis of accusations. Neither justices nor witnesses altered the central responsibility of the chosen men of the neighborhood. The neighborhood had become the county and personal acquaintance between petty juror and defendant had become unusual, but the flow of legal process essentially remained the same. Although jurors no longer justified their power through the intimacy of provinciality, they had not surrendered their authority into the hands of more formal legal officials.

The exact influence of judges upon juries is difficult to determine. The most common judicial interventions were probably impromptu and unrecorded observations made during trials. Serious disagreements between juries and the Bench produced written evidence that suggests that while angry judges

[38]   At the Assizes, 65 percent of the cases tried with the committing magistrate present ended with convictions and 64 percent of the cases tried without the magistrate present ended the same way. The appropriate justices were absent from the proceedings in about 1 case in 5.

did not hesitate to deride petty jurors, intimidation was the exception and not the rule. Of the 178 petty juries known to have returned verdicts in the Elizabethan Assizes in Sussex, only five (3 percent) were ordered to explain those verdicts. Three of the five disagreements, moreover, originated at one meeting of the court (March 1568). Neither the records of later Assizes and Quarter Sessions nor the records of the Court of the Star Chamber, which had jurisdiction over such complaints, reveal additional disagreements. In fact, the records of the Jacobean Star Chamber include only twelve complaints against juries anywhere in the five counties of the Home Circuit. Most of these contended not that judges and jurors were at odds, but that verdicts had been returned against the evidence. In response to one such charge, the fore-man of a jury impaneled to try a dispute over land in western Sussex explained that he and his fellows had done their job as they understood it, to "well and carefully regard the evidence that was given then at the Bar on both sides according to his said oath taken in that behalf so near as his and their small skill could attain."[39]

As Cockburn suggests, the lack of evidence of contention between judges and petty jurors at the Assizes does not prove the latter's independence. Silence can illustrate successful domination as easily as it can the acceptance of shared power. But the passivity of petty jurors does not fit the evidence from eastern Sussex very easily. Several means other than direct intimidation would allow judges and justices to neutralize or to qualify verdicts with which they disagreed. Judicial recourse to such mechanisms confirms the continued discretionary powers of jurors, while also suggesting the limits of such powers. If petty jurors convicted someone of a felony that was not clergyable, the Bench could intervene on the felon's behalf for a pardon, or it could offer to exchange service in the military, galleys, or distant colonies for a reprieve from execution. If a jury transformed a nonclergyable offense into one that was eligible for clerical privilege, judges and justices could guide the decision as to what constituted literacy. Even when jurors eliminated the possibility of execution by acquitting a suspect or finding him guilty only of petty larceny, presiding officials could qualify delivery by insisting upon a bond for good behavior (which meant a second appearance in court and perhaps jail until the defendant produced acceptable sureties), by having the defendant escorted to his place of birth or last residence (called passporting), by apprenticing him to a local resident, or by sentencing him to a stay in the

---

[39] PRO STAC 8/105/07. No evidence has been found in the years studied here of juries bound over to explain verdicts returned in the Quarter Sessions in eastern Sussex or in crown pleas at the Assizes for the shire. A list of complaints from Sussex registered in the Star Chamber against verdicts of all sorts can be found in Herrup, diss., pp. 388–9, n. 73; for the rest of the Home Circuit, see *List and Index*, ed. Barnes; cf. Cockburn, *Introduction*, pp. 70–1; Lawson, pp. 191–2.

nearest House of Correction. Judges and justices in eastern Sussex made use of almost all of these alternatives at one time or another.[40]

About one third of the extant verdicts from eastern Sussex reflect the influence of both jurymen and judicial personnel; that percentage is large enough to confirm that juries were independent of the legal establishment, but it is small enough to suggest that the atmosphere of the courtroom was normally one of balance and negotiation, not oppression and compliance. No known case exists, for instance, in which a petty jury assured a defendant's eligibility for benefit of clergy, but the Bench denied the plea. Nor did the Bench usually allow convicts to be executed if grand juries had earlier reduced the charges. Even if the Bench intended to show dissatisfaction with every acquittal to which it added a disciplinary measure (an exaggeration to be sure), only about one in seven deliveries could be included in this category.

The pressures that worked to undermine the power of petty juries by the end of Elizabeth I's reign elsewhere seem to have less impact in Sussex, but the shire was hardly a rural Arcadia. Some differences consistently characterized the way that jurors and the Bench used their discretionary powers. The formal and informal sources of legal authority in the shire did not always value the same types of evidence or the same qualities of character in defendants. The distinctions highlight how judges, justices and juries protected the differing sources of their authority. The behavior of judges and justices shows their respect for the technicalities of the law. They added minor disciplines or bonds to keep the peace to the acquittals of defendants accused of felonies without clergy, statutory offenses, or disrespect towards legal officials. They were skeptical of anyone who had been accused by several witnesses or who had a history of misbehavior.[41]

If judges and justices showed greater concern than petty jurors for technically serious cases, jurors showed greater concern than judges and justices about defendants who might endanger the local peace. The Bench

---

[40] Judges and justices seem to have used more exotic measures sparingly, although since such additions were listed on gaol delivery calendars rather than on indictments the evidence is incomplete. Among the verdicts in eastern Sussex, 16 convictions ended with pardons or remands to wait for pardons and 3 ended with military service. Among the acquittals 19 cases were qualified by recognizances, 16 by stays in the House of Correction and 8 by passports out of the shire. An unspecified number of acquitted suspects were forced by the requirement that all fees must be paid before delivery to serve *de facto* sentences in jail. On the general uses of such penalties, see Bodleian Tanner MS 76/18/160; *CSPD* 1625–6, pp. 197, 299; 1635–6, pp. 143, 437; 1637–8, pp. 400–1; Cockburn, *Introduction*, pp. 115, 126–9.

[41] Judges qualified verdicts in at least 14 percent of the acquittals in cases where the alleged crime would have been unclergyable (11 of 78), 19 percent of cases where the offense was statutory (3 of 16), and 38 percent of the cases with legal officers as victims (3 of 8). They qualified acquittals in 23 percent of the cases in which there had been 3 or more witnesses (8 of 35) and in 22 percent of the cases in which suspects had a traceable previous appearance before a court (30 of 137).

handled almost all of the mitigations provided to defendants from outside of eastern Sussex, and almost all of those offered to defendants convicted of committing several crimes in a single day. It was also the source of much of the mercy accorded to defendants of particularly high social status or to those from outside of the agricultural population.[42] These differences outline an interaction between juries and the Bench that was neither predominantly consensual nor conflictual; the Bench stiffened verdicts in some cases and eased them in others. The fact that so many cases ended with resolutions reached partly by jurors and partly by judges or justices testifies to the basically collaborative nature of the legal process.

However, the situation in eastern Sussex was not inviolable. Several changes in the 1630s suggest a new vulnerability for petty juries in the shire and a new willingness among judicial personnel to sidestep such juries. The same number of juries that tried 115 prisoners at the Assizes between 1613 and 1618 handled 174 defendants between 1634 and 1640. In these seven years, four of the six Assizes between 1592 and 1640 that were staffed by a single jury met; only one session of the court swore enough men for more than two panels of jurors. In Sussex, the courts of the 1620s and the 1630s, not those earlier, made the most extensive use of confessions and plea bargaining.[43] These meetings of the Assizes had the highest number of qualified acquittals as well as the highest number of partial verdicts. The pattern discerned by Cockburn for the Home Circuit as a whole may simply have surfaced more slowly in Sussex than elsewhere, but the spectacular rise in business that inspired the changes of the late sixteenth century had no local parallel in the 1630s. On average, the Assizes handled fewer triable cases than in earlier decades and in both courts among the cases tried juries returned more acquittals.[44] The apparent peculiarity of Sussex is puzzling but, perhaps

[42] The Bench was responsible for all of the mitigations offered to defendants from western Sussex (17 cases) and for 87 percent of those offered to defendants whose recognizances suggest a home outside of Sussex (13 of 15). It handled 95 percent of the mitigations for defendants accused of committing several crimes in one day (20 of 21), all of the mitigations offered to yeomen or gentlemen (4) and 94 percent of those offered to men identified as from outside of the agricultural community (15 of 16).

[43] The percentage of cases dealt with through confession as a percentage of all cases tried or confessed in eastern Sussex was: 6 percent in the sample of Elizabethan courts; 7 percent in the sample of Jacobean courts; 23 percent in the sample of transitional courts; and 20 percent in the sample of Caroline courts. In the Assizes, the decade of highest confessions was the 1630s, when 15 percent of the cases bypassed trial; see Cockburn, *Introduction*, pp. 65–70 and conclusion, *passim*.

[44] The average number of cases concerning eastern Sussex tried or confessed before the Assizes dropped steadily throughout the period from an average of 20 cases per court in the 1590s to 9 cases per court in the late 1630s. In the sample of Elizabethan courts and of transitional courts, juries at the Assizes acquitted 33 percent of the cases brought before them; in the sample of Jacobean courts, that percentage rose to 49 percent; and in the sample of Caroline courts, it was 47 percent. See above, Chapter 3, pp. 62–6.

in the 1630s, "Thorough" inspired a judicial activism reminiscent of the 1580s and 1590s. The symbiotic relationship between juries and judicial personnel was never smooth, but neither party could permanently undermine its partner. Their interdependence was part of the legitimacy of the legal structure, a given of the authority for its operation. In shires such as Sussex, where jurors had maintained at least some of their autonomy, the judiciary met jurors who had their own notions of proper governance.

Verdicts in eastern Sussex were not the product of clear standards of evidence such as applied in decisions by grand juries. Grand jurors heard only the complaints of prosecuting parties and indictments reflected the grand jurors' opinions of the coherence of the accusations more than of the character of the suspect. Petty juries, whose decisions were final rather than preliminary, reversed these priorities; they used their impressions of the defendant as a guide through the normally conflicting evidence offered by accuser and accused. To them, a defendant's attitude often revealed culpability and character was crucial evidence of the potential for repentance.

In every session of a court, the property holders of the shire, by direct participation and through the legal establishment, reaffirmed their idea of criminality. The most severely judged defendants were executed, but guilt alone did not bring execution. Dangerous convicts were purged from the community, but the less bothersome were allowed to return home. Through their verdicts, jurors identified the men and women that they were willing to allow to die; through their sentences, judges and justices chose the criminals from among the convicts. Two extremes, executed felons and repeatedly convicted defendants, reveal most clearly the way that villagers and the judiciary in early modern England defined crime, accepted it as a part of daily life, and set limits beyond which integration was not feasible.

7

Becoming a criminal

Most convictions in eastern Sussex were for felonies and all common law felonies shared the single punishment of execution.[1] The central paradox of the early modern English penal system was that, while allegedly only hanging avenged crime and instructed people about the dangers in a sinful life, routine recourse to executions seemed to do little to educate anyone about either royal justice or royal mercy. Life was too complex and humanity too imperfect to conform easily to a legal structure that defined almost every crime as a felony and penalized all felonies with death.[2] The law relied too heavily upon communal participation to function except where the penal structure could express both modulated degrees of popular outrage and the finality of official power. The administrators of the criminal law in early modern England maintained their legitimacy by enforcing the law as a blend of technical rigidity and practical flexibility. Eighty percent of the persons found guilty in eastern Sussex could have been hanged for their crimes, but at least two-thirds were saved from the gallows through grants of benefit of clergy, remands, pardons, or more exotic disciplinary alternatives such as impressment into military service or transportation overseas.[3] Most convicted or confessed felons proceeded with their lives and never reappear in the surviving records.

---

[1] Of the 405 known convictions 330 (82 percent) were for felonies (including accessory to felony). Across the Home Circuit between 1559 and 1624, between 37 and 45 percent of the convicted or confessed felons at the Assizes were ordered executed; Cockburn, *Introduction*, p. 125; in Essex between 1620 and 1640, rates of execution seem to have been slightly, but not significantly, lower: Sharpe, *Essex*, pp. 96, 109, 134, 136; cf. Lawson, p. 197; Sharpe, *Crime in Early Modern England*, pp. 64–5; Philip Jenkins, "From Gallows to Prison? The Execution Rate in Early Modern England," unpubl. paper, 1985, pp. 5, 12–15.

[2] There was disagreement, moreover, on the effectiveness of execution as a deterrent; see Coke, *Third Part of the Institutes*, p. 244; Babington, p. 53; *England as Seen by Foreigners*, p. 269, n. 108; Radzinowicz, *History of English Criminal Law*, 1, pp. 259–61; cf. Pieter Spierenburg, *The Spectacle of Suffering: Executions and the Evolution of Repression: From a Preindustrial Metropolis to the European Experience* (Cambridge, 1984), chs. 3–4.

[3] In eastern Sussex, 118 of the 363 felonies for which there was either a confession or a conviction seem to have ended on the gallows (33 percent). Estimates of execution must be inferential since no positive proof exists that such sentences were carried out. Felons are

The high rate of reduced punishments shows that people used the law to differentiate two different sorts of convicts: those who were too dangerous to remain in the community, and those who dispite misbehavior still deserved some sympathy. Even among persons who committed nonclergyable offenses, more convicts than not escaped the gallows. Comparing the cases of felons who were sentenced to death with those of felons spared through mitigation illustrates the difference between tolerable and intolerable criminality. Contrasting the allegedly executed felons with a small group of identifiably chronic miscreants (recidivists) brings these distinctions into high relief.

Despite the importance of sentencing for law enforcement, surprisingly little is known about it. Sentencing was the stage of legal process dominated most completely by the Bench; through their control of benefit of clergy and various sorts of reprieves, judges and magistrates could mitigate penalties against the desires of any jury. However, the way that members of the judiciary decided who among the convicts were proper recipients of mercy and who were not often remains unclear. The pattern of judicial interventions is recoverable, but the pressures such decisions reflect are not. The patterns of sentencing at the Assizes were similar, but not identical through the entire Home Circuit. Judges and magistrates had definite ideas about proper punishment, but, at least on occasion, they seem to have listened to advice offered by jurors or other local residents about the best resolution of a case.[4]

In examining cases that Bench and jury dealt with differently, some sense of judicial priorities emerges. Little can be inferred from the routine use of benefit of clergy, but exceptional cases are more revealing. They confirm the picture sketched earlier; judges, magistrates and petty jurors had generally complementary, but not identical, ideas about justice. Judges, justices and juries seem to have agreed as to the proper sentence in the vast majority of cases convicted in the Assizes or the Quarter Sessions. Each group was willing to intervene when necessary and the Bench, not the jurors, seems to have had the greatest reservoir of patience.

The Bench controlled the granting of benefit of clergy, but, by convicting a defendant of a felony without clergy, juries could prevent the use of the miti-

---

categorized here as executed if a sentence of death was noted on their indictment and no sign of mitigation could be found in the gaol delivery calendars, the crown docket books, or the patent rolls: PRO ASSI 35/34–82; C 66; C231/1–5; ESRO Q/R/E 1–50; WSRO Q/R/WE 16, 31.

[4]   The most extensive discussions of sentencing have focused on its social purpose and particularly on the uses of discretion in the eighteenth century; Hay, "Property, Authority and the Criminal Law"; John H. Langbein, "*Albion*'s Fatal Flaws," *P & P* 98 (February, 1983): 96–120; P. J. R. King, "Decision Makers and Decision Making in the English Criminal Law, 1750–1800," *HJ* 27 (1984): 25–58; Beattie, *Crime and the Courts*, chs. 8–10; Jenkins, "From Gallows to Prison," *passim*; and, for the seventeenth century, Herrup, "Law and Morality," pp. 102–23.

gation. In the late sixteenth century, judges at the Assizes occasionally ignored the restrictions on benefit of clergy and spared defendants anyway but, by the early seventeenth century, such flexibility was rare.[5] In most cases of nonclergyable felony in eastern Sussex (106 of 129 convicted), by not intervening, juries left the defendant to the gallows. And in 80 percent of the cases in which jurors expressed no preference for mercy (85 out of 106), the Bench concurred. The Bench could save a defendant convicted of a felony without clergy by returning the convict to custody to await some sort of reprieve. Evidence of such intervention survives in only twenty-one cases of nonclergyable felony in eastern Sussex. A similar judicial deference is clear in the response of the Bench to the interventions of juries in clergyable felonies. Judges or justices granted benefit of clergy to all eleven of the defendants whose charges juries reduced for that purpose. The Bench was the routine source of mitigation only in cases of grand larceny; grants of benefit of clergy were so common here that jurors probably considered mitigation rather than execution to be the normal sentence. In most cases, ordinary thieves did not need protection from the gallows.

The cases that prompted judicial intervention were not those for which jurymen had no middle ground between conviction for felony and acquittal. Fifteen of the twenty-one judicial mitigations concerned cutpursing, burglary, highway robbery or murder, all accusations that jurors could have reduced to clergyable offenses. Nothing clearly characterizes the cases in which the Bench intervened, but many of the remanded convicts had some quality that jurors in other cases had responded to sympathetically. For example, jurors often reduced the culpability of defendants who confessed but, despite their apparent confessions, Henry Gibbs and Anthony Wells each found themselves convicted of nonclergyable thefts. Jurors were usually lenient towards defendants who were receivers of stolen goods but, although Richard Martin was a receiver, he was convicted without mercy. Without the judge's intervention, these three men would have hanged. Judges and justices used their powers not to counteract the rigidities of the law, but rather to offset specific opinions of juries.[6] In these cases and others, the Bench and the jurors seem to have sensed different degrees of danger in the conflicts; the judiciary responded to defendants who left the jurymen unmoved. On occasion, the passivity of the jurors may have been simply a special case of the maxim that familiarity breeds contempt; at least four times, judges spared

---

[5] Cockburn, *Introduction*, pp. 119–21, but cf. Lawson, pp. 197–226.
[6] PRO ASSI 35/38/8/26, 27, 123, 140v (Gibbs); 35/38/8/22, 23, 58, 101–2 (Wells); 35/76/9/29, 77 (Martin); see also Lawson, pp. 204–6; Sharpe, *Essex*, pp. 147–8.

defendants who had been convicted of similar crimes in previous sessions of the court.[7]

Not surprisingly, the distribution of mercy reveals generally similar priorities to those suggested earlier. Punishment reflected popular perceptions both of particular crimes and of the nature of criminality. Both the specific felony and the demeanor of the convicted individual influenced the court. The inherent harmfulness, not the prevalence of a crime, determined its heinousness, and in certain circumstances heinousness could be offset by the defendant's behavior. The perceived remorsefulness, not the history, of a convict determined his criminality.

Tables 7.1 and 7.2 illustrate which accusations ended most regularly in orders for execution. Table 7.1 shows the distribution of sentences of death according to cases convicted or confessed in specific categories of crime. Table 7.2 lists the number of felons who were ordered executed. Sentences of hanging rarely touched people charged with simple theft; execution was generally reserved for convicts whose misbehavior violated the sanctity of home, person, or status. Even these crimes generally brought execution only if they were combined with a particular style of behavior. Decision-makers recognized dangerous criminals by their fondness for profit, their calculated approach to illegal activity and their lack of contrition.

The theft of horses was the epitome of a crime founded in avarice and calculation. Since jurors had no way to reduce the penalty for someone guilty of stealing horses, petty juries were relatively cautious about returning convictions for this crime, but almost everyone who was convicted was sentenced to the gallows. Defendants could rarely claim that they had stolen horses directly out of need. Unlike sheep or cattle, horses had no easy value as food nor, in Sussex, were they favored as good farm animals. The theft of horses was inextricably linked to resale for profit and, moreover, to resale through a network of professional criminals. John Brasier was typical of the men convicted in eastern Sussex for stealing horses. Brasier confessed that he had taken five horses from victims in three different parishes in the six months before he was arrested. He had passed each animal to a middleman who in turn carried it away from the immediate vicinity to be sold. Two of the animals stayed in Sussex, one went to a butcher in London and two were sold

---

[7]   Three of the repeating defendants (Elizabeth Jove, Thomas Tisdale and Robert Leigh) are discussed below as recidivists; see pp. 182–92. The fourth repeater, William Madgewick, was acquitted of theft at the Assizes in July, 1628, but the gaol delivery calendar for that court reads, "[Madgewick] is set at work in the house of correction until the next Assize because [we] hold him a common thief." At that next meeting, Madgewick was convicted of another theft and reprieved. He was still in jail in July, 1629, but had disappeared from the records by the next extant court in July, 1630; PRO ASSI 35/70/8/21, 59v; 35/71/9/35; 35/71/10/73.

Table 7.1. *Executions ordered according to category of felony*

Category of crime	% of convictions and confessions ordered executed	No. of cases convicted or confessed
Murder	65	17
Infanticide	88	8
Felonious killing	36	11
Theft without clergy	76	51
Highway robbery	43	7
Breaking/entering	50	8
Horse theft	94	32
Cutpursing	50	4
Burglary	56	54
Food, poultry	31	16
Household goods	62	13
Money, jewels, plate	58	12
Cloth	80	5
Clothing, shoes	67	6
Miscellaneous	100	2
Grand larceny	11	210
Food, poultry	15	20
Household items	28	18
Money, jewels, plate	25	16
Iron goods	14	7
Cloth	6	16
Sheep, pigs	5	65
Cattle	17	30
Clothing, shoes	6	31
Miscellaneous	—	7
Other felonies	43	7
Accessory to felony	—	5
Totals	33	363

in Essex. Although Brasier claimed that he slept in barns and stole small animals for food, his stealing of horses was, in effect, a business.[8]

Alone among serious crimes, the theft of horses was denounced not simply for the fear intrinsic in the crime, but also for its profitability. Brasier notwithstanding, the reputation of horse thieves was that they were notoriously

---

[8]   ESRO Q/R/E 12/30–30v, 49. Seven of the twenty convicted horse thieves in eastern Sussex had at least two victims each.

successful at selling their booty quickly and well. The Elizabethan statute against the theft of horses acknowledged this ability by complaining that stolen animals changed hands so very quickly that "the owner cannot by pursuit possibly help" – that is, he could not stop the sale of his stolen property. Such impotence must have been particularly frustrating in regions such as eastern Sussex, where the prosecutors of horse thieves were not primarily gentlemen or yeomen. The avarice perceived in such thefts and the quality of luxury about the stolen property made horse thieves the least likely of all criminals to elicit sympathy from either juries or the Bench. Such convicts seemed the most likely of all offenders to steal again, and the least likely of all offenders to be dissuaded by a change of environment or circumstances. The professional aura surrounding the theft of horses made it the single most severely punished crime in eastern Sussex.[9]

In other crimes, the priorities suggested by sentences generally paralleled those suggested by verdicts; burglars and killers ended their lives on the gallows far more often than did thieves. Burglary in the early seventeenth century differed technically from grand larceny in two important ways: burglars broke into a residence, and they struck at night. These two components, violation and darkness, justified the legislation denying burglars benefit of clergy. The concurrence of local jurors in this view of the seriousness of burglary can be seen in their willingness to follow the statutory guideline rather than to sidestep it by reducing charges of burglary to clergyable thefts or petty larceny. The peculiar nature of burglary resulted from both pragmatic and psychological considerations. Someone who broke into a home was clearly involved in intentional, not simply opportunistic, behavior. Deliberate criminal purpose, aided by darkness, almost always gave the burglar an advantage of surprise over his victim. On the most basic level, burglary violated physical security. A person victimized outside his home or one whose doors, windows or lands were open to intruders might accept some blame for his misfortune; he had tempted the individual of weak character with an easy opportunity. An individual whose closed residence was violated at a time when most persons would be sleeping was blameless. Burglary, then, struck at both private property and personal vulnerability. This combination may explain why burglars were more likely to be hanged than people convicted of most other types of theft without clergy. Highway

---

[9] 31 Elizabeth I, c. 12. Ten of the 25 known victims in horse thefts have left recognizances stating their social statuses: 1 was listed as a widow, 3 as husbandmen, 3 as local retailers, 2 as yeomen and 1 as a gentleman. The distaste for horse thieves was not peculiar to eastern Sussex; see Sharpe, *Essex*, pp. 97–8; J. S. Morrill, "The Army Revolt in 1647," in A. C. Duke and C. A. Tamse (eds.), *War and Society: Papers Delivered to the 6th Anglo-Dutch Historical Conference* (Britain and the Netherlands, 6, The Hague, 1977), pp. 62–3; Eyre, "Diurnall," pp. 16, 76; Sharpe, *Crime in Early Modern England*, pp. 106–7.

Table 7.2. *Felons ordered executed according to category of felony*

Crime	No. of felons ordered hanged
Horse theft	18
Murder	11
Burglary – household items	7
Infanticide	7
Burglary – money, jewels, plate	6
Felonious killing	4
Breaking and entering	4
Burglary – food, poultry	4
Burglary – mix of goods	4
Mix of crimes*	4
Burglary – miscellaneous goods	3
Grand larceny – household goods	3
Grand larceny – mixed goods	3
Cutpursing	2
Grand larceny – money, jewels, plate	2
Grand larceny – cattle	2
Bigamy	2
Highway robbery	1
Burglary – cloth	1
Grand larceny – food, poultry	1
Coining	1
Total	90

*This includes men ordered executed after convictions for burglary and grand larceny (1), grand larceny and horse theft (1) and grand larceny and highway robbery (2).

robbery, breaking and cutpursing were all crimes of violation but, as they lacked the added element of vulnerability associated with the night, their practitioners earned more leniency (see Tables 7.1 and 7.2).[10]

Even the sentences ordered for larcenists and burglars who took similar sorts of property were very different. Most thieves who stole from houses received lessened punishments but, despite the fact that their ill-gotten gains had no higher commercial value, most burglars who favored household items were sentenced to hang. A similar pattern can be traced for felons who fancied money, plate or jewels; three times as many burglars as larcenists apparently died for such covetousness. Moreover, while thefts of food rarely brought sentences of death, a burglar who took food might well be ordered hanged. Burglars of food were treated more leniently than other burglars, but no type of burglary routinely earned mitigated punishments. The heinousness

[10]   23 Henry VIII, c. 1; 1 Edward VI, c. 12, s. 9; 18 Elizabeth I, c. 7; 39 Elizabeth I, c. 15.

of the burglary clearly did not lie in the value of the appropriated property; part of the threat was the act of burglary itself.

However, not all burglars were sent to the gallows and seven of the fifteen known recidivists in eastern Sussex committed burglaries. Even within crimes such as burglary, a line existed between the forgivable and the unforgivable. For burglary that line seems to have divided burglars who stole different types of goods for different destinations; burglary for need was more forgivable than burglary for profit. Recidivists favored food or small household items in their burglaries; felons who were ordered hanged had concentrated on goods that were more profitable. Six of the eight burglaries involving items estimated at a value greater than £5 were answered with condemnations. Two-thirds of the convictions for burglaries of food ended with mitigations, while approximately two-thirds of the convictions for burglaries of items probably intended for resale ended with sentences of death. Even in a category such as household goods, criminals often were distinguished from forgivable offenders by the quantity and value of the goods they stole. Henry Briggs, who was convicted in 1596 for taking twenty-five yards of woollen cloth (valued at twenty shillings) from the house of a fuller, worked on a different scale and probably to a different purpose from Thomas Tisdale, who was convicted earlier that year for taking a dozen table napkins (valued at five shillings) from the home of a local magistrate. Both juries were willing to see the convicts hanged, but the court remanded Tisdale's sentence despite his three previous criminal accusations. The desires of Tisdale's victim, Edward Culpepper, probably influenced this decision, but Culpepper's opinion undoubtedly reflected his knowledge both of Tisdale and of the most likely motive for such crimes.[11]

The differences between persons executed for homicides, and those found guilty and yet saved from death reinforce this interpretation of the priorities suggested in the punishment of burglars. The court was particularly unsympathetic to killers who took advantage of a victim's trust or defenselessness. Malice and deliberateness on the part of the defendant distinguished the nonclergyable crime of murder from the clergyable crime of felonious killing or manslaughter, but not all murderers were ordered hanged and not all other killers were spared the gallows. The ancient notion that the most heinous slayings were not only malicious but also unexpected still had resonance; even in homicide, it seems, there was to be a modicum of fair play.

Fifteen people in eastern Sussex, eleven who had been convicted of murder

---

[11] The 6 condemnations involving items valued at £5 or more included 3 burglaries of money or plate, 1 of cloth, 1 of clothing and 1 of miscellaneous household goods. Both of the dearly valued burglaries that were mitigated concerned clothing. For Briggs and Tisdale, PRO ASSI 35/38/9/28, 51 (Briggs); 35/38/8/81; 35/37/9/59; 35/37/9/60; ESRO Q/R/E 1/27 (Tisdale). On recidivists, see below, pp. 182–92.

and four who had been convicted of felonious killing, were ordered hanged for killing other adults. At least six of these homicides (all murders) were brutal surprises for their victims: a death by poisoning, an assault at night, an attack on a woman inside her home, a strangulation in a wood and two cases where the defendants attacked members of their own households. In contrast, none of the ten individuals spared from execution (three after convictions for murder, seven after convictions for felonious killing) seems to have killed in a situation of unquestioned advantage. No evidence exists of prior intimacy or unfair advantage between the defendants and those killed. In at least two cases, the coroner's inquisitions explicitly detailed sudden and unexpected quarrels. The situations in most of the cases seem to have been ones of immediacy and anger.[12]

This concern for the defenselessness of victims may also explain the harshness with which the court treated women convicted of infanticide. Like horse theft, infanticide was a crime in which petty juries had little control over punishments and, like horse theft, it was a crime with a relatively high rate of acquittal. Among the convicted, however, almost no one escaped the death penalty; seven of the eight women found guilty of the crime in eastern Sussex were ordered hanged. The one woman who was spared, moreover, differed from her fellows in three separate ways: her method of killing (drowning) was less direct and less decisive than the means chosen by other women (i.e. strangulation, stabbing, cutting the throat); the coroner's inquest into the matter was dated more than two months after the alleged death and her plea of pregnancy was made more feasible by the fact that fully five months had elapsed between the birth of her last child and the meeting of the Assizes.[13]

In homicide, as in burglary, criminality was defined on at least two levels; everyone found guilty by a petty jury might be guilty, but not everyone guilty was dangerous enough to deserve full punishment. The felons who earned such harshness had in common not particular crimes as much as a particular criminal style. Their actions breached basic needs for physical security, above all within one's home or among one's friends and family. The attitudes necessary to avoid that degree of vulnerability, if left on an individual level, approached those of a Hobbesian state. The execution of invasive criminals, therefore, reassured residents that officials were vigilant and concerned about

---

[12] PRO ASSI 35/59/7/13, 20; 35/38/9/14, 34–5, 43–4; 35/34/9/8; 35/77/7/3, 9; 35/36/8/13, 61; 35/37/7/23; for similar concerns elsewhere, see Sharpe, *Essex*, pp. 123–35; Lawson, pp. 228ff. The final verdict in three additional cases in eastern Sussex is uncertain. The defendants were women who received temporary reprieves because they were pregnant; Cockburn, *Calendar, Sussex: Elizabeth I*, entries 1328, 1361, suggests that 2 of the 3 eventually were hanged. The cases were murders committed within the families of the defendants and, as such, not likely tȯ prompt much mercy.

[13] PRO ASSI 35/37/9/41v, 70; 35/38/8/140; 35/38/9/80 for the remanded Elizabeth Lyndsey; see also Sharpe, *Essex*, pp. 135–8; Hoffer and Hull, *Murdering Mothers, passim.*

the basic expectations of civilized life. Many residents of England in the six-teenth and seventeenth centuries believed that chaos lurked around every corner; the distinction drawn to divide forgivable criminals from unforgiv-able ones complemented that picture of the world by assuring some degree of order within civilization.

More than half of the felons punished in eastern Sussex had been convicted of grand larcenies, but the larcenists guilty in only 11 percent of these cases seemed dangerous enough to deserve sentences of death. Execution was not manipulated as a means to deter the most commonly reported thefts in the shire. Although such larcenies were easy to accomplish and accounted for almost half of the acknowledged larcenies, almost no one who stole only items integrally related to agriculture (sheep, cattle) was hanged. And, while the taking of food or clothing made up almost another quarter of the larcenies, only a handful of these felons were ordered to the gallows. But the executions ordered in grand larcenies do reveal a greater sensitivity to the victim's wealth and power than was evident in other stages of the formal legal process. Fifteen felons held responsible for grand larcenies in eastern Sussex were ordered executed. Their thefts covered most types of goods and a wide range of valuations. Of the twelve of their victims whose statuses can be traced, eight identified themselves in recognizances as esquires, gentlemen or yeomen.

Despite this apparent sensitivity to status, however, it was the felons rather than the felonies or the victims that really distinguished those ordered hanged for grand larceny from those who were spared. Ten of the fifteen felons who were ordered hanged had been convicted of more than one crime before the court that sentenced them (seven had committed multiple larcenies, three combined grand larceny with burglaries or highway robberies). Eleven of the fifteen (including seven of the ten with multiple convictions) had partners in their crimes. Three of the last seven even had a variety of partners. Such collegiality was dangerous for both local residents and convicted felons.[14]

The immorality of theft did not itself warrant execution. Whether the temptations of theft were excused because of an awareness of social con-ditions or because of a belief in the universal frailty of humanity, the inexcusable criminals were only those whose acts by their specific quality suggested not crimes bred of weakness but misbehavior deliberately adopted as a way of life. Most executions in eastern Sussex punished persons involved in intrusive crimes that suggested calculated rather than opportunistic behavior. The audience to whom the exemplary lesson of execution was most directly addressed was probably not the general population; the thrust of the

---

[14] A similar set of concerns seems to have influenced the punishment of thieves in Hertfordshire and Essex; see Lawson, pp. 199–202; Sharpe, *Essex*, pp. 92–114.

disciplinary message may have been directed most specifically at other convicts. Executions were a grisly warning of the fine line between tolerable and intolerable misbehavior.

Because it was so unusual to order someone hanged for grand larceny, the cases of grand larceny that ended in orders of execution reveal something of the fears that underlay the penal structure. Guilt alone rarely led to the gallows, but guilt associated with deliberation was a deadly mixture. The qualities that isolated particular thieves from their fellows also influenced more serious cases; no matter how heinous the crime, a distinction was made between dangerous felons and others who had committed felonies. The definition of danger in serious felonies paralleled the definition implied by the disposition of grand larcenies.

In nonclergyable felonies, an order of execution was most likely if a convict's booty was valued at £5 or more; fifteen of seventeen such cases ended in sentences of death. Tables 7.3 and 7.4 trace the distribution of orders for capital punishment according to categories of crime and stated social status. Most of the changes between rates of conviction and rates of ordered execution reflect the particular crimes attributed to different sorts of defendants, but status was not irrelevant. Although men identified as laborers and women identified as spinsters were more likely than anyone else to be labeled as felons, they were also likely to elicit sympathy in sentencing. Felons identified as laborers were ordered hanged in a smaller proportion of cases than other men in almost every category of crime, and no one identified as a spinster was sentenced to death except for committing infanticide. Among women, matters of status were complicated by the relationship of respectability to gender. Despite the low rate of execution for women generally, only one woman received benefit of clergy from the judges in eastern Sussex, and none received a remand except after proof of pregnancy. Since wives and widows probably could not plead pregnancy as freely as could spinsters, the peculiarities of the status of women before the law may unintentionally have had the effect of increasing the vulnerability of wives and widows to execution. But, if this was so, the behavior of grand jurors and petty jurors may have offset it; the vulnerability of married and widowed women may help to explain their low rate of both indictment and conviction.[15]

---

[15] The 2 non-spinsters hanged were a widow convicted of cutting purses and a wife convicted of stealing household goods. The widow was 1 of 3 felons identified as widows; the wife was 1 of 3 felons identified as wives. In contrast, 17 spinsters were convicted, or confessed to felonies apart from infanticide. The determination of pregnancy was left to juries of local matrons and there were complaints that many women became impregnated in prison before trial; see above, pp. 48–50, 143. A similar distinction in punishment between spinsters and other women occurred in Essex in property offenses, but not in violent crimes; cf. Sharpe, *Essex*, pp. 95, 108, 124.

Table 7.3.* *Executions ordered according to category of felony and convict's stated status†*

	Gentlemen	Yeomen	Husbandmen	Laborers	Non-agricultural	Women	Overall rate of executions ordered	No. of cases convicted and confessed
Murder	—	—	80%	75%	100%	—††	63%	16
Felonious killing	—	—	—	33%	67%	—	36%	11
Infanticide	—	—	—	—	—	88%	88%	8
Theft without clergy	—	—	67%	65%	79%	20%	66%	105
Grand larceny	—	—	9%	9%	24%	7%	12%	210
Overall rate of executions ordered	—	—	28%	31%	47%	29%	32%	
No. of cases convicted or confessed	2	2	47	209	59	31		350

*Qualifications about the uses of tables such as this are discussed above, p. 116. Following the order of the table, the number of convictions and confessions in each category is: gentlemen (1, 0, 0, 0, 1); yeomen (0, 2, 0, 0, 0); husbandmen (5, 0, 0, 9, 33); laborers (4, 6, 0, 72, 127); non-agricultural (3, 3, 0, 19, 34); women (3, 0, 8, 5, 15). The categories are explained in Appendix 2 below.
†This table excludes one case of murder in which the suspect's status is unknown.
††Cockburn, *Calendar, Sussex: Elizabeth I*, 1328, 1361, says 2 of the 3 women spared because of pregnancy were eventually hanged.

The relationship between the stated statuses of victims of felony and the likelihood of capital punishment suggests again the crucial link between specific crimes and specific rates of execution. Certain social groups were particularly vulnerable to certain sorts of crimes, and, once this is taken into account, the relationship of status and execution is unsurprising. For example, although felons who threatened women were more likely to be ordered hanged than felons who threatened most men, the prominence of women as victims of nonclergyable thefts explains much of this pattern. Among males, the high rate of executions ordered for felons whose victims worked outside of agriculture and the low rate of executions ordered for

Table 7.4.* *Executions ordered according to category of felony and victim's stated status†*

	Gentlemen	Yeomen	Husbandmen	Laborers	Non-agricultural	Women	Overall rate of executions ordered	No. of cases convicted or confessed
Murder	—	—	—	100%	75%	33%	63%	8
Felonious killing	—	—	—	100%	—	—	33%	3
Theft without clergy	75%	57%	60%	—	86%	63%	71%	42
Grand larceny	19%	21%	9%	—	17%	25%	15%	72
Overall rate of executions ordered	38%	33%	17%	40%	57%	47%	38%	
No. of cases convicted or confessed	24	21	30	5	30	15		125

*Qualifications about the uses of tables such as this are discussed above, p. 116. Following the order of the table, the number of convictions and confessions in each category is: gentlemen (0, 0, 8, 16); yeomen (0, 0, 7, 14); husbandmen (0, 2, 5, 23); laborers (1, 1, 0, 3); non-agricultural (4, 0, 14, 12); women (3, 0, 8, 4). See Appendix 2 below.

†This table excludes victims of infanticide (2 male and 5 female infants), the victims of 2 miscellaneous felonies (both wives whose husbands were executed for bigamy) and 3 victims (all clerks) whose status fell into an "other" category.

those who threatened the safety of husbandmen is striking, but again the disparity is deceptive. Although men from outside of the agricultural community do seem to have been slightly more successful than husbandmen at avenging themselves, most felonies with tradesmen, craftsmen, or industrial workers as victims were burglaries or highway robberies while most felonies with husbandmen as victims were grand larcenies. And while genteel victims prompted more executions than did husbandmen, that prominence contrasts markedly with the relatively low rate of conviction for felons who chose genteel victims. The shift suggests that the Bench, itself composed of gentlemen, was more likely than a petty jury to demand full satisfaction for such crimes.

Sentencing decisions did not rely only upon categories of crime or status; styles of criminality also influenced punishments. The felons most likely to be sent to the gallows were strangers in eastern Sussex, they were likely to have been convicted or at least accused within a brief period of time of several similar crimes, and they often acted with a partner rather than alone. As with those ordered executed for grand larceny, these qualities suggested a deliberateness absent from convicts who earned mitigated punishments. It is worth elaborating briefly on each of these distinctions since together they outline a contemporary view of criminality more complex than one based only upon crimes or status.

The prejudice of residents of early modern England towards strangers is well known. Recent studies of mobility showing how routine at least limited migration was for much of the population have cast this prejudice into a new light, but, even if most people did not live out their lives in the parishes of their births, the suspicion of outsiders seems to have been deep seated and ubiquitous. As defendants, strangers were particularly vulnerable because they had no local family or neighbors to vouch for them and because the popular belief in a criminal underworld sabotaged their credibility. If an outsider was suspected of misbehaving, local residents attributed an element of calculation to the acts that significantly compromised any claim to mercy.

The most reliable records for discovering the residences of defendants are the recognizances used to ensure the appearances of witnesses, accusers and suspects before the courts. Because they were composed near the day and scene of the alleged crime, recognizances normally provide more trustworthy information than indictments. The recognizances indicate that convicts from outside of eastern Sussex, or those who wandered without any settled residence, were less likely to receive mercy than were local convicts. Details in indictments can be checked against recognizances or other independent sources for forty-four felons, nine of whom were ordered executed and thirty-five of whom were spared full punishment. For nineteen of the convicts spared from immediate execution (54 percent), the pertinent information about the defendant (residence, status, crime) in the recognizance was identical with the information in the indictment. The geographical details matched for twenty-eight of the thirty-five felons. In 80 percent of these situations, then, the evidence suggests a local residence for felons who earned the mercy of the court. Moreover, in five of the seven cases where the defendant's home was misstated, the locale cited in the recognizance was still in eastern Sussex. The available information for the nine persons ordered executed is very different. Only three of the recognizances sworn for these felons confirm details in the indictments, and all six of the erroneous indictments misstate the residences of the defendants. None of the felons indicted in these six cases took property from anyone in their own parishes, and at least three felons apparently lived outside eastern Sussex.[16]

The impression that outsiders were particularly dependent upon local tolerance is reinforced by the information about defendants taken from the few cases identifying suspects as residents of places other than eastern Sussex. Since the parishes named in these instances fit neither the sites of the alleged crimes nor the venues of the courts, it is safe to assume a general degree of accuracy. Thirteen convicts who committed crimes in eastern Sussex were indicted as residents of western Sussex or other counties. Eight of the thirteen were ordered hanged.[17] Last, it is worth noting that the handful of convicts escorted back to their residences or birthplaces by being passed from constable to constable all went home to parishes within eastern Sussex. Although the sample is so small it may be unrepresentative, passporting as a mitigation was apparently not available to felons who were also strangers. The inference from these bits and pieces is clear: in eastern Sussex, as elsewhere, residents were considerably less charitable to outsiders than to near neighbors.[18]

Fear of a hardened group of criminals also is apparent in the way that different patterns of felonious behavior influenced decisions about punishment. Individuals found guilty of several crimes were treated far more harshly than either felons convicted of single errors or recidivists sentenced for crimes committed over a period of years. Only 51 percent of the defendants convicted in one court of several crimes escaped a sentence of death even temporarily. In contrast, 69 percent of the felons charged with a single misdeed, and an even larger percentage of recidivists (87 percent), had some mitigation offered to them. The contrast is further heightened if the fates of persons whose indictments indicate crimes limited to a single day are separated from the fates of those whose misbehaviors allegedly spanned days, weeks, or months. Crimes committed all of a sudden implied dire need, irresistible opportunity, or a sudden imbalance in behavior; crimes committed over time suggested premeditation and surrender to a life of crimi-

---

[16] The residences stated in indictments and recognizances differed in 7 cases for felons spared from execution; 5 of these errors were minimal, but 2 involved cattle thieves who, according to their recognizances, came from outside of the shire (1 from Kent, 1 from Hampshire). Five of the 6 errors in cases where felons were ordered hanged reveal homes outside of eastern Sussex, although 4 of the 5 suggest residences in western Sussex.

[17] Ten of the 13 felons were from western Sussex (4 from the rape of Arundel, 4 from the rape of Bramber and 2 from Chichester); 1 felon each came from Kent, Hampshire and Surrey. Those spared had all committed grand larcenies; 4 of those hanged had committed burglaries, 2 had committed horse thefts, and 2 had committed bigamy.

[18] Only 3 convicted felons were passported home, but 3 of the 4 suspects passported after convictions for petty theft or after acquittals also returned to parishes in eastern Sussex. For examples of the hostility towards outsiders at work elsewhere, see Ingram, "Law and Disorder," pp. 129–33; *A Royalist's Notebook*, pp. 27, 46; Holmes, *Lincolnshire*, p. 111; Beier, *Masterless Men*, *passim*.

nality. One-third of the felons whose indictments suggested sprees of a single day were ordered executed; among those whose lapses were apparently more sporadic, the rate of executions ordered was 51 percent.[19]

Most persons found guilty of several felonies in one court had been convicted of the sorts of crimes that were often answered with sentences of death but, even in the cases normally accorded mercy, individuals with several counts proved against them were punished severely. It was the "professional" rather than simply the perpetual criminal for whom the full harshness of the law was reserved. Recidivists merited greater mercy than felons with several pending accusations because most repeaters appeared before any single court accused of only one moment of weakness. Lapses interspersed with upright conduct suited contemporary expectations of behavior. In contrast, defendants who arrived in court to face multiple charges showed nothing suggesting a desire for rehabilitation. There was no impetus for the jury or the court to delay final punishment.[20]

The frequency with which partnerships in crimes involved persons convicted of multiple crimes before a single court suggests one reason why such persons were more likely than others to be considered dangerous to the community. Sixty-two percent of these felons were accused with companions; only 31 percent of the persons charged with one illegal act worked with known associates. Individuals suspected of several crimes often enlisted different partners for separate exploits, and traceable ties of blood or friendship rarely connected the associates. In addition, all but one case involving four or more defendants together included a multiple offender as one of the accused. Most persons indicted as partners of defendants responsible for several crimes were not multiple offenders themselves; consequently, they received less severe sentences than their incorrigible associates. The rate of executions ordered for felons with concurrent convictions and partners was more than three times as high as the rate of executions ordered for similarly incorrigible convicts who acted independently. Even within criminal associations, legal authorities tried to single out offenders whose behavior suggested deliberate and obstinate irresponsibility.[21]

---

19 Twenty-three of 45 felons with multiple convictions before one court were spared as compared to 148 of 214 felons with one conviction and 13 of 15 recidivists. Among the 45 with multiple convictions, 2 of the 6 felons whose indictments suggested the odd spree but 20 of the 39 whose exploits were more frequent and serious were ordered executed.

20 On recividists, see below, pp. 181–92. Six of the 22 felons with multiple convictions specialized in horse thefts and 6 in grand larcenies. Of the remainder, 8 committed at least one burglary and 2 combined grand larceny with highway robbery.

21 Twenty-eight of the 45 felons who had multiple convictions worked with partners, while only 66 of the 214 felons with one conviction did. Six of the 28 had a variety of partners. Only 2 of the 28 (7 percent), but 12 of the 66 (18 percent) had the same surname as any of their partners. Seventeen of the 28 felons with concurrent convictions and partners were ordered

One additional feature distinguished the treatment of persons convicted of numerous crimes in one court from the treatment of other sorts of felons; courts and juries were less responsive to a confession if a defendant was guilty of several crimes. Among persons held responsible for only one crime, confession normally meant a reprieve from death, but five of the fourteen confessed criminals with multiple accusations (36 percent) were ordered hanged. This was almost four times the rate for felons who admitted a single crime and more than four times the rate of execution for confessed recidivists. Defendants with several counts against them were no less likely than other felons to admit their guilt, but the act of confession did far less to protect them from the gallows. The rate of execution for offenders with multiple convictions who did not confess was 48 percent; for those who submitted it was 36 percent. In contrast, the rate for persons who committed one crime was 34 percent if they were convicted and only 10 percent if they had confessed.[22] Almost all thieves with concurrent indictments, furthermore, faced charges of grand rather than petty larceny. Since half the persons indicted for petty larcenies had confessed and since few stolen items were undeniably worth less than twelve pence, it is clear that confession frequently encouraged officials to undervalue stolen goods. Where criminality stretched over days, weeks or months, however, confessions prompted no such consideration. Only one defendant, a spinster, entered more than one confession for petty larceny before a single meeting of the court. Courts viewed the remorse implied by confession skeptically when it came from persons they suspected of acting like hardened criminals.[23]

No single quality defined criminality in early modern England, but the stigma attached to particular crimes and particular patterns of behavior is unmistakable. Felons who planned rather than pilfered, who traveled rather than stayed near home, who tempted others rather than acting in isolation and who committed one crime after another rather than being stricken by remorse after misbehaving were treated differently from those perceived to be

---

executed (61 percent), while only 3 of the 17 felons with concurrent convictions who worked alone were ordered executed (18 percent). Eight of the 17 felons ordered executed were men with concurrent convictions who were partners of one another; among the partners of the remaining men, 5 of the 6 tried were convicted, but all were spared from the gallows. Among the partners of those executed after only one conviction, fewer were convicted (8 of 13 who were tried) but more of those convicted were sentenced to death (6 of 8).

[22] Two of the 21 felons who confessed to a single crime were ordered executed (10 percent); only 1 recidivist who had confessed was given a sentence of death and that was after a second accusation and conviction: see below, pp. 186–8. The rate of confession for persons facing one indictment was 10 percent; for those with multiple crimes, it was 11 percent.

[23] Fifty-five of the 109 persons guilty of petty larceny (50 percent) confessed their crimes, but only 1 confession concerned acts committed over more than a single day. The relationship between confession and undervaluation was not unique to Sussex; see Cockburn, *Introduction*, pp. 65–70; Lawson, pp. 133–4.

needy, weak and submissive. More than half of the felons ordered executed can be associated with at least one of the qualities identified above as criminal. In crimes of property, almost three-quarters of the felons can be so classified and every person ordered executed for grand larceny either took exceptionally valuable property, committed several thefts, worked with a partner, or apparently lived outside the county.[24]

This profile of felons punished by sentences of death contrasts generally with the characteristics of felons spared, but perhaps the most interesting contrast is between the felons ordered executed and a small group of local convicts who repeatedly escaped the gallows. Fifteen individuals appeared in court after earlier convictions and were again found guilty of criminal misbehavior. In fact, five of the fifteen were held responsible during their lives for at least three crimes each. Obviously, these men and women were as incorrigible as the convicts dangerous enough for execution, but almost all of them repeatedly received mitigated punishments. A smaller percentage of reecidivists was ordered executed than the proportion of felons ordered hanged after either multiple convictions or single misdeeds. Why did individuals who clearly breached the rules of proper behavior, and whose repentances, however sincere, were only temporary, so regularly escape sentences of death?[25]

The answer lies in the fact that these recidivists were almost a mirror image of the executed felons. The fifteen repeaters studied here committed crimes of opportunity rather than invasion – their booty was modest, and many were established, albeit marginal, local residents. Recidivists, by definition, committed several crimes, but their lapses were sporadic rather than concentrated, and most of them acted without involving others. Most repeaters counterbalanced the severity of their crimes at least once by confessing. Jurors, judges and magistrates tailored the penalties meted out to recidivists to correspond with the seriousness of each new accusation. Without resorting to execution, the authorities often managed to convey the waning patience of the community.

[24] Forty-six of the 65 felons (71 percent) held responsible for crimes against property can be linked to one of the characteristics discussed above; 29 of the 46 can be linked to 2 traits or more. Two of the 3 felons ordered hanged for bigamy or coining fall into this category as well. In contrast, only 3 of the 22 felons ordered executed for crimes of violence had any of these characteristics.

[25] Recidivists here include only persons held responsible by 2 separate courts for at least 2 separate crimes and who can be identified with information beyond the names used in indictments. At least 36 persons beyond the 15 cited here faced repeated accusations, but earned only 1 conviction each. For narrative entries on the career of each recidivist, see Herrup, diss., pp. 479–83. The rate of apparent execution for recidivists was 17 percent (2 of the 12 who were found guilty of felonies at least twice). The rate for those with multiple convictions at one court was 49 percent and for defendants with a single conviction, 31 percent.

No recidivist was accused of homicide, cutpursing or stealing horses. Almost 80 percent of the forty-five crimes attributed to recidivists were simple larcenies, and more than half of these concerned the theft of either food or clothing. Although seven of the fifteen repeaters were convicted of burglaries, close to half of these break-ins were also directed at food, and two of the burglars immediately confessed to their captors. Most accusations that did not concern edibles or clothing alleged the thefts of sheep, small tools, or miscellaneous bits and pieces of household property. Only one case concerned the theft of money, only two cases concerned expensive items such as cattle, and no case touched goods valued at £5 or more. Most repeaters obviously committed crimes of opportunity, not planning, and they were pilferers rather than major thieves.[26]

The willingness to let acknowledged felons rejoin their communities arose in part from the fact that at least some recidivists had lived a considerable time among the people whom they victimized. All five of the fifteen recidivists who came from parishes with registers still extant can be traced through these records. The three from Heathfield, where a fairly full register has survived, all recorded either a marriage or the baptism of a child at least four years before they appeared as a defendant in the courts. All three throughout their "careers" had their children baptized in the parish. Francis Pankhurst apparently died on the gallows, but John Ashburnham and Robert Walcott were both buried in the sanctity of the local churchyard. It is a mark both of their integration into local life and of the tentativeness of that integration that Ashburnham and Walcott, although they were themselves convicts, stood at various times as sureties for the appearance in court of Francis Pankhurst. Moreover, recidivists tended to find their victims close to home. Only one of the fifteen was held responsible for two crimes more than fifteen miles apart, while more than one third of the felons with multiple crimes who were ordered executed were that mobile. At least in Heathfield, not all defendants were strangers, and established residence may have been as responsible as any other fact for the opportunities given to felons to redeem themselves. It is quite plausible that those allowed to become recidivists were, like Ashburnham, Walcott and Pankhurst, well-known, if not necessarily well-respected, members of their villages.[27]

---

[26] The 45 crimes attributed to recidivists were 27 grand larcenies (7 of food, 7 of clothing, 4 of household goods, 3 of iron, 2 of sheep, 2 of cattle, 1 of feathers, 1 of cloth), 8 petty larcenies (3 of food, 2 of iron, 1 each of sheep, cloth and clothing), 9 burglaries (4 of food, 3 of household goods, 1 of hides, 1 of money) and 1 breaking and entering.

[27] ESRO PAR 372/1/1/1 (Heathfield); Q/R/E 40/32–3, 41; 43/28, 37. The recognizance assured by Walcott was defaulted. For biographical details from the register of Heathfield, see Herrup, diss., pp. 401–2, n. 53. For the much thinner register from East Grinstead, *The Parish Register of East Grinstead 1558–1661*, ed. R. P. Crawfurd, SRS 24 (Lewes, 1917). Although only 1 recidivist committed more than one crime in the same parish, 10 of the 15

Tolerated criminals in eastern Sussex favored different acts and different geographical perimeters from their counterparts who were executed. They also displayed a distinctive pattern of behavior. Most repeaters stood accused of only one crime before any single meeting of the court, and most made no more than two appearances in any three or four meetings. Recidivists were more likely to be found guilty of crimes committed with partners than were felons who earned only one conviction, but their sociability was not as marked as among persons found guilty before a single court of multiple crimes. Nine recidivists acted illegally with other individuals, but only two used partners every time they breached the peace. In most trials involving repeaters and their companions, petty jurors split verdicts in a way that implies that the recidivist was the recruited, rather than the recruiting, party in the association.

In fact, recidivists' partners, who often faced multiple convictions, routinely received harsher penalties than the known repeaters. John Rootes, William Wattle and John Ashburnham, for example, all appeared in court with companions who had to answer several concurrent charges of felony. Rootes, Wattle, and Ashburnham were spared execution by grants of benefit of clergy, but their associates were all ordered to the gallows. A fourth repeater, William Marner, had a partner who was not a multiple offender, but the court nevertheless allowed Marner to plead clerical privilege and sent his associate to hang. When, however, Marner reappeared within less than eighteen months with a second partner, the court did not discriminate between them. Both were ordered executed.[28]

Only two examples of recidivists apparently luring others into illegal acts can be detailed. The two repeaters, Francis Pankhurst and Michael Brockett, were the only recidivists who, having earned convictions, then began to tempt others. Pankhurst's companions, a couple who ran a local alehouse, were merely accomplices who were willing to buy property without asking too many questions. Pankhurst was convicted; the couple was acquitted. Michael Brockett, sometimes known as Michael Ifold, went much further than Pankhurst did in encouraging immorality. Brockett's career was one that by all expectations should have ended upon the gallows; he appeared in court only twice, but he was accused of eleven separate crimes, ten of which were dealt with in a single session of the Assizes. Brockett worked with ten different partners and his crimes covered eleven different local parishes. At least two of

---

recidivists worked within an area of 10 miles or less, 7 in adjacent parishes. Four of the 22 criminals with multiple concurrent convictions concentrated on a single parish, but 8 of the remaining 18 moved between parishes at least 15 miles apart.

28 With the exceptions of Francis Pankhurst and Michael Brockett, discussed below, no recidivist received a harsher penalty than a partner; in 4 of the 6 cases where both partners were tried, the repeater's punishment was the lighter of the two.

his companions were men who lived outside of Sussex (Brockett's home is unknown). One was later hanged for acts committed elsewhere. Brockett escaped execution because he was granted benefit of clergy in each of the Assizes where he was indicted. Although a repetition of clerical privilege was in itself illegal, the lenient treatment allowed Brockett probably resulted from his cooperation with the court. Brockett not only confessed many of the crimes attributed to him or to his partners, but also claimed to have heard the confessions of five other felons. Brockett's reliability as an informant did not impress the petty jurors but, for assessing his proper punishment, his willingness to talk rather than the ability to make good his stories may have been what counted.[29]

Brockett's cooperativeness illustrates the clearest distinction between recidivists and other convicted criminals; ten of the fifteen known repeaters avoided trials by offering confessions at least once, and two more who had trials also admitted misbehavior. Recidivists were far more likely to confess than were felons with either one conviction or many convictions. Although almost all of those who confessed condemned themselves in felonies, no recidivist was ordered executed for a crime that he admitted. No one except Brockett seems to have used the occasion to implicate other individuals. The willingness of recidivists to admit lapses openly was essential to their ability to avoid capital punishment repeatedly. Confession in law paralleled confession in religion. God forgave those who were contrite, and in most cases the law would not demand a life from those who had asked their peers to forgive them.[30] Confession was perhaps particularly important because recidivists seem to have been more likely than other felons to defy accepted notions of deference by choosing a knight or an esquire as a victim. Recidivists accounted for four of the nine known thefts against current members of the commission of the peace. It is unclear whether recidivists preyed upon the gentry more frequently than did other felons or if gentlemen were just less tolerant than others of recidivists. Two of the three recidivists who victimized the powerful immediately confessed. Recidivists combined cooperation with repeated error. Nothing in their backgrounds, attitudes, or behavior was provocative or threatening. To the general population, such men and women probably represented weakness, not depravity, and this attitude was reinforced by the remorse expressed so freely by so many of the repeaters.

While Michael Brockett was held responsible for more crimes than any

[29] Brockett's information against others is noted in PRO ASSI 35/38/8/119, 132–3. His own crimes can be studied at PRO ASSI 35/35/7/1, 55; 35/38/8/4, 7, 13–14, 16, 52, 59–62, 65–6, 70, 80, 82, 107–10, 112–13, 115, 126–7; for Pankhurst, see below, n. 32.
[30] Some ecclesiastics even argued that the decline of auricular confession in the church brought an increase in crime, see Thomas, *Religion and the Decline of Magic*, p. 158.

other known recidivist in eastern Sussex, Francis Pankhurst was the focus of more accusations than Brockett, almost as many convictions, and a "career" that spanned fourteen documented years as opposed to Brockett's three. Pankhurst's ubiquity has already brought him into this study in several places, so it is fitting to illustrate the interplay between persistent crime and escalating punishments with his full story. Because criminality was not synonymous with breaking the law in the early seventeenth century, and because convicts worthy of execution differed so thoroughly from other felons, it is not surprising that most felons escaped execution. Since what divided dangerous criminals from all others was their deliberateness, the punishment of persistent, but not deliberate, felons offered opportunities for rehabilitation. Since in early modern English society everyone was assumed to be a sinner, only a hardened criminal deserved a punishment that protected the community but ignored the convict's soul.[31] The sentences provided for recidivists in eastern Sussex suggest more than simple mitigation; they suggest a carrot and stick philosophy that not only expressed varying degrees of communal outrage, but also offered opportunities for repentance. Mitigations such as benefit of clergy were not always warnings to the first offender; they could also be penultimate disciplines in a series of mitigations ranging from reduced accusations and partial verdicts to informal exile from the shire, enforced apprenticeship and military service. A change in the seriousness of crimes committed or in the defendant's attitude would be paralleled by the responses of the court.

Francis Pankhurst was one of only two known recidivists in eastern Sussex who seems to have been hanged, but Pankhurst was sentenced to die only after at least fifteen appearances in court. Over fourteen years, he was convicted or confessed to eleven thefts: four of household goods, three of food, one of a sheep, two of iron tools, and one involving several sacks of feathers. Grand juries spared him from two other charges of stealing food. Petty juries delivered him from further accusations of taking household goods and cattle and of highway robbery. All but one of these crimes occurred within one of three adjacent parishes. All but one involved Pankhurst alone as a defendant.

---

[31] The popular linking of crime and sin is ubiquitous, but for some examples see Thomas, *Religion and the Decline of Magic*, pp. 475, 523–4; Seaver, *Wallington's World*, esp. pp. 28ff, 65, 120; Mervyn James, *Family, Lineage and Civil Society: A Study of Society, Politics and Mentality in the Durham Region 1500–1640* (Oxford, 1974), pp. 54–5; *Diary of Ralph Josselin*, pp. 52, 349, 605; Michael Walzer, "Puritanism as a Revolutionary Ideology," *History and Theory* 3 (1963), p. 80; Wrightson, *English Society*, p. 176; *Life of Adam Martindale*, p. 125; "Diary of Robert Beake," p. 128; J. A. Sharpe, " 'Last Dying Speeches': Religion, Ideology and Public Execution in Seventeenth-Century England," *P & P* 107 (May 1985): 144–67; Lacey Baldwin Smith, "English Treason Trials and Confessions in the Sixteenth Century," *Journal of the History of Ideas* 15 (1954): 471–98.

His victims ranged from widows to local gentlemen, but most were members of the general agricultural population. Pankhurst had been living in Heathfield for at least four years before his first known difficulty with the law, and the willingness of his neighbors to guarantee his appearances in court assured him of freedom before most of his indictments.

The first known charge against Francis Pankhurst was in 1616 for stealing cattle. The jury at the Assizes acquitted him. When Pankhurst was accused and acquitted of highway robbery just six months after that delivery, however, the judges at the Assizes ordered him to spend a month in the House of Correction. At the Quarter Sessions at Michaelmas, 1624, a petty jury convicted Pankhurst of stealing various goods from the home of Richard Horsecrofte; since this was a felony, the convict avoided death only through a successful plea of benefit of clergy. The courts meeting in 1625 and 1626 heard three new indictments against Francis Pankhurst, all categorized as petty larcenies, and all of which Pankhurst readily confessed. By the late 1620s, Pankhurst was known in the Heathfield area as a thief, and he had exhausted all of the routine non-capital penalties. It is not surprising that in 1628, next to the notice of the baptism of Pankhurst's fifth child in the parish register, the father's identification as "an honest man" was crossed out as an error. In 1629, Pankhurst was again accused of a petty theft and convicted by a petty jury at the Quarter Sessions. Three years later a grand jury dismissed suspicion against him for stealing sheep. The first half of the 1630s seems to have been a time of relative calm for Pankhurst.

Pankhurst's eldest son, Robert, died in July, 1635. Robert's mother followed seven months later. It is probably more than coincidence that, within a year of these two events, Pankhurst was once again indicted and that his alleged crimes now focused on the theft of items immediately usable as food. He was accused of three such thefts at Quarter Sessions held in 1637; a grand jury dismissed one charge and petty juries reduced the other two to petty larcenies. The juries at the Quarter Sessions in January, 1638, heard three more accusations against Pankhurst, all for felonies, but none for stealing food. He was convicted on two of the three counts, allowed a second, technically illegal, plea of benefit of clergy, and once again sent to a House of Correction. Although the rules limiting clerical privilege had been abrogated for him, Pankhurst's luck was clearly running out. Perhaps recognizing this, when ordered to answer yet another charge of theft in September, 1638, Pankhurst took the drastic step of breaking his promise to appear. He had earlier been absolutely reliable about appearing on recognizances. His disappearance in the fall of 1638 was an unusual, and probably fatal, step. By the next Quarter Sessions, in January, 1639, Pankhurst had been captured, sent to jail to await trial, and ordered to answer not one but now two charges of theft. Although he confessed to at least one of the two victims, there were no more mitigations. The petty jury convicted Pankhurst and the Bench condemned him to death.[32]

Francis Pankhurst's experience is so vivid that it is difficult not to romanticize him. Whatever the motives behind his actions or behind the responses of those who confronted him, the legal authorities in eastern Sussex clearly offered Pankhurst repeated chances for reform and rehabilitation. He was ordered hanged only when his appetite for misbehavior seemed to be escalating and when he violated the trust accorded him. Pankhurst may have been a hardened criminal, a victim of the realities of early modern economic life, the unfortunate scapegoat for every crime in his area or a bit of all three; it is certain, however, that he was not ordered executed simply for the theft of a few smocks from some hedges.

The lives of the three other men eventually excluded from eastern Sussex, while neither so diverse nor so extended as Francis Pankhurst's, reveal the same interplay of persistence and tolerance. William Marner was the only recidivist besides Pankhurst to be sentenced to hang. Although his exploits were fewer than Pankhurst's, from the very start he was charged in matters considerably more dangerous. Marner's initial appearance was before the Quarter Sessions in January, 1626, when he confessed to stealing cattle from a local gentleman. His partner in the misdeed was ordered hanged, but Marner was allowed to plead benefit of clergy. Less than two years later, he was again in court; this time accused at the Assizes not only of the more serious charge of burglary, but also of being in partnership with a dangerous felon. His associate, William Sharpe, was indicted for five separate burglaries, two with Marner and three with other partners. By his second appearance, then, Marner exhibited many of the characteristics of the hardened criminal: he was suspected of several sporadic thefts within a brief period of time, he worked with an incorrigible partner, and he was indicted for invading the sanctity of two people's homes. Not surprisingly, both Marner and William Sharpe were ordered to hang.[33]

The cases of William Wattle and Richard Potter are very different, for their careers did not evince a growing professionalism. Unlike Francis Pankhurst and William Marner, they remained amateurs in the eyes of the court, and as a consequence they were removed from the shire not by hanging, but by the time-honored solution of sending criminals off to war. A grand jury at the Assizes indicted Wattle, along with several other men, in 1635 for a burglary and for stealing pieces of iron. One of Wattle's associates was ordered hanged, but Wattle and two other companions, found guilty only of petty

[32] PRO ASSI 35/58/7/28; 35/58/8/14, 40v; 35/67/8/65, 87v; ESRO PAR 372/1/1/1; Q/R/E
      22/53, 121, 123; 30/74; 37/102; 39/8, 98, 109; 39/49, 98, 109; 40/32, 44; 40/33, 43–4, 64,
      94–94v; 40/34, 41, 94v; 43/28, 37; 44/31, 63, 69; QI/EW1.
[33] ESRO Q/R/E 22/50, 78, 90, 101, 110, 116, 126, 128; PRO ASSI 35/69/6/11; 35/69/6/9.

larcenies, were whipped and then freed. In 1638, Wattle appeared at the Assizes again, this time confessing to the petty theft of clothing. He was again sent home after a whipping. Sometime between 1638 and 1640, Wattle was impressed into the military, but, by the meeting of the Assizes in the summer of 1640, he was in jail accused of desertion. He was ordered directly down to Maidstone, "to be employed in royal service in the wars."

Richard Potter was also sent to Maidstone and overseas, but his background differed from Wattle's. In 1636, Potter had confessed to stealing a capon and two hens from two local gentlemen. He was passported to his father's home in Maresfield after a whipping at the Assizes. In 1639, a jury at another Assizes acquitted him of another theft of hens, but convicted him of stealing other animals for food. Potter's conviction was for felony. He escaped the gallows by pleading benefit of clergy. One year later, Potter, this time brought to the Quarter Sessions, confessed to yet another theft and earned yet another whipping, and in July, 1640, he was back at the Assizes again. On this last occasion, he was again accused of stealing poultry. Although he was acquitted, the court ordered Potter sent with Wattle and others to serve as soldiers.[34]

Most recidivists were less persistent than Pankhurst, Marner, Wattle, or Potter, but each earned slightly harsher penalties for every new conviction. Robert Leigh, Richard Cade, John Rootes, and Robert Walcott each elicited pity from petty juries for the first charges lodged against them; the jurors turned felonies into petty larcenies and saved the convicts from execution. Leigh followed a daytime break-in, in 1627, with a full-fledged burglary early in 1628, and in 1628 the jurors at the Assizes condemned Leigh to be hanged. The court remanded Leigh's sentence. Leigh's claim to mercy is not clear, but, as noted earlier, the depositions concerning his initial indictment refer to him repeatedly as "a boy." Richard Cade also followed a theft with a burglary, although several years separated his appearances. On both occasions, juries found Cade guilty only of simple theft, but in the first instance the grand jurors at the Quarter Sessions transformed felony into petty larceny; in the second case, the petty jurors at the Assizes reduced burglary to clergyable theft. The jurors who tried Robert Walcott and John Rootes reacted in the same manner as those that handled Leigh and Cade, progressing from interventions that limited penalties to whipping to those that allowed the possibility of death.[35]

34 PRO ASSI 35/77/6/21; 35/77/6/5; 35/80/8/3; 35/82/5/36v (Wattle); PRO ASSI 35/78/8/21–2, 52; 35/81/5/17; 35/82/5/12, 36v; ESRO Q/R/E 48/24 (Potter).
35 ESRO Q/R/E 25/35, 60, 67; PRO ASSI 35/70/3/2 (Leigh); ESRO Q/R/E 15/5; PRO ASSI 35/82/4/8, 37v (Cade); PRO ASSI 35/77/6/15, 48; 35/77/6/21; 35/78/8/1, 52v; 35/78/9/4; 35/78/9/5 (Rootes); ESRO Q/R/E 35/14, 17; 46/45, 58–9; PRO ASSI 35/77/6/20 (Walcott).

In two other cases, the Bench rather than the jury controlled the mitigating process, but the results were the same. Elizabeth Jove confessed at the Quarter Sessions to a petty theft of cloth in 1639. Within a year, she was indicted at the Assizes for the felonious larceny of various linens. Edward Gilbert confessed to two crimes: the petty theft of several geese in 1637, and the taking of miscellaneous sheets, smocks and aprons from a local yeoman in 1638. Neither first crime was heard at the Quarter Sessions as a felony, so some escalation in penalties was only natural. Since both Jove and Gilbert confessed their thefts and since each indictment valued the stolen property at ten pence (the standard amount used in undervaluations), the goods stolen in these first crimes probably received sympathetic rather than realistic evaluations. In her second appearance, a jury tried and convicted Jove, but the Bench intervened with a remand to save her life. Gilbert confessed to his second crime as well as to his first. For this second crime, a felony, the justices at the Quarter Sessions allowed Gilbert benefit of clergy.[36]

The tailoring of punishment to persistence is also apparent in the penalties provided when repeaters were accused of second crimes that were less disruptive than the original misbehaviors. John Frankwell and John Ashburnham were each indicted for felonious thefts in their first appearances in court; they were convicted and allowed benefit of clergy. Frankwell's second indictment, a year after his first, was again for theft, but whereas he had earlier favored linen and money, this time he had helped himself to less than a bushel of grain. The petty jury at the Assizes reduced his culpability from sixteen pence to eight pence. Ashburnham received similar treatment. He moved from the substantial accusation heard at the Assizes of stealing cattle to an accusation heard at the Quarter Sessions concerning an iron chain valued at a bit more than three shillings; the petty jury decreased the value to ten pence, and Ashburnham, like Frankwell, only earned a whipping. Francis Terry was also indicted for two thefts, but it was the Bench rather than a jury that determined Terry's second sentence. The petty jurors at the Quarter Sessions had reduced Terry's first case, a theft of wheat, to petty larceny; he avoided a second trial, for taking a sheep, by confessing. The sheep was valued at ten pence and so Terry stood responsible only for a second petty larceny.[37] In almost every instance, then, both the Bench and jurors tailored punishments to fit a defendant's apparent success at controlling his behavior. Obstinacy brought escalating penalties; even moderate reform earned lighter sentences. Despite the formal rigidity of the penal structure, only recidivists

---

[36] ESRO Q/R/E 44/27, 58; PRO ASSI 35/82/4/6, 37v; 35/82/5/36 (Jove); ESRO Q/R/E 37/31, 42, 62, 74; 42/56, 93; 47/7, 29 (Gilbert).

[37] PRO ASSI 35/37/7/9; 35/38/8/38–9, 95 (Frankwell); PRO ASSI 35/77/6/17; ESRO Q/R/E 47/19; 49/43, 87 (Ashburnham); ESRO Q/R/E 25/36, 56–7, 79; 29/29, 89v; WSRO Q/R/WE 16/19, 44 (Terry).

whose attitudes or crimes suggested a shift from tolerable to intolerable criminality were ordered executed.[38]

Why were these repeaters treated so differently from other criminals? The recidivists were hardly bastions of virtue with lives blemished by a single moment of weakness. In their own way, the recidivists were every bit as obstinate as were the felons who died for their behavior. The contrast in treatment of recidivists and criminals who were immediately ordered executed suggests a basic distinction built upon social, psychological and moral substance. Illegal behavior was tolerable, even if repeated, so long as it was conducted by certain rules of fair play, and as long as need, direct or indirect, seemed more prominent than avarice as the motivating force. Everyone struggled against the forces of evil within. Most persons were too aware of their own shortcomings to end someone else's life for the loss of a few shillings worth of food or household goods.[39]

Crimes were sins, yet sinning was universal. In a religious milieu that repeatedly emphasized that everyone was a sinner, equating sinning with criminality would have made everyone either a known or an unknown criminal. In an age notorious for economic aggressiveness and litigiousness, drawing the line between the respectable and the criminal simply on the basis of illegal acts would have been similarly unacceptable. The common law had always stressed the importance of *mens rea* in determining a felony; in the seventeenth century, the concurrence of the notion that humans were imperfect, yet redeemable, with the notion that economic mobility was dangerous, but desirable, necessitated two interpretations of law-breaking and law-breakers. Intention was the quality that distinguished not only accidents from felonies but also offenders from real criminals. Attempts to control one's behavior were as important a measure of criminality as success or failure in such attempts. The important difference between executed felons and spared felons was the perceptual difference between weakness and evil. What most distinguished criminals from mere law-breakers was that, unlike

[38] The record of only one recidivist, Thomas Tisdale, varied from this pattern. Tisdale was convicted of theft in 1594 at the Quarter Sessions and allowed benefit of clergy. The next year, he was acquitted at the Assizes on 2 separate charges of larceny. In the winter of 1596, he was convicted of burglary at the Assizes, his sentence was remanded and he was eventually pardoned. The explanation for the lenience shown him is unclear. Tisdale stole household goods and he does not seem to have confessed to any of his crimes. His fate may be linked to the fact that both crimes for which he was held responsible were committed against justices of the peace. If these men took mercy on Tisdale, their opinions probably held sway. ESRO Q/R/E 1/27; PRO ASSI 35/37/9/59–60; 35/38/8/81.

[39] These attitudes were not unique to eastern Sussex, although they have not been systematically studied elsewhere; see Richard Gough, *The History of Myddle*, ed. David Hey (Harmondsworth, 1981), *passim*; Samaha, "Hanging for Felony"; and the works cited in n. 31 above; but cf. Lawson, pp. 200–2, 309–12.

other sinners, criminals appeared to have abandoned even the quest for self-discipline.

The penal structure in eastern Sussex was manipulated repeatedly and consistently to contain temptation and misbehavior within certain limits. The law worked to prevent the shire being made a target for outsiders, for intensive spreed or for felonies of particularly brutal intrusiveness. The operation of the law, perhaps more than its rules, defined and reinforced proper behavioral boundaries. Every punishment was public "to the end it may advance the more good to the Prince in profit, to the Justices in credit, and to the People in example." Even the defendant was expected to concur in the fairness of his treatment. Before judges declared sentences upon convicted felons, the prisoners were brought before the Bar and asked to agree, tacitly at least, that justice had been done. The judge inquired:

You do remember that before this time you have been severally indicted for several felonies, upon your indictments you have been arraigned and have severally pleaded not guilty and for your trials have severally put yourselves upon God and the country, which country hath found you guilty. Now what can you say for yourselves why according to law you should not have judgment to suffer death?

This ceremony, known as the *allocutus*, provided the opportunity for convicts to plead benefit of clergy, pregnancy, or any other mitigating facts. Psychologically, however, the *allocutus* confirmed for the court and for all spectators that a felon understood his situation and accepted it.[40]

---

[40] T. W., *Clerk of the Assizes*, p. 93; Baker, "Criminal Courts and Procedure," *Crime in England*, p. 41; for the similar purpose given to speeches on the scaffold, see BL Harleian MS 1603/30v–31; Bodleian Rawlinson MS D399/90; Sharpe, "Last Dying Speeches"; Smith, "English Treason Trials"; cf. Spierenburg, *Spectacle of Suffering, passim.*

8

The common peace

More than a century ago, the American jurist and legal scholar Oliver Wendell Holmes wrote, "The life of the law has not been logic, it has been experience."[1] As it operated in early modern England, the criminal law involved logic in the common rather than in the scientific sense. The enforcement of the law was an exercise of choices, not of categorizations. And this exercise routinely modified the theories of legal science to suit the specific complexities of daily life. The gap between law as written and law as lived did not betoken ignorance or incompetence; the divergence created room for the manipulation of authority to fit circumstances, and ensured that mercy remained a gift, never an unquestioned right. The criminal law fundamentally concerned the maintenance of morality; it could not routinely be abrogated without losing its validity. Morality was supposed to be unchanging, and the formal law reflected that constancy. To deny flexibility in the operation of the law, however, was to place an unmanageable burden on both the governed and the governors. As a consequence, the criminal law as written worked as an ideal, as a moral standard that was enforced or waived as seemed appropriate.

The maintenance of two levels of law paralleled the two distinct scriptural inheritances of early modern England. The formal law, inflexible and awesome in its demands and punishments, reflected the God of the Old Testament, the patriarch whose insistence upon adherence to His Commandments was so complete that he denied his own emissary Moses entrance to the Promised Land because of a youthful transgression. The law as enforced followed the gentler mood of the New Testament. The older law was still authoritative, but its implementation was didactic as well as directive. In practice it valued repentance as well as compliance. Many seventeenth-century sermons for the Assizes spoke to the text, "He bears not the sword in vain; for he is the minister of God, a revenger to execute wrath upon him that does evil," but the actual practices of the Assizes and Quarter Sessions could

---

[1] Oliver Wendell Holmes, *The Common Law*, ed. Mark De Wolfe Howe (Cambridge, Mass., 1963), p. 5.

as easily come closer to another statement from Paul, "The letter kills, but the spirit gives life."[2]

The rituals of legal process repeatedly emphasized the foundation of the criminal law in morality and religion: the splendid processions of officials to and from court, the stylized confrontations between defendants and jurors, the gruesome spectacles of public punishments; all these provided eloquent lessons for the populace. The intimate interweaving of criminal law and morality found expression not only in legal ceremonies, but also in contemporary sermons, literature, and legal dicta. The ingrained awareness of the link between good order and good conscience can even be traced in early modern epitaphs. The inscription upon the memorial carved in 1613 for Ralph Maynard, an esquire from Hertfordshire, states:

> The man that's buried in this tomb,
> In heavenly Canaan hath a room . . .
> His body by will here under lies
> Still harkening for the great Assizes
> When Christ the judge of quick and dead
> Shall raise him from this earthly bed,
> And give him heaven's eternal bliss
> To live and reign with saints of his.[3]

The Last Judgment itself could be likened to a special meeting of the major criminal tribunal in the shires. The definition of the common law as common justice and the identification of both with divine notions of virtue infused the legal and social structures of early modern England.

The hubris of the early modern gentry allowed them to envision divine judgment as a replica of an English institution, but few persons were so confident as individuals about their worthiness. The view that humanity was unavoidably flawed made a law that lacked room for more than occasional mercy a mockery of justice. The social gulf between magistrate and miscreant, or between constable and criminal was substantial, but in the struggle to control behavior, everyone was believed to share an enemy. John Milton voiced perhaps the most common personal concern of propertied Englishmen when he wrote:

There is not that thing in the world of more grave and urgent importance throughout the whole life of man, than is discipline . . . Discipline is not only the removal of disorder, but if any visible shape can be given to divine things, the very visible shape and image of virtue.

The quest for discipline ended only in death. No victory in the battle for self-

---

[2] Romans, xiii, 4, cited by Cockburn, *Assizes*, p. 86; II Corinthians, iii, 6.
[3] St Alban's Cathedral, apse, south side, erected by Maynard's son Robert. This parallel was a common theme for sermons at the Assizes at least into the eighteenth century. See Beattie, *Crime and the Courts*, p. 317.

control was more than temporary.[4] If the rigidity of English criminal law reflected its moral underpinnings, the flexibility of enforcement reflected a realization of the frailty of humanity. Legal results could not dovetail with legal ideals until human strength outwitted human weakness; only in a world of saints would every thief truly be a felon and every felon deserve execution.

The effectiveness of law, therefore, cannot be measured by its adherence to legal formulae; its power is best understood through the options exercised by legal officials and other individuals and through the choices made at different stages of the legal process. The authority to enforce the law and to punish persons who refused to obey its dictates was not confined to members of the judiciary or magistracy. The propertied segments of the community shared real power over the implementation and effectiveness of the law. Not every participant earned equal gratitude or respect, but each was relatively autonomous in his specific area of responsibility. Successful prosecution required that victim and neighbors, headboros and hundredal constables, grand jurors and petty jurors, and magistrates and judges reach generally complementary conclusions about both culpability and criminality. When no broad agreement existed, suspects were left unapprehended, unindicted, unconvicted, or unpunished.

Moreover, the people who controlled the legal system were in some sense representatives of their communities. The obligation to participate in prosecutions went deep into the ranks of propertied society, assuring not only the involvement of a fair number of persons but also their interest in upholding deference to the law. For example, of one hundred and eleven individuals from the parish of Heathfield in eastern Sussex who contributed to the collection for the relief of the Irish Protestants in 1642, at least forty participated in the legal process as prosecuting victims, witnesses, sureties, constables, or jurors. An additional eleven individuals, while not personally involved, had fathers who were active in enforcing the criminal law. Almost half of the contributors in this village in 1642, then, had close experience with the criminal courts of the shire.[5]

---

[4] Cited in Christopher Hill, *Society and Puritanism in Pre-Revolutionary England*, p. 225. Seaver provides a particularly vivid example of this concern in his analysis of the writings of Nehemiah Wallington. For examples linking discipline more explicitly to criminality, see T. C. Curtis and F. M. Hale, "English Thinking about Crime 1530–1620," in Knafla, ed., *Crime and Criminal Justice*, pp. 111–26; Anthony Fletcher and John Stevenson, eds., *Order and Disorder in Early Modern England* (Cambridge, 1985); Lincoln B. Faller, *Thieves and Murderers Turn'd to Account: The Forms and Functions of Criminal Biography in Late Seventeenth and Early Eighteenth-Century England* (Cambridge, forthcoming).

[5] This included 9 men acting as sureties for recognizances, 8 as victims, 5 as grand jurors and hundredal constables at the Quarter Sessions, 4 as petty jurors at the Quarter Sessions, 4 as witnesses, 1 as a hundredal constable never called as a juror and 9 as part of 2 or more of these categories. This list underestimates true participation even in the extant records because of the impossibility of positively identifying jurors, witnesses and sureties in the Assizes. The

The enforcement of the criminal law reflected local property holders' perceptions of morality. The participation of a variety of private persons in criminal prosecutions ensured that the legal process remained not only authoritative and flexible, but also responsive to the concerns of the propertied population. Individual decisions might be capricious or unjust, but the pattern of decisions made at each formal stage of criminal procedure reveals the imagined boundaries between harmony and discord in the shire and the functional division between tolerable and intolerable misbehavior.

Well before any legal official received a criminal complaint, the friends and neighbors of the aggrieved victim worked to isolate a suspect from the rest of the population. In almost all detection, the victimized individual, rather than the headboro or hundredal constable, initiated investigation. Most investigative successes were the accomplishments of private persons, and most victims identified their suspects with the help of servants, family or neighbors. Even without personal interest in a particular crime, residents were expected to report eccentric behavior to authorities. Local officials normally helped to conclude investigations rather than to organize them and were most useful in confronting recalcitrant suspects, making arrests, and escorting accused persons to the nearby magistrates. But, even in these situations, constables relied on private help for added muscle. Since they normally were not men of exceptional status, leisure, or training, constables and headboros could not hope to apprehend criminals without support from local villagers.

Once a suspect was arrested, he was taken to a justice of the peace for interrogation. Although the testimony of the victim and witnesses was influential, magistrates essentially controlled the escalation of a complaint into a formal accusation. A magistrate could try to arbitrate between two parties, or he could decide that the problem necessitated an appearance at the Assizes or Quarter Sessions. If a justice of the peace determined upon prosecution, he then decided whether to allow the suspect to remain free until the meeting of the court or to order him detained in jail. The decision to arbitrate a dispute, or to dismiss, bind over, or jail a suspect was one of the few choices in prosecution regularly made by individuals acting alone (a solitude, moreover, not sanctioned by the government).[6] However, since private persons acted as sureties, witnesses, and escorts for the journey to prison, the availability of willing helpers still influenced magisterial decisions.

1642 collection provides the most comprehensive local listing available for this period of men of some means; such men, of course, never constituted the majority of the population. Cf. the religious censuses of 1603 and 1676 where the number of local communicants is said to be, respectively, 600 and 390; "Ecclesiastical Returns," p. 11; J. H. Cooper, ed., "A Religious Census of Sussex in 1676," *SAC* 45 (1902), 145.

[6] Marian legislation demanded that more than one magistrate certify most grants of bail, but the restriction was generally ignored; see above, p. 90 n. 38.

Neither the suspicion of interested parties, nor the concurrence of local officials and magistrates in that suspicion guaranteed the trial or conviction of an accused criminal. The choice of indicting or dismissing a suspect belonged to the grand jurors; the conviction of a suspect or his return to innocence was left to a second, discrete, group of jurors. The grand jurors examined the evidence against each suspect and decided which accusations seemed to be sustained by reasonable levels of proof. Twelve assents turned a charge into an indictment.

Many indictments concerned offenses that could be handled summarily, and others named defendants who spared themselves trial by confession, but most cases proceeded to yet another group of decision-makers, the twelve "good men and true" who sat as symbols of the country. The petty jury in its ability to redefine charges and to deliver verdicts of partial guilt had a voice not merely in deciding guilt or innocence but also in defining the appropriate punishment for each convict. Its verdicts rested upon information from defendants, witnesses, victims, and probably presiding judicial officers, but jurors retained their right to decide cases autonomously. Judges and justices of the peace, however, had important discretionary powers. By their control over benefit of clergy and their influence over grants of pardon, judicial officials modified the decisions of juries. Even after acquittals, judges invoked disciplinary measures that limited the freedom of acquitted defendants.

Given this complex and participatory process, how was criminality defined? What marked persons as worthy of suspicion, confinement, indictment, and punishment? Criminality, like the law, existed on two levels, the forgivable and the unforgivable. The surviving records of the Quarter Sessions in eastern Sussex show that three out of four accusations presented to grand jurors became indictments, and in both the Quarter Sessions and the Assizes well over half of the known indictments brought some punishment to the defendant. Every person judged culpable of an action that violated the criminal law was guilty of a crime, but the responses of courts and juries indicate that not every person who committed a crime was considered to be a dangerous criminal. While most persons accused before a grand jury of misbehavior were indicted, and most of those indicted were disciplined, relatively few persons whose actions made them liable for capital punishment were actually sent to the gallows. Most felons who were ordered hanged, moreover, shared certain attributes of background, attitude and behavior that set them apart from other transgressors. The line between forgivable and unforgivable misbehavior was broadly consistent; it can be traced not only in the sentences of the courts, but also in the choices made over arrests, committals, indictments, and convictions.

Both concrete evidence and more impressionistic information inferred

from a defendant's demeanor affected legal decisions. The social and legal
implications of an alleged crime were the most important influences upon
local sympathies toward a suspect, but at every point, not only the actual
proof against a defendant, but also his position in the wider community
counted. Each prosecution was an assessment of the trustworthiness of a
defendant rather than simply a test of guilt or innocence. These subjective
judgments of character relied upon the attitude and behavior of a suspect as
much as upon social status. The balance between facts and impression
differed at each stage of the legal process, but in the context of the seventeenth century judgments based on facts alone would not have been considered just.

The first confrontations between individuals and the law in the criminal
process – encounters that ended in freedom or arrest, recognizance or confinement – were those most intimately affected by social standing. Although
successful detection ideally depended upon evidence linking the alleged crime
and the suspect, often no firm clues were available. In such uncertain cases,
suspicion fell quickly upon persons of questionable reputation, those who
lived idly, persons whose behavior or life underwent sudden improvements,
and persons who acted eccentrically or boasted carelessly. Such attitudes
ensured that strangers and peddlers, laborers and servants, were particularly
vulnerable to accusation. However, social position, of itself, did not determine any decision; victims and neighbors devoted considerable time and
effort to making the evidence collected against a suspect as cohesive and com-
pelling as possible. They followed trails left after alleged crimes; they
matched footprints from the scene of alleged felonies with the accused; they
compared suspicious goods with identifiable items. They conducted formal
and informal searches and elaborate stakeouts. Their efforts were worth-
while, if successful, for the concreteness of the case assembled against a
suspect discernably influenced decisions about both arrest and bail.

A suspect's response to the evidence gathered against him was also an
essential part of the determination of trustworthiness. The accused's attitude
toward legal scrutiny was almost as important as the objective information.
Innocent people were supposed to submit to legal questioning without either
fear or discomfort; those who blushed, answered slowly, or refused to look
interrogators directly in the eye were considered disingenuous. It was
presumed that anyone caught in a direct attempt to evade or to mislead an
investigation had something to hide. Decisions about arrest and recognizance, then, were based upon a combination of impressions taken from the
evidence surrounding an alleged crime, information about the accused, and
the way in which the suspect responded to his own dilemma. Social position
probably carried considerable weight in these initial choices, but even these

decisions reflected the availability of objective information and the behavior of defendants.

The choices made by grand jurors in their indictments and those made by petty jurors in their verdicts counterbalanced the preliminary concern about a suspect's history with a strong focus on the details of each defendant's recent past. A comparison of the indictments returned by grand juries to the Quarter Sessions in eastern Sussex with the accusations they rejected reveals an overriding concern for objective linkages between alleged crimes and alleged criminals. Grand jurors were sensitive to accusations based upon social prejudice, upon convenience or opportunity, and upon maliciousness or desperation. They consistently rejected such allegations as well as many accusations leveled against persons whose age or family ties mitigated their responsibility for their actions. In charges of theft, grand jurors required that stolen property be clearly identified and linked directly to the intentional misbehavior of a suspect. They shied away from circumstantial charges and from cases in which confusion or intimidation might have influenced the actions of the accused. Grand jurors reinforced the caution of constables, magistrates and coroners by taking particular care over accusations that could end upon the gallows. While grand jurors were not oblivious to social differences, the nature of the alleged crime and the strength of the evidence assembled against the defendant were the most persuasive reasons for indictment.

Petty jurors, in making their choices over guilt or innocence, combined this concern for information with concern for a defendant's motive and demeanor. When facts linked a defendant to a crime, petty jurors rarely contravened the evidence, but they did redefine accusations to mitigate verdicts in cases that were apparently born of need rather than of avarice. The greater the chance of execution upon conviction, the more caution jurymen took before returning a verdict of guilty. The defendant's own performance before the jurors, moreover, had a greater influence upon decisions than did the speeches of magistrates or witnesses. As in the earlier choice of indictment or dismissal, social status had only a secondary impact on verdicts. The concerns of both grand and petty juries moderated earlier decisions in the legal process. The accused's history often did as much as current evidence to determine a suspect's treatment before trial. The role of the two juries was to weed out the truly substantial cases from the chaff of prejudicial or simply illproven charges.

Although juries mitigated charges against some defendants, the Bench was the most active source of such alterations. If the early stages of decisionmaking focused upon the qualities of character suggested by a defendant's past, and the jurors' decisions concentrated on the realities of a defendant's present, the final legal choice, to execute a convict or to mitigate his penalty, seems to have been made with a steady eye on the possibilities of a defendant's future. Both the autonomous and the joint mitigations made by juries and judicial officers show a clear desire to remove from the community anyone who seemed committed to a life of crime. However, the decisions also reveal a concern to spare individuals whose need or weakness repeatedly brought them into conflict with their neighbors.

Many of the subjective concerns that underlay earlier choices to arrest, to dismiss, to bind over, or to jail suspects resurfaced in this last stage of decision-making. Once again, strangers and persons of marginal status were exceptionally vulnerable. Once again, a defendant's attitude, expressed through confession or defiance, sporadic recidivism or concentrated involvement in crime, was important. Once again, the associations of a felon, and particularly his interest in tempting others, was of particular interest. The system penalized incorrigible criminals, but it eliminated only those who, by their crimes and their attitudes, seemed to violate the most basic rules of ethical behavior. It was the criminal who struck at the sanctity of home, person or social status that threatened communal harmony most deeply. It was this sort of crime, when committed by someone considered to be a hardened criminal, that brought execution.

All five stages of decision-making – arrest/dismissal, confinement/bail, indictment/delivery, conviction/acquittal, and execution/mitigation – provided forums in which legal representatives could try to sift sinful persons from unfortunate ones. At every point, evidence, social prejudice and the demeanor of the opposing parties all affected the opinions of the authorities. The choices made throughout prosecution reinforced the common convictions of the propertied community: idleness, wanderlust, greed and insolence were the signposts on a road that led to anarchy and damnation. Crimes bred of these qualities were very different from those born from need, confusion or intimidation. The first were committed by true criminals; the perpetrators of the second were errant brethren who might still be redeemed.

Because so many people participated in the legal process and because their decisions were always partially impressionistic, some common definition of a desirable peace was necessary if the structure was to function. However, nothing demanded absolute concord. Tension between different authorities within the legal process and between the individuals who made up those authorities was common, but, since prosecution was a series of discrete decisions not a single collective effort, specific disagreements did not undermine the broad consensus that kept the structure working. Authority in enforcement moved between independent levels of decision-making like a baton passed in a relay. The movement not only ensured the goal, but also smoothed over differences by implicating the wider propertied community in the endeavor. The sharing of legal obligations breathed life into the system because, while the social and professional elites participated in the legal process, they did not control it. A structure so decentralized both encompassed and to some extent neutralized the self-interest of its participants.

How typical was the system outlined here for eastern Sussex? The idiosyncrasies of documentation and scholarly interests make a comprehensive comparison with other jurisdictions impossible. Without fully comparable sets of legal records any conclusions must be speculative, but several points seem clear. The legal patterns traced here were a variant on a theme rather than *sui generis*. No shire seems to have had a system identical to that of eastern Sussex, but no part of the structure in eastern Sussex was unique. The way that the law was enforced in any county emerged from the interaction of particular property holders with particular offenses within particular administrative structures. The intermingling of these influences, not any single feature, produced the distinctive history of the criminal law in a community. Consequently, while the system was generally similar, every shire in England was peculiar. In eastern Sussex, prosperity, cohesiveness, religious intensity and administrative decentralization each contributed to the local definition of good order.

The agendas of the criminal courts in eastern Sussex reveal fewer reported thefts and more reported cases of violence than elsewhere. Perhaps fewer thefts of all sorts occurred here than in other places, but, more likely, the low rate of reported theft means that victims were more willing to settle such matters privately. The relatively even prosperity of eastern Sussex may partially explain why local men of property were less anxious than their compatriots elsewhere in the Southeast to prosecute cases of not only theft, but also witchcraft or arson. Moreover, it is not surprising to find a high rate of prosecutions for violent crimes coupled with a low rate of prosecutions for theft. Where the population had reached the natural limits of easy expansion, tensions of competition were likely to erupt into disorder.

However, prosperity and economic aggressiveness do not alone explain the pattern of prosecutions. The link between economic life and reported crime was forged through the peculiarities of the local social structure. Relatively, eastern Sussex was not only economically prosperous but also socially stable. Most of the major families had been local residents for centuries and the forests and mud limited the number of immigrants both rich and poor. This stability may have heightened the distrust of outsiders while making forgiveness more likely for locally known miscreants. This intimacy suggests as well one reason why, despite the presence of enthusiastic and active Puritans, comparatively little sustained enthusiasm existed for a legally imposed reformation of manners.

The social environment affected who enforced the law as well as which laws were chosen for enforcement. From victims through to magistrates, the willingness of individuals to participate in enforcing the law seems to have been greater in eastern Sussex than it was in many other places. The longevity of genteel families locally and the rough balance between the gentry and the yeomanry may have encouraged a participatory structure that, while keeping the commission of the peace relatively small, also accorded authority to offices beyond the magistracy. Since duties such as serving on grand or petty juries were respectable, they were a logical focus for men of middling status interested in an active role in governance. This willingness dovetailed with the firmly geographical basis of the administrative structure to set the tone of the enforcement of the criminal law in eastern Sussex. If economic conditions helped determine which sorts of behavior would inspire prosecutions, and social conditions helped guarantee which sorts of people would participate in the legal system, the firmly geographical basis of the local administrative structure made the system not simply participatory, but also wide ranging. Because most tasks fell upon not just any residents but upon those of a specific region, the burden of service in eastern Sussex was naturally limited. The rotation of obligations ensured that one might be active without being overwhelmed.

Most of the shires for which extensive evidence from the early modern period survives (Kent, Surrey, Essex, Hertfordshire and Cheshire) resemble one another generally in the sorts of crimes reported and the treatment of those crimes, but eastern Sussex seems to share more with Cheshire than with nearer neighbors. In Cheshire, too, violence was particularly prominent on the agendas of the courts and thefts were less important than in other shires. In Cheshire, too, mundane problems of rural life concerned grand jurors more regularly than did complaints about the poor. In Cheshire, too, legal duties were a proper focus for local activism. And Cheshire was relatively prosperous, had a social structure resembling that of eastern Sussex, contained a community of enthusiastic Puritans and based recruitment for many local offices upon residence. These parallels suggest that the character of the enforcement of the law as well as the pattern of local crimes can be plotted on a rustic–urban continuum, but such a conclusion may only parody reality. For example, in Worcestershire, which had a large urban population, an active industrial economy, a central location, and no large concentration of either old gentry families or active Puritans, the tenure of many legal offices also depended on residence; men of local standing often served on juries and both grand and petty juries were active bodies of opinion.[7]

---

[7] On general trends in reported crime, see Sharpe, *Crime in Early Modern England, passim*; Lawson, ch. 7. On Cheshire, see Sharpe, *ibid.*; T. C. Curtis, "Some Aspects of the History of Crime"; Morrill, *Grand Jury, passim*; J. S. Morrill, *Cheshire 1630–1660: County Govern-*

The complexities of the relationship between local societies and the enforcement of the criminal law were not static, but the span of fifty years covered
in this study is both too long and too short for effectively tracing how criminal
prosecution changed over time. The values embodied in the legal system
shifted to match changes in economic conditions, social life and administrative structure as well as to respond to schemes concocted in the Inns of
Court or the Privy Council. Business, personnel and verdicts could change
drastically with each session of the courts, but the records extant from eastern
Sussex are not complete enough to make close annual comparisons valuable.
The contrasts that bring the particular qualities of early seventeenth-century
enforcement into clearest relief encompass centuries rather than decades. In
1500, roughly one hundred and fifty years before the terminal date of this
study, the agendas of the courts contained a greater number of violent crimes
than in 1640. The middling freeholders were fewer, poorer and less important to government than in the seventeenth century. And the mechanisms for
prosecuting felons were more limited. Magistrates were not legally required
to provide the court with written evidence of their investigations; the distinction between the jurisdictions of the Quarter Sessions and the Assizes was
uncertain; benefit of clergy, while less restricted than in the early seventeenth
century, was more genuinely part of an ecclesiastical system of punishment.[8]

By 1800, roughly one hundred and fifty years after the terminal date of this
study, the crimes, the decision-makers, and the legal structure had changed
again. Crimes of property overwhelmed crimes of violence on the dockets of
most courts; a new notion of crime and criminality separated the law-abiding
from the law-breakers. The proportion of middling men had shrunk in many
places, although the survivors were wealthier and even more central to the
government than they had been in 1640. But the importance of such men was
greater outside the courtroom than inside; middling property holders were

---

ment and Society during the English Revolution (Oxford, 1974), pp. 1–31. On Worcestershire, see *Worcester County Records*, pp. iv–ccxxxiii; Silcock, "Worcestershire," *passim*.
The only other English jurisdiction for which extensive early documentation survives is
Middlesex. Although London and Middlesex were separate jurisdictions, even in the sixteenth century, the business of the courts in Middlesex had a decidedly urban flavor. Not
much has been written about Middlesex, but some of its records have been calendared and
published; *Middlesex County Records*, ed. J. F. C. Jeaffreson, 4 vols., Middlesex County
Record Society, 1886–92, and *County of Middlesex Calendar to the Sessions Records*, new
series, ed. W. Le Hardy, 4 vols., Middlesex County Record Society, 1935–41.

[8] Sharpe, *Crime in Early Modern England, passim*; Stone, "Interpersonal Violence"; Green,
Verdict, chs. 1–3; J. G. Bellamy, *Criminal Law and Society in Late Medieval and Tudor
England* (New York, 1984), *passim*; Langbein, *Prosecuting Crime*, chs. 4–5; Gabel,
Benefit of Clergy.

more prominent as prosecuting victims in the courts of the late eighteenth century than they had been earlier, but even petty gentlemen were less likely than they had been to be impaneled as grand jurors. New punishments matched the burst of new felonies; transportation and the growth of prisons revolutionized the old system of execution and mitigation. A smaller proportion of convicts was sentenced to hang in 1800 than in 1640, but a far larger proportion of those spared from the gallows suffered some other form of lasting punishment. The structure of enforcement in 1800 will be more familiar to modern readers than the system of a century and a half earlier; by 1800, felons used counsel, judges chose punishments from a range apart from execution, legal scholars discussed both how criminal trials should be conducted and the proper division of labor within the courtroom. The reliability of the case was replacing the reliability of the criminal as the central question in the trial process. The structure of enforcement in 1800 was more professional, more rational and more uniform than in 1640; whether it offered better justice is an open question.[9]

In the early seventeenth century, the procedures of the law frequently mixed ancient practices with innovations. Investigations combined echoes of the hue and cry with newer notions of the responsibilities of parochial officials; juries stood between their traditional role as local experts and a newer position as assessors of evidence; punishments provided a moral education for the public but also often offered felons a public chance at rehabilitation. But this was not a system harking back into the past or looking forward into the future; it was very much a system of its own place and time. The late sixteenth and early seventeenth centuries were years of economic tension at most levels of society; poor and rich alike felt the concurrent pressures of bad harvests, high inflation and increased governmental expenditures. Not surprisingly, such strains provoked an intense concern for order, and that concern is reflected in the high national rate of criminal prosecutions and capital convictions. Its influence can be seen as well in attempts to construct a system of relief, to broaden the role of the magistrate in the com-

---

[9] The literature on changes in society and in the law in the 150 years after 1640 is vast; some of the works most pertinent here include: Beattie, *Crime and the Courts*; Langbein, "The Criminal Trial before the Lawyers"; Hay, "War, Dearth and Theft"; Hay, "Property, Authority and the Criminal Law"; Norma Landau, *The Justices of the Peace 1679–1760* (Berkeley, 1984); Barbara Shapiro, *Probability and Certainty in Seventeenth-Century England* (Princeton, 1983), pp. 163–93; King, "Decision Makers and Decision Making"; Green, *Verdict*, chs. 7–8, and on developments concerning punishment see also Jenkins, "From Gallows to Prison?"; Michael Ignatieff, *A Just Measure of Pain: The Penitentiary in the Industrial Revolution 1750–1850* (New York, 1978); Margaret DeLacy, *Prison Reform in Lancashire 1750–1800* (Stanford, 1986); E. Roger Ekirch, *Bound for America: Convict Transportation, Crime and Society in the Eighteenth Century* (Oxford, forthcoming).

munity and to continue to reduce the use of benefit of clergy.[10] Inevitably, this last policy meant that for many felons the power of juries to return partial verdicts and the power of judges to recommend convicts for pardons replaced benefit of clergy as the major hope of mitigation.

This unintentional partnership of jurors and judges as mitigating parties was complicated by an economic irony; the inflationary pressures that brought misery to so many English men and women qualified a new range of modest property holders for legal authority. Men who would have been unable to meet property qualifications in 1500 and who would have been excluded by increased property qualifications in 1800, found themselves among the governing population in 1600. For many such men, the timing of this change was particularly propitious. Discretion had traditionally been considered a crucial component of justice in English law and the uses of discretion mirror the concerns of those who used it. For the period between 1590 and 1640, these concerns were intensely religious. Even minor parochial offices could seem a God-given opportunity to implement reform. The zeal for reform had different results in different settings, but everywhere it revealed a mix of worldliness and otherworldliness, of smugness and insecurity, of commonality and distance that belonged peculiarly to the late sixteenth and early seventeenth centuries.

Cockburn and Langbein have chronicled the efforts of both judges and privy councillors in the sixteenth and early seventeenth centuries to rationalize criminal procedure; the preceding chapters have analyzed both how and why such innovations were adopted, adapted, or resisted in eastern Sussex. Since any innovation affected such a wide variety of people, most attempts brought tension rather than simply change and, because so many influences could inspire change, the system of enforcement was always a system in transition. But the story of criminal enforcement in eastern Sussex has implications beyond the history of the legal system. It deepens our understanding of the responses to the Civil War and Revolution that broke across England in the 1640s and 1650s because it reveals something of men's expectations and experiences of administration. It adds nuance to our idea of how Puritanism translated into daily life and how the cooling of that activism changed local governance. It offers a picture of social relations in a shire less industrialized, less urbanized, and less polarized than its more frequently studied fellows in the southeastern part of England. But, most importantly, it shows how the legal system exemplifies the participatory nature of English government in the seventeenth century. Effective government could not do without the willingness of men to act as agents of central institutions. Ruling

[10] Sharpe, *Crime in Early Modern England*, chs. 3 and 8. On efforts to provide relief, see Beier, *Masterless Men*, ch. 9; Slack, "Poverty and Politics in Salisbury"; Pound, *Poverty, passim.*

was a repeated exercise in compromise, cooperation and cooptation because, in the absence of a large salaried bureaucracy, the need for participation set strict limits on the capabilities of administration. The amorphous collection of modest property holders who made up the middling sort in the late sixteenth and early seventeenth centuries were not only the jurors and the constables and the victims and the witnesses who were key to any court; they were also the churchwardens and the assessors and the freeholders who were key to the business of the parish, to the collection of taxes and to the winning of elections. The early seventeenth century was a time of great opportunities and great burdens for such men, but, by the 1630s, interference from Westminster threatened to restrict much of the freedom in that responsibility. Men of modest property found themselves scrutinized as churchwardens by agents of Archbishop Laud, bypassed as assessors by royal appointees and disciplined as militia members by professional soldiers. The prosopographical and substantial changes evident in the Assizes in eastern Sussex in the 1630s suggest a parallel disruption. An additional peculiarity of the late-sixteenth- and early-seventeenth-century legal structure may be that middling men found themselves both newly active in the legal process and newly threatened in their activism.

In the first half of the seventeenth century, the lessons of the law revealed the commonality of men as well as the deference due to those with economic power and, as long as that was so, the maintenance of two levels of the law and two levels of criminality reinforced the strength of the legal system. In a society where many of the propertied considered life to be a test that most individuals must fail, discretion was the necessary link between law and justice and the moral foundations of the law constrained as well as inspired the men whose decisions determined punishment. In most places, the intimacy of these relationships did not survive the seventeenth century; the gap between victim and sinner grew into a chasm. New ideals of social responsibility emerged, but they were based upon the distance between the privileged and the unprivileged rather than upon their similarities. Inevitably, new standards for enforcing the law arose to suit the new complexion of society. Just as inevitably, they changed the meaning of the common peace.

APPENDIX 1

Summary of sampled courts*

Time	Quarter Sessions	Assizes
Elizabethan	Epiphany 1594–Michaelmas 1595 6 courts/128 cases	Winter 1592–Summer 1597 11 courts/327 cases
Jacobean	Easter 1614–Epiphany 1618 10 courts/236 cases	Summer 1613–Winter 1618 8 courts/147 cases
Transitional	Easter 1625–Epiphany 1628 11 courts/415 cases	Winter 1623–Summer 1629 9 courts/223 cases
Caroline	Easter 1636–Trinity 1640 18 courts/662 cases	Winter 1634–Summer 1640 14 courts/274 cases
Total	45 courts/1,441 cases	42 courts/971 cases

*A full listing of the extant files for eastern Sussex can be found in Herrup, diss., Appendix 1, pp. 406–11.
Source: Assize 35 files, Public Record Office; Quarter Sessions files, East Sussex Record Office, West Sussex Record Office.

APPENDIX 2

Status categories

In general, the categorizations shown below follow those laid out by R. H. and A. J. Tawney in their essay on seventeenth-century occupations.[1] But it must be remembered that the only constant in the social structure of early modern England seems to be its rich local variation over both time and space. These categories would be most useful as part of a statistical description of the social structure of individual communities in eastern Sussex, but such a project is fraught with difficulties. No contemporary local analysis tying status to population exists, and modern analyses favor the more concrete categories of income or tenurial status to the vaguer labels of social position. The accuracy as well as the local applicability of contemporary national descriptions are, as a result, questionable.[2]

Another book would be necessary to delve fully into the complexities of the social structure in eastern Sussex; all that can be attempted here is a summary of some of the information most pertinent to legal administration. Population density in the region varied widely, with the least populous parishes in the Downs and the densest concentrations of people in the Weald. The eighty-one parishes for which the ecclesiastical returns of 1603 survive show adult communicants ranging per parish from eight (at East Aldrington, in the Downs) to six hundred (at Heathfield, in the Weald). Since parishes were not uniform in geographical size, Colin Brent has used the more complete 1676 ecclesiastical census to plot the number of adults per square mile for 121 rural parishes, and his figures show a range of from fewer than ten adults per square mile at several places in the Downs or the Marshlands to more than eighty adults per square mile at several parishes in the Weald. The average distribution was twenty-nine adults per square mile.[3]

But how many of those adults, roughly half of them male, were part of any

---

[1] "An Occupational Census of the Seventeenth Century," R. H. Tawney and A. J. Tawney, *EcHR* 5 (1934): 25–64.

[2] The best recent discussions of the social structure in early modern England can be found in Wrightson, *English Society*, ch. 1, and in Palliser, *The Age of Elizabeth*, ch. 3.

[3] "Ecclesiastical Returns"; Brent, "Employment," Table 9.

specific social grouping? As a general rule, men farming more than fifty acres may be classified as yeomen, men farming between five and fifty acres may be classified as husbandmen, and men with more modest holdings may be classified as laborers. Distinctions of acreage, rather than of tenure, seem to have dictated local status as well as official obligations. Analyzing 953 holdings on eighteen Wealden manors, Brent found the breakdown of acreage between 1567–1650 to be:

101 acres or more	8%
51–100 acres	12%
21–50 acres	22%
5–20 acres	27%
4 acres or less	30%
Unknown	1%
	100%

This distribution complements the earlier findings of Julian Cornwall for eastern and western Sussex as well as estimates made in other counties.[4]

Crudely, this suggests that in a parish with one hundred resident male landholders, probably at least half would qualify to serve as constables and jurors (as well as in a variety of positions not connected with the courts). To have a true estimate of eligibility, however, one would need to know not only local customs concerning office, but also how many male adults held no land, how many had some exemption from official obligations, and how many of the landholders were absentees. Nevertheless, this rough estimate provided by Brent's investigations is reinforced by what we know about the moveable wealth of yeomen and husbandmen in seventeenth-century Sussex. In his survey of inventories, Julian Cornwall found that 65 percent of the yeomen and 24 percent of the husbandmen left estates valued at more than one hundred pounds; Brent found similar evidence of affluence among 27 percent of those surveyed in the Downs, and among 14 percent of those surveyed in the Weald. The equation of acreage and office is far too simple, but it does roughly accord with at least some observed patterns of participation.[5]

It is even more difficult to estimate the proportion of established members of the non-agricultural community. The line between trade and farming was an exceptionally fluid one; even in Lewes in the early seventeenth century, about one third of the residents were involved in farming. Without an exten-

---

[4] Brent, "Employment," Tables 34–6; Cornwall, "Sussex," Table 2; Wrightson, *English Society*, pp. 31–2; Palliser, *The Age of Elizabeth*, pp. 71–2, 174–5.
[5] Cornwall, "Sussex," p. 361; Brent, "Employment," pp. 232–5; see also Palliser, *The Age of Elizabeth*, Table 4.2.

sive study of probate or taxation records, there is no guide to help distinguish the successful businessman from his less established colleague. Some information on the distribution of trades in eastern Sussex, however, provides information on the broader category of the non-agricultural occupations. G. Cowley used marriage licenses and wills to analyze the occupations of 629 residents of Lewes between 1586 and 1636; he divided their occupations as follows:

agriculture	31%
cloth and leather	26%
food and drink	16%
retail	12%
building	5%
professions	3%
miscellaneous	7%
	100%

The occupations most regularly cited, in descending order of importance, were: farmer, tailor, cordwainer, innholder, butcher, mercer, saddler, weaver, blacksmith, draper, merchant, grocer, haberdasher and vintner. Brent used a slightly more varied group of records to analyze the distribution of trades in rural eastern Sussex in the early seventeenth century. The pattern he discovered was less diverse than the one in Lewes, but its outlines were generally the same; among individuals whose living did not rely primarily on agriculture, occupations involving cloth and leather were the most numerous, followed by those concerned with food and drink, retailing, and construction. The most frequently mentioned specific occupations were weaving, butchering, tanning and making gloves.[6]

[6] Cowley, "Sussex Market Towns," p. 188; Brent, "Employment," Table 20.

Status category	Definition
Gentlemen	persons identified as esquires, gentlemen, clerics, peers, or barbers
Yeomen	persons identified as yeomen
Husbandmen	persons identified as husbandmen
Laborers	persons identified as laborers, shepherds, gardeners, soldiers, sailors or coachmen
Legal officers	persons identified as bailiffs, jailers, constables, headboros, justices of the peace, parish clerks, warreners, or informers
Women	persons identified as spinsters, widows, or wives
Non-agricultural	cloth and leather: persons identified as weavers, cloth-workers, shearmen, fullers, hempdressers, tanners, curriers, collarmakers, saddlers, sheathmakers, or cordwainers
	iron: persons identified as pinners, colliers, smiths, founders, forgemen, finers, hammermen, metalmen, edgetoolmakers, or gunsmiths
	building: persons identified as coopers, carpenters, joiners, shipwrights, wheelwrights, sawyers, masons, shinglers, bricklayers, glaziers, thatchers, millwrights, or stone-healers
	food and drink: persons identified as butchers, bakers, brewers, rippiers, millers, vintners, victuallers, innkeepers, or tipplers
	retail: persons identified as shoemakers, tailors, glovers, hosiers, drapers, mercers, chandlers, ladlemakers, pewterers, tinkers, or petty chapmen
Other	persons identified as masters, paupers, children, musicians, diviners, lightermen, lunatics, fletchers, carriers, or lime-burners

BIBLIOGRAPHY

MANUSCRIPTS

Bodleian Library, Oxford
    Rawlinson MS B431 Precedent Book of a Sussex JP, 1630s
      MS D399 Exhortation to Condemned Thieves (fos. 193–4)
      MS D720 Charge of Ld Keeper Finch, 1640 (fos. 36–53)
    Tanner MS 76/18 Privy Council Order Sending Felons to the Galleys, 1602
      (fo. 160)
      MS 233/7 Reasons against Punishing Crimes by Death (fo. 134)
      MS 288/18 Queries between the JPs and Judges at the Norfolk Assizes, 1632
      (fos. 266–71)
British Library, London
    Additional MS 11,571 Dr Burton's Journey Through Sussex, 1751 (fos. 116–22)
      MS 12,496 Book of Orders (fos. 262–91)
      MS 23,007 Orders for Setting up Meetings of Divisions (fos. 38–41)
      MS 33,058 Pelham Correspondence, 1642–5
      MS 33,145 Pelham Accounts, 1620s
      MS 33,174–7 Pelham Court Books
      MS 38,139 Liber Pacis, 1604 (fos. 159v–160v)
    Harleian MS 38 Treatise Concerning and a General Description of the Nobility
      According to the Laws of England
      MS 703 Sir Walter Covert's Letter Book
      MS 1603 Early Seventeenth-Century Notes on Common Law
    Lansdowne MS 49 The Course of the Assizes, 1586 (fos. 59–60)
      MS 53 Report on JPs, 1596
      MS 72 Justice Popham's Views on the Punishment of Recusancy (fo. 41)
      MS 160 Charges of Ld Bacon (fos. 81–2v, 331–2)
      MS 569 A Collection of Law Tracts
      MS 1218 Liber Pacis, 1559, 1561 (fos. 29v–30v, 80v–81, 90–2)
East Sussex Record Office, Lewes
    ABER 1–3 Manorial Records
    Accession 2189 Lewes Gaol Petition, 1579
    ADA MSS 56; 73; 143; 157 Sackville Court Books
    BT XE 1/302/2 Bishop's Transcript of the Parish Register of Dallington
    Dyke Hutton 1121–3 Court Rolls, Lewes Borough
    FRE MS 520 John Everenden's Account Book
    FRE MS 4223 Samuel Jeake's Letter Book

Index of ecclesiastical deponents
PAR 372/1/1/1 Parish Register of Heathfield
QCP/EW4 Statement Respecting the Ancient Custom of Dividing Sussex, 1853
QI/EW1 Quarter Sessions Indictment Book, 1620s
Q/R/E 1–50 Quarter Sessions files
SAS MSS 19F; RA/70–5 Misc. Court Books of Ld Dorset
W/A7–28 Registers of Wills, Archdeaconry of Lewes
Kent Archives Office, Maidstone
Sackville MSS
U522/04 Recognizance Book, Sir Thomas Walsingham, 1638–44
Public Record Office, London
ASSI 35 Home Circuit Assize files
ASSI 45/1/1 Northeastern Circuit Depositions
C 66 Chancery, Patent Rolls
C 231/1–5 Chancery, Crown Docket Books
E 101 Exchequer, Sheriff's Accounts
E 137 Exchequer, Estreats
E 178 Exchequer, Special Commissions
E 179 Exchequer, Subsidies
E 215 Exchequer, Commission on Fees
E 368 Exchequer, Memoranda Rolls
KB 9 King's Bench, Ancient Indictments
PROB 11 Wills, Prerogative Court of Canterbury
SP 12; 14; 16 State Papers, Elizabeth I, James I, Charles I
STAC 8 Star Chamber files, James I
West Sussex Record Office, Chichester
Ep II/5/3–17 Deposition Books, Archdeaconry of Lewes, 1547–1641
Ep II/9/7–23 Detection Books, Archdeaconry of Lewes, 1593–1639
Ep II/10/1–3 Roll Call of Visitations of Clergy and Churchwardens, 1600–41
PAR 301/7/2 Parish Book, Cuckfield
Q/R/WE16; 31 Quarter Sessions files
STC I–III Consistory Court, Wills and Inventories

PRINTED SOURCES

Acts of the Privy Council 1542–1628. ed. John Roche Dasant. 43 vols. London, 1890–1949.

Alumni Cantabrigienses. 10 vols. eds. and comps. J. and J. A. Venn. Cambridge, 1922–54.

Alumni Oxonienses 1500–1714. ed. and comp. J. Foster. 4 vols. Oxford, 1891–2.

Babington, Zachary. *Advice to Grand Jurors in Cases of Blood.* London, 1677.

Bernard, Richard. *A Guide to Grand Jury Men, Divided into Two Books.* London, 1627.

Beverley Borough Records 1575–1821. ed. J. Dennett. Yorkshire Archaeological Society Record Series 84 (1933).

The Book of John Rowe. ed. W. H. Godfrey. *SRS* 34. Lewes, 1928.

Brinkelow, Henry. *The Complaint of Roderick Mors . . .* London, 1548.

Bullein, William, "A Dialogue against the Pestilence" in *Everyone a Witness: The Tudor Age.* comp. A. F. Scott. New York, 1977.

Calendar of Assize Records: Home Circuit Indictments. Elizabeth I and James I. ed. J. S. Cockburn. 11 vols. London, 1975–85.

Calendar of State Papers. Domestic. ed. M. A. E. Green. 11 vols. (to 1625). London, 1857–72. ed. John Bruce. 23 vols. (to 1649). London, 1858–97.

Calendar of Sussex Marriage Licences Recorded in the Consistory Court of the Bishop of Chichester for the Archdeaconry of Lewes August 1586 to March 1642/3. ed. E. H. W. Dunkin. SRS 1. Lewes, 1902.

Camden, William. *Camden's Britannia: Surrey and Sussex.* ed. Gordon J. Copley. London, 1977.

Coke, Sir Edward. *The Lord Coke, his Speech and Charge.* London, 1607.
   The Third Part of the Institutes of the Laws of England: Concerning High Treason and Other Pleas of the Crown and Criminal Causes . . . London, 1644.

The Constables' Accounts of the Manor of Manchester from the Year 1612 to the Year 1647 and from the Year 1743 to the Year 1796. ed. J. P. Earwaker. 2 vols. Manchester, 1891–2.

County of Middlesex. Calendar to the Sessions Records, new series. ed. William Le Hardy. 4 vols. Middlesex County Record Society. 1935–41.

Dalton, Michael. *The Countrey Justice.* 5th ed. London, 1635.
   The Office and Authority of Sheriffs. 2nd ed. London, 1628.

Defoe, Daniel. *A Tour through the Whole Island of England and Wales, 1722.* London, 1927.

Depositions from the Castle of York Relating to Offences Committed in the Northern Counties in the Seventeenth Century. ed. James Raine, Jr. Surtees Society 40 (1861).

The Diary of Ralph Josselin 1616–1683. ed. Alan Macfarlane. British Academy, Records of Social and Economic History. new series, 3 (1976).

"The Diary of Robert Beake, Mayor of Coventry, 1655–1656." ed. Levi Fox. Dugdale Society, *Miscellany.* ed. Robert Bearman. 1 (1977): 111–37.

E., T. *The Law's Resolution of Women's Rights: Or the Law's Provision for Women.* London, 1632.

"Ecclesiastical Returns for 81 Parishes in East Sussex Made in 1603." ed. Walter C. Renshaw. SRS 4. Lewes, 1905: 1–17.

The Elizabethan Underworld. ed. A. V. Judges. London, 1930.

England as Seen by Foreigners in the Days of Elizabeth and James I, with Extracts from the Travels of Foreign Princes and Others. ed. W. B. Rye. reprint. New York, 1967.

Eyre, Adam. "A Diurnall or Catalogue of all my Accions and Expences from the 1st of January 1646." ed. H. J. Morehouse in *Yorkshire Diaries and Autobiographies in the Seventeenth and Eighteenth Centuries.* Surtees Society 65 (1875): 1–118.

Fortescue, Sir John. *Learned Commendation of the Political Laws of England.* London, 1567.

Gough, Richard. *The History of Myddle.* ed. David Hey. Harmondsworth, 1981.

A Guide to Juries: Setting forth their Antiquity, Power and Duty, from the Common Law and Statutes . . . London, 1699.

The Harleian Miscellany. ed. W. Oldys. 12 vols. London, 1808–11.

Harrison, William. *The Description of England.* ed. George Edelen. Ithaca, 1968.

Hawarde, John. *Les Reportes del Cases in Camera Stellata 1593 to 1609.* ed. W. P. Baildon. London, 1894.

Hawles, Sir John. *The Englishman's Right: A Dialogue Between a Barrister at Law and a Juryman.* London, 1732.

Hext, Edward. "To Burghley on the Increase of Rogues and Vagabonds" in *Tudor Economic Documents.* eds. R. H. Tawney and Eileen Power. III. London, 1924: 339–46.

An Homily against Disobedience and Wilful Rebellion. London, 1571.

Jonson, Ben, Chapman, George, and Marston, John. *Eastward Ho!.* ed. C. G. Petter. London, 1973.

Journal of Nicholas Assheton of Downham . . . ed. F. R. Raines. Chetham Society. old series, 14. Manchester, 1848.

Kitchin, John. *Jurisdictions or the Lawful Authority of Courts Leet, Courts Baron, Court of Marshalsea, Court of Piepowder and Ancient Demesne.* London, 1651.

Lambard, William. *The Duties of Constables, Borsholders, Tithingmen and Suche Other Lowe Ministers of the Peace.* London, 1591.

Eirenarcha, or of the Office of the Justice of the Peace in Four Books. London, 1591.

The Letters and the Life of Francis Bacon . . . comp. James Spedding. 6 vols. London, 1872.

The Life of Adam Martindale Written by Himself. ed. Richard Parkinson, Chetham Society, old series, 4. Manchester, 1845.

List and Index to the Proceedings in Star Chamber for the Reign of James I (1603–1625) in the Public Record Office, London, Class STAC 8. comp. and ed. Thomas G. Barnes and the staff of the Legal History Project. 3 vols. Chicago, 1975.

Middlesex County Records. ed. J. F. C. Jeaffreson. 4 vols. Middlesex County Record Society. London, 1886–92.

Minutes of Proceedings in the Quarter Sessions Held for the Parts of Kesteven in the County of Lincoln 1674–1695. ed. S. A. Peyton. Lincoln Record Society 25–6. Lincoln, 1931.

More, Sir Thomas. *Utopia.* Complete Works, IV. eds. Edward Surtz, SJ, and J. H. Hexter. New Haven, 1964.

"Notebook of a Surrey Justice." ed. Granville Leveson-Gower. Surrey Archeological Collections 9. London, 1888: 161–232.

The Official Papers of Sir Nathaniel Bacon of Stiffkey, Norfolk, as Justice of the Peace 1580–1620. ed. H. W. Saunders. Camden Society. 3rd series, 26. London, 1915.

The Parish Register of Brighton in the County of Sussex 1558–1701. ed. Henry D. Roberts. Brighton, 1932.

The Parish Register of East Grinstead 1558–1661. ed. R. P. Crawfurd. SRS 24. Lewes, 1917.

The Parish Registers of Cuckfield, Sussex 1598–1699. ed. W. C. Renshaw. SRS 13. Lewes, 1911.

Parliamentary Debates. Commons. 5th series, vol. 261 (2 Feb.–19 Feb.) 1932. London: Her Majesty's Stationery Office.

Quarter Sessions Indictment Book, Easter, 1631 to Epiphany, 1674. eds. S. C. Ratcliff and H. C. Johnson. Warwick County Records 6. Warwick, 1941.

Quarter Sessions Order Book 1642–1649. ed. B. C. Redwood. SRS 54. Lewes, 1954.

The Records of the Honourable Society of Lincoln's Inn: Admissions. ed. W. P. Baildon. 2 vols. London, 1896.

A Register of Admissions to Gray's Inn 1521–1889 . . . ed. J. Foster. London, 1889.

Register of Admissions to the Honourable Society of the Middle Temple from the Fifteenth Century to the Year 1944. ed. H. A. C. Sturgess. 3 vols. London, 1949.

"A Relation of a Short Survey of the Western Counties Made by a Lieutenant of the Military Company in Norwich in 1635." ed. L. G. Wickham Legg. Camden Society. 3rd series, 52, *Miscellany* 16 (1936).

"A Religious Census of Sussex in 1676." ed. J. H. Cooper. *SAC* 45 (1902): 142–8.

The Reports of Sir John Spelman. ed. J. H. Baker. Selden Society 93–4. London, 1977–8.

Royal Proclamations of King James I 1603–1625. ed. James F. Larkin and Paul L. Hughes. Oxford, 1973.

A Royalist's Notebook: The Commonplace Book of Sir John Oglander, Kt of Nunwell . . . ed. Francis Bamford. London, 1936.

Smith, Sir Thomas. *De Republica Anglorum.* London, 1609.

Somerset Assize Orders 1629–1640. ed. Thomas G. Barnes. Somerset Record Society 66. London, 1959.

Somerset Assize Orders 1640–1659. ed. J. S. Cockburn. Somerset Record Society 72. London, 1971.

The Staffordshire Quarter Sessions Rolls. ed. S. A. H. Burne. William Salt Archaeological Society 53–4, 56, 59, 64, 70. Kendal, 1931–3, 1936, 1940, 1950.

Statutes of the Realm. 9 vols. London, 1810–22.

Students Admitted to the Inner Temple 1547–1660. ed. W. H. Cooke. London, 1878.

The Visitation of Sussex, Anno Domini 1662 . . . ed. and ann. A. W. Hughes Clarke. Harleian Society 89. London, 1937.

The Visitations of the County of Sussex . . . 1530 and 1633/4. ed. W. Bruce Bannerman. Harleian Society 53. London, 1905.

W., T. *The Office of the Clerk of the Assize . . .* London, 1676.

Western Circuit Assize Orders 1629–1648: A Calendar. ed. J. S. Cockburn. Camden Society. 4th series, 17. London, 1976.

The Wigginton Constable's Book 1691–1836. ed. F. D. Price. Banbury Historical Society 11. Chichester, 1971.

William Lambarde and Local Government: His "Ephemeris" and Twenty-Nine Charges to Juries and Commissions. ed. Conyers Read, Ithaca, 1962.

Wilson, Thomas. *A Discourse upon Usury . . .* ed. and intro. R. H. Tawney. New York, 1925.

Worcester County Records. Calendar of Quarter Sessions Papers 1591–1643. ed. J. W. Willis Bund. 2 vols. Worcestershire County Records, 11 and 12. Worcester, 1899–1900.

SECONDARY WORKS

Albery, William. *A Millennium of Facts in the History of Horsham and Sussex 947–1947.* Horsham, 1947.

Baker, J. H. *An Introduction to English Legal History.* 2nd ed. London, 1979.

Barnes, Thomas G. *Somerset 1625–40: A County's Government during the "Personal Rule".* Cambridge, Mass., 1961.

Barnes, Thomas, G., and Hassell Smith, A. "Justices of the Peace from 1558 to 1668: A Revised List of Sources." *BIHR* 32 (1959): 221–42.

Beattie, J. M. *Crime and the Courts in England 1660–1800.* Princeton, 1986.

"The Pattern of Crime in England 1660–1800." *P & P* 62 (February 1974): 47–95.

"Towards a Study of Crime in Eighteenth Century England: A Note on Indictments" in Paul Fritz and David Williams, eds. *The Triumph of Culture: Eighteenth Century Perspectives*. Toronto, 1972: 299–314.

Beier, A. L. *Masterless Men: The Vagrancy Problem in England 1560–1640*. London, 1985.

"Poor Relief in Warwickshire, 1630–1660." *P & P* 35 (December, 1966), 77–100.

Bellamy, John G. *Criminal Law and Society in Late Medieval and Tudor England*. New York, 1984.

Blackstone, Sir William. *Commentaries on the Laws of England*. 4 vols. Chicago, 1979.

Blatcher, Marjorie. *The Court of King's Bench 1450–1550: A Study in Self-Help*. London, 1978.

Brent, Colin. "Devastating Epidemic in the Countryside of Eastern Sussex between Harvest Years 1558 and 1640." *LPS* 14 (Spring, 1975): 42–8.

"Employment, Land Tenure and Population in Eastern Sussex 1540–1640." Ph.D. diss. University of Sussex, 1973.

Brewer, John, and Styles, John, eds. *An Ungovernable People: The English and their Law in the Seventeenth and Eighteenth Centuries*. London, 1980.

Campbell, Mildred. *The English Yeoman under Elizabeth and the Early Stuarts*. reprint. New York, 1968.

Chartres, J. A. "Road Carrying in England in the Seventeenth Century: Myth and Reality," *EcHR*. 2nd series, 30 (1977): 73–94; 33 (1980): 92–9.

Clark, Peter. *The English Alehouse: A Social History 1200–1830*. London, 1983.

English Provincial Society from the Reformation to the Revolution: Religion, Politics and Society in Kent 1500–1640. Rutherford, NJ, 1977.

"Popular Protest and Disturbance in Kent 1558–1640." *EcHR*. 2nd series, 29 (1976): 365–81.

Cockburn, J. S., ed. *Crime in England 1550–1800*. London, 1977.

"Early Modern Assize Records as Historical Evidence." *Journal of the Society of Archivists*, 5 (1975): 215–31.

A History of English Assizes 1558–1714. Cambridge, 1972.

"Trial by the Book: Fact and Theory in the Criminal Process 1558–1625" in J. H. Baker, ed. *Legal Records and the Historian*. London, 1978: 60–79.

Collinson, Patrick. *The Religion of Protestants: The Church in English Society 1559–1625*. Oxford, 1982.

Cooper, W. V. *A History of the Parish of Cuckfield*. Hayward's Heath, 1912.

Cornwall, Julian. "The Agrarian History of Sussex, 1560–1640," M.A. thesis. University of London, 1953.

Cowley, G. O. "Sussex Market Towns 1550–1750." M.A. thesis. University of London, 1965.

Cressy, David. *Literacy and the Social Order: Reading and Writing in Tudor and Stuart England*. Cambridge, 1980.

Curtis, T. C. "Some Aspects of the History of Crime in Seventeenth-Century England with Special Reference to Cheshire and Middlesex." Ph.D. diss. Manchester University, 1973.

Cust, Richard, and Lake, Peter G. "Sir Richard Grosvenor and the Rhetoric of Magistracy." *BIHR* 54 (1981), 40–53.

DeLacy, Margaret. *Prison Reform in Lancashire 1750–1800*. Stanford, 1986.

Ekirch, E. Roger. *Bound for America: Convict Transportation, Crime and Society in the Eighteenth Century*. Oxford, forthcoming.

Erikson. Kai. *Wayward Puritans: A Study in the Sociology of Deviance*. New York, 1966.

Erredge, J. A. *History of Brighthelmston*. Brighton, 1862.

Faller, Lincoln B. *Thieves and Murderers Turn'd to Account: The Forms and Functions of Criminal Biography in Late Seventeenth and Early Eighteenth-Century England*. Cambridge, forthcoming.

Farrant, John and Sue. "Brighton 1580–1820: From Tudor Town to Regency Resort." *SAC* 118 (1980): 331–50.

Fisher, F. J. "The Development of the London Food Market 1540–1640." *EcHR*, 5: 2 (April, 1935): 46–64.

Fletcher, Anthony J. *A County Community in Peace and War: Sussex 1600–1660*. London, 1975.

    The Outbreak of the English Civil War. New York, 1981.

    Puritanism in Seventeenth-Century Sussex. Studies in Sussex Church History, 1. London, 1981.

Fletcher, Anthony J., and Stevenson, John, eds. *Order and Disorder in Early Modern England*. Cambridge, 1985.

Fuller, G. Joan. "A Geographical Study of the Development of Roads through the Surrey and Sussex Weald to the South Coast, during the period 1700–1900." Ph.D. diss. University of London, 1950.

Gabel, Leona C. *Benefit of Clergy in England in the Later Middle Ages* in S. B. Fay and H. U. Faulkner, eds. Smith College Studies in History 14, 1928–9.

Gatrell, V. A. C., Lenman, Bruce, and Parker, Geoffrey, eds. *Crime and the Law: The Social History of Crime in Western Europe since 1500*. London, 1980.

Given, James Buchanan. *Society and Homicide in Thirteenth-Century England*. Stanford, 1977.

Gleason, John H. *The Justices of the Peace in England 1558–1640: A Later Eirenarcha*. Oxford, 1969.

Goebel, Julius, and Naughton, T. R. *Law Enforcement in Colonial New York: A Study in Criminal Procedure 1664–1776*. New York, 1944.

Goring, Jeremy. "The Expansion of the Sussex Gentry 1525–1600." *Sussex Family Historian* 5 (1982): 76–86.

    "The Fellowship of the Twelve in Elizabethan Lewes." *SAC* 119 (1981): 157–72.

Green, Thomas A. "The Jury and the English Law of Homicide 1200–1600." *Michigan Law Review* 74 (1976): 414–99.

    Verdict According to Conscience: Perspectives on the English Criminal Trial Jury 1200–1800. Chicago, 1985.

Hammer, Carl I. "Patterns of Homicide in a Medieval University Town: Fourteenth Century Oxford." *P & P* 78 (February, 1978): 3–23.

Hanawalt, Barbara A. *Crime and Conflict in English Communities 1300–1348*. Cambridge, Mass., 1979.

Hassell Smith, Alan. *County and Court: Government and Politics in Norfolk 1558–1603*. Oxford, 1974.

    "The Elizabethan Gentry of Norfolk: Officeholding and Faction." Ph.D. diss. University of London, 1959.

Hay, Douglas. "Property, Authority and the Criminal Law" in Douglas Hay, Peter Linebaugh, John G. Rule, E. P. Thompson and Cal Winslow, eds. *Albion's Fatal Tree: Crime and Society in Eighteenth-Century England*. New York, 1975: 17–63.

    "War, Dearth and Theft in the Eighteenth Century: The Record of the English Courts." *P & P* 95 (May, 1982): 117–60.

Helmholz, R. H. "The Early History of the Grand Jury and the Canon Law." *The University of Chicago Law Review* 50 (1983): 613–27.

Herrup, Cynthia Brilliant. "The Common Peace: Legal Structure and Legal Substance in East Sussex 1592–1640." Ph.D. diss. Northwestern University, 1982.

"The Counties and the Country: Some Thoughts on Seventeenth Century Historiography." *Social History* 8 (1983): 169–81.

"Law and Morality in Seventeenth Century England." *P & P* 106 (February, 1985): 102–23.

Hill, Christopher. *Society and Puritanism in Pre-Revolutionary England.* 2nd ed. New York, 1967.

The World Turned Upside Down: Radical Ideas during the English Revolution. New York, 1975.

Hirst, Derek. "Court, Country and Politics before 1629" in K. Sharpe, ed. *Faction and Parliament: Essays on Early Stuart History.* Oxford, 1978: 105–37.

The Representative of the People?: Voters and Voting in England under the Early Stuarts. Cambridge, 1975.

Hoffer, Peter C., and Hull, N. E. H. *Murdering Mothers: Infanticide in England and New England 1558–1803.* New York, 1981.

Holmes, Clive. "The County Community in Stuart Historiography." *JBS* 19: 2 (Spring, 1980): 54–73.

Seventeenth-Century Lincolnshire. History of Lincolnshire 7. Lincoln, 1980.

Holmes, Oliver Wendall. *The Common Law.* ed. Mark DeWolfe Howe. Cambridge, Mass., 1963.

Horsfield, T. W. *The History and Antiquities of Lewes and its Vicinity.* 2 vols. Lewes, 1824–7.

The History, Antiquities and Topography of the County of Sussex. 2 vols. London, 1835.

Hughes, Ann Laura. "Politics, Society and Civil War in Warwickshire 1620–1650." Ph.D. diss. University of Liverpool, 1979.

Hunt, William. *The Puritan Moment: The Coming of Revolution in an English County.* Cambridge, Mass., 1983.

Hurstfield, Joel. "County Government: Wiltshire c.1530–c.1660" reprinted in Hurstfield, *Freedom, Corruption and Government in Elizabethan England.* Cambridge, Mass., 1973: 236–93.

Ignatieff, Michael. *A Just Measure of Pain: The Penitentiary in the Industrial Revolution 1750–1850.* New York, 1978.

Illich, Ivan. *Deschooling Society.* Harmondsworth, 1971.

Ingram, M. J. "Ecclesiastical Justice in Wiltshire 1600–1640 with Special Reference to Cases Concerning Sex and Marriage." D.Phil. diss. Oxford University, 1976.

Isaac, Rhys. *The Transformation of Virginia.* Chapel Hill, 1982.

James, Mervyn. *Family, Lineage and Civil Society: A Study of Society, Politics and Mentality in the Durham Region 1500–1640.* Oxford, 1974.

Jenkins, Philip. "From Gallows to Prison? The Execution Rate in Early Modern England." Unpublished paper, 1985.

Kent, Joan. "Attitudes of Members of the House of Commons to the Regulation of 'Personal Conduct' in Late Elizabethan and Early Stuart England." *BIHR* 46 (1973): 41–71.

"The English Village Constable 1580–1642: The Nature and Dilemmas of the Office." *JBS* 20: 2 (Spring, 1981): 26–49.

King, P. J. R. "Decision Makers and Decision Making in the English Criminal Law, 1750–1800." *HJ* 27 (1984): 25–58.

King, Walter J. "Prosecution of Illegal Behavior in Seventeenth Century England with Emphasis on Lancashire." Ph.D. diss. University of Michigan, 1977.

Knafla, Louis A., ed. *Crime and Criminal Justice in Europe and Canada*. Calgary, 1981.

Kussmaul, Ann. *Servants in Husbandry in Early Modern England*. Cambridge, 1981.

Landau, Norma. *The Justices of the Peace 1679–1760*. Berkeley, 1984.

Langbein, John H. "*Albion*'s Fatal Flaws." *P & P* 98 (February, 1983): 96–120.

"The Criminal Trial before the Lawyers." *University of Chicago Law Review* 45 (1978): 263–316.

Prosecuting Crime in the Renaissance: England, Germany, France. Cambridge, Mass., 1974.

Larminie, V. M. *The Godly Magistrate: The Private Philosophy and Public Life of Sir John Newdigate 1571–1610*. Dugdale Society. Occasional Papers 28. Oxford, 1982.

Larner, Christina. *Enemies of God: The Witch-hunt in Scotland*. London, 1981.

Lawson, Peter G. "Crime and the Administration of Criminal Justice in Hertfordshire 1580–1625." D.Phil. diss. Oxford University, 1982.

Leppard, M. J. "Replies. East Grinstead Assizes III." *Sussex Notes and Queries* 17 (1969): 130–1.

Macfarlane, Alan. *The Justice and the Mare's Ale: Law and Disorder in Seventeenth-Century England*. Cambridge, 1981.

Review of J. S. Cockburn, ed. *Calendar of Assize Records: Essex Indictments Elizabeth I*. *The American Journal of Legal History* 24 (1980): 171–8.

Witchcraft in Tudor and Stuart England: A Regional and Comparative Study. New York, 1970.

Manning, Brian. *The English People and the English Revolution 1640–1649*. London, 1976.

Manning, Roger B. *Religion and Society in Elizabethan Sussex: A Study of the Enforcement of the Religious Settlement 1559–1603*. Leicester, 1969.

Marchant, R. A. *The Church under the Law: Justice, Administration and Discipline in the Diocese of York 1560–1640*. Cambridge, 1969.

Meynell, Esther. *Sussex*. London, 1947.

Milsom, S. F. C. *Historical Foundations of the Common Law*. 1st ed. London, 1969. 2nd ed. London, 1981.

Morrill, J. S. "The Army Revolt in 1647" in A. C. Duke and C. A. Tamse, eds. *War and Society: Papers Delivered to the 6th Anglo-Dutch Historical Conference*. Britain and the Netherlands, 6. The Hague, 1977: 54–78.

Cheshire 1630–1660: County Government and Society during the English Revolution. Oxford, 1974.

The Cheshire Grand Jury 1625–49: A Social and Administrative Study. Leicester, 1976.

The Revolt of the Provinces: Conservatives and Radicals in the English Civil War 1630–1650. 2nd ed. London, 1980.

Mousley, Joyce. "Sussex Country Gentry in the Reign of Elizabeth I." Ph.D. diss. University of London, 1956.

Munsche, P. *Gentlemen and Poachers: The English Game Laws 1671–1821*. Cambridge, 1981.

Oldham, James. "On Pleading the Belly: A History of the Jury of Matrons." *Criminal Justice History* 6 (1985): 1–64.

Palliser, D. M. *The Age of Elizabeth: England under the Later Tudors 1547–1603*. London, 1983.

Palmer, Robert C. *The County Courts of Medieval England 1150–1350*. Princeton, 1982.

Pollock, Sir Frederick, and Maitland, Frederic. *The History of English Law before the Time of Edward I.* 2 vols. reissue. Cambridge, 1968.

Pound, J. F. *Poverty and Vagrancy in Tudor England.* London, 1971.

Quintrell, B. W. "The Government of the County of Essex 1603–42." Ph.D. diss. University of London, 1965.

"The Making of Charles I's Book of Orders." *EHR* 95 (1980): 553–72.

Radzinowicz, Sir Leon. *A History of English Criminal Law and its Administration from 1750.* vol. 1: *The Movement for Reform 1750–1833.* New York, 1948.

Roberts, Stephen K. "Initiative and Control: The Devon Quarter Sessions Grand Jury, 1649–1670." *BIHR* 57 (November, 1984): 165–77.

Recovery and Restoration in an English County: Devon Local Administration 1646–1670. Exeter, 1985.

Rosenheim, James M. "Robert Doughty of Hanworth: A Restoration Magistrate." *Norfolk Archaeology* 38 part 3 (1983): 296–312.

Russell, Conrad. *Parliaments and English Politics 1621–1629.* Oxford, 1979.

Samaha, Joel. "Hanging for Felony: The Rule of Law in Elizabethan Colchester." *HJ* 21 (1978): 763–82.

Law and Order in Historical Perspective: The Case of Elizabethan Essex. New York, 1974.

Seaver, Paul S. *Wallington's World: A Puritan Artisan in Seventeenth-Century London.* Stanford, 1985.

Shapiro, Barbara J. *Probability and Certainty in Seventeenth-Century England.* Princeton, 1983.

Sharpe, J. A. *Crime in Early Modern England 1550–1750.* London, 1984.

Crime in Seventeenth-Century England: A County Study. Cambridge, 1983.

"Domestic Homicide in Early Modern England." *HJ* 24 (1981): 29–48.

" 'Last Dying Speeches': Religion, Ideology and Public Execution in Seventeenth-Century England." *P & P* 107 (May, 1985): 144–67.

Silcock, R. H. "County Government in Worcestershire 1603–1660." Ph.D. diss. University of London, 1974.

Simpson, H. "The Office of Constable." *EHR* 40 (1895): 625–41.

Skipp, Victor. *Crisis and Development: An Ecological Case Study of the Forest of Arden 1570–1674.* Cambridge, 1978.

Slack, Paul. "Books of Orders: The Making of English Social Policy 1577–1631." *TRHS* 5th series, 30 (1980): 1–22.

"Poverty and Politics in Salisbury, 1597–1666" in Peter Clark and Paul Slack, eds. *Crisis and Order in English Towns 1500–1700: Essays in Urban History.* London, 1972.

"Vagrants and Vagrancy in England, 1598–1664." *EcHR* 2nd series, 27 (1974): 360–80.

Smith, Lacey Baldwin. "English Treason Trials and Confessions in the Sixteenth Century." *Journal of the History of Ideas* 15 (1954): 471–98.

Spierenburg, Pieter. *The Spectacle of Suffering: Executions and the Evolution of Repression: From a Preindustrial Metropolis to the European Experience.* Cambridge, 1984.

Steer, David. *Uncovering Crime: The Police Role.* Royal Commission on Criminal Procedure Research Study 7. London, 1980.

Stephen, Sir James F. *A History of the Criminal Law of England.* 3 vols. London, 1883.

Stone, Lawrence. "Interpersonal Violence in English Society 1300–1980." *P & P* 101 (November, 1983): 22–33.

Straker, Ernest. *Wealden Iron*. London, 1931.

Styles, John. "An Eighteenth Century Magistrate as Detective: Samuel Lister of Little Horton." *The Bradford Antiquary* new series, 47 (1982): 98–117.

Tawney, R. H. and A. J. "An Occupational Census of the Seventeenth Century." *EcHR* 5 (1934): 25–64.

Thirsk, Joan. "The Farming Regions of England" in Joan Thirsk, ed. *The Agrarian History of England and Wales, IV, 1500–1640*. Cambridge, 1967: 1–112.

Thomas, Keith. *Religion and the Decline of Magic*. New York, 1971.

Thomas-Stanford, Charles. *Sussex in the Great Civil War and the Interregnum 1642–1660*. London, 1910.

Thompson, E. P. *Whigs and Hunters: The Origins of the Black Act*. New York, 1975.

"Ticehurst Parishioners in 1635." *Sussex Genealogist and Family Historian* 4 (1983): 137–8.

Tite, Colin G. C. *Impeachment and Parliamentary Judicature in Early Stuart England*. London, 1974.

The Victoria History of the County of Sussex. 6 vols. W. Page, ed. vol. 1; L. F. Salzman, ed. vols. 3, 4, 7–9. London, 1905–53.

Walter, John, and Wrightson, Keith. "Dearth and the Social Order in Early Modern England." *P & P* 71 (May, 1976): 22–42.

Walzer, Michael. "Puritanism as a Revolutionary Ideology." *History and Theory* 3 (1963): 59–90.

Webb, Sidney, and Beatrice. *The Parish and the County*. English Local Government, vol. 1. 1906; reprint London 1963.

Whitelock, Dorothy. *The Beginnings of English Society*. Harmondsworth, 1952.

Wrightson, Keith. *English Society 1580–1680*. London, 1982.

    "Infanticide in Earlier Seventeenth-Century England." *LPS* 15 (Autumn, 1975): 10–22.

    "The Puritan Reformation of Manners with Special Reference to the Counties of Lancashire and Essex 1640–1660." Ph.D. diss. Cambridge University, 1974.

Wrightson, Keith, and Levine, David. *Poverty and Piety in an English Village: Terling 1525–1700*. New York, 1979.

Wrigley, E. A., and Schofield, R. S. *The Population History of England 1541–1871: A Reconstruction*. Cambridge, Mass., 1981.

Young, Arthur. *General View of the Agriculture of the County of Sussex*. London, 1808.

INDEX

accomplices, *see* receivers

ad hoc commissions, 43

age: of enforcers of the law, 55, 105, 107, 108, 140; as a factor in legal decisions, 129, 158, 189

alehousekeepers, 75, 128, 146, 184

alehouses, 33, 34, 82, 105, 110, 115, 128

Alfrey, Richard, 102 n16

alibis and disclaimers, 80, 81–2, 87, 120, 123, 124, 128, 147–8

allocutus, 192

amateurs in law enforcement, 3–6, 68, 92, 159, 195, 200–1, 204; *see also* participation, communal

Amherst, Richard, 81

appeal of felony, 68

apprentices, 161, 162 n40; *see also* servants

approvers, 86, 127–8, 185

arrest of suspects, 73, 85, 151; *see also* detection of suspects

arson, 31

Ashburnham, John, 183, 184, 190

assault, 39, 108

Assizes: records of, 7, 67 n1, 112; places and frequency of meeting in Sussex, 24, 42, 56, 58, 101; authority of, 42–3, 51, 57, 194; jurisdiction of, 43–51, 62–5; advantages of, 44, 47–51; disadvantages of, 50, 55–8; non-judicial functions of, 51–3; changes over time in, 62–5, 159, 163–4, 203; estimated rate of indictment at, 113; trial business at, 132, 156, 159; *see also* ceremonies; clergy, benefit of; judges; juries; jurors; trial

Avington, Richard, 73, 79–80

Babington, Zachary, 94, 96, 133–4

Bacon, Sir Francis, 52, 57, 71, 91

bail, *see* recognizances

bailiffs, 70

Baker, J. H., 121

Ball, Ann, 129

Ball, John, 129

Barcombe, 30 n26

Barham, William, 105

Bartlett, Richard, 102 n16

Barton, Agnes, 80

Battle, 30

belly, benefit of the, 143, 173, 175

Bexhill, 37 table, 74

Bexhill hundred, 125 n42

Bishop of Bangor, son of the, 140

Bishop's Ordinary, 48

Bishopstone hundred, 125 n42

Blackstone, Sir William, 129

Blaker, Arthur, 158

Bodiam, 30 n26

Bolney, 126

Book of Orders, 52

Boorner, John, 74

Brasier, Anne, 155

Brasier, John, 168–9

breaking, 30, 48, 171, 189

Breecher, Roger, 123

Brent, Colin, 208–9

Breton, Nicholas, 136

Briggs, Henry, 172

Brightling, 30 n26

Brighton, 16, 17, 81, 108; crimes reported from, 29, 30; legal participation from, 68–9, 108, 138, 139–40

Brockett alias Ifold, Michael, 184–6

Brockett, Thomas, 140

Brown, Ned, 71

Brown, Thomas, 82

burglary, *see* criminal offenses

Burleigh Arches hundred, 125 n42

Burt, John, 81–2

Buttinghill hundred, 104, 106–8, 109, 138, 139

Buttinghill liberty, 107, 137

Buxted, 80

Cambridge Studies in Early Modern British History